The Federation of Alberta Naturalists

FIELD GUIDE TO ALBERTA BIRDS

W. Bruce McGillivray
Glen P. Semenchuk

Federation of Alberta Naturalists

ISBN 0-9696134-2-3

Printed June 1998
Published by the Federation of Alberta Naturalists
P.O. Box 1472, Edmonton, Alberta, T5J 2N5

Additional copies of the Alberta Bird Guide, The Atlas of Breeding Birds of Alberta, or permission to use of FAN's data base for scientific research or other purposes, may be obtained by contacting FAN at the above address.

Printed and bound at Friesen Printers
Altona, Manitoba

Electronic Layout and Design by
Karen Richards

All photographs of birds courtesy of the Edgar T. Jones collection at the Provincial Museum of Alberta, unless otherwise indicated.

Canadian Cataloguing in Publication Data

McGillivray, W. Bruce (William Bruce). 1954-
  Federation of Alberta Naturalists field guide to Alberta birds

  Includes index.
  ISBN 0-9696134-2-3

  1. Birds—Alberta—Identification. I. Semenchuk, Glen P. (Glen Peter), 1949-
II. Federation of Alberta Naturalists. III. Title. IV. Title: Field guide
to Alberta birds.
QL685.5.A86M32 1998Á   Á598'.097123Á   ÁC98-091571-1

Printed in Canada

Contents

Acknowledgments

The authors would like to dedicate this book to the thousands of birders who through their efforts have contributed to the knowledge base of Alberta's birds. We are pleased to acknowledge the generosity and talent of the many amateur photgraphers who allowed us to reproduce their work.

We appreciate the support and assistance of our two sponsoring organizations the Federation of Alberta Naturalists and the Provincial Museum of Alberta, Department of Community Development. Thanks go to Dr. Jocelyn Hudon, Curator of Ornithology, Provincial Museum of Alberta and chairman of the Alberta Rare Bird Committee, for his assistance in developing species lists.

We are grateful to our dedicated team that worked long hours to bring the concept for this book to life. Thanks go to:

Copy Editor
Dr. Jim Burns

Desktop Publishing
Karen Richards
Bryan Kulba
Karen Seto-Wagg

Maps and Graphics
Bryan Kulba
Erik Ellehoj
Barbara Redmond
Karen Richards
Trevor Wiens

Photo Research and Preparation
Bryan Kulba

Digital Photograpy of Bird Eggs
Graham Mitchell-Lawson
Kim Chapman

Bird Illustrations
Allan Whincup

INTRODUCTION

What is birding?

Birders, like birds, come in all sizes, ages and shapes. Their motivation for an interest in birds is equally variable but most begin the pastime because they have an appreciation for the diversity of birdlife in our part of the world. It is hard not to be moved by the reappearance of life in Alberta after a cold, long winter. We are fortunate to experience some of the most dramatic migratory events in North America every spring and fall on our sloughs and lakes. The diversity of birds in Alberta cannot compete with that farther south but we have a big advantage over tropical rain forest environments; we can see our birds. Most of the spectacular displays of birdlife in Alberta are right out in the open on our grasslands, parkland and lakes. For those who make the effort to battle the elements and our insect biodiversity to look for birds in the boreal forest, you will be rewarded with glimpses of tropical species who visit us briefly to breed before heading back to Central and South America.

Field guides would not exist if we did not have an interest in the name of the bird we happened to be looking at. Knowing what you are looking at and then reading about the life history of that species challenges you to learn and discover more. In the past, birdwatchers seemed content to list species; it was enough to see it, identify it, put in on a life list and move on to the next bird. This is a sport and it is fun but it does not bring the knowledge and the understanding of birds that are both compelling and critical for maintenance of healthy populations. Today, birders help study birds, they monitor breeding through atlassing programs, they participate in breeding-bird and Christmas-count surveys, they truly make a difference in bird management across the continent. With better application of current technologies, we would be able to make birders key partners in virtually all monitoring and censussing programs carried out by wildlife agencies.

What are we looking at?

Bird taxonomy has passed through phases in which species were split based on minor plumage differences, then lumped when it was apparent that differently plumaged forms managed to interbreed, then split again when sophisticated genetic studies showed that interbreeding was restricted to a narrow area, leaving the parent populations distinct. And so it goes. The trend now is to splitting as sequences of mitochondrial DNA tell ornithologists that different forms of what was thought to be a single species have been split for thousands, even millions, of years. A sign of the future is the recent splitting of the Solitary Vireo (*Vireo solitarius*) into three species—the Blue-headed Vireo (*Vireo solitarius*), Cassin's Vireo (*Vireo cassinii*) and the Plumbeous Vireo (*Vireo plumbeus*). Both the Cassin's and the Blue-headed occur in Alberta but unless you know their song differences, you will not be able to tell them apart. Unfortunately, in the bird world, genetic differences between species are not always correlated with plumage differences. This guide introduces you to some of the species that are likely to be split in the future to give you a head start on telling them apart.

Alberta, by virtue of having the Rocky Mountains as its western border (at least in the south), is a meeting place of different forms of birds. This makes our part of the world one of the best in which to study geographic and genetic variation among bird populations. We have many species with a distinct "eastern" form and an equally distinct "western" form. Some of these, like the Blue Jay/Steller's Jay pair, or Baltimore Oriole/Bullock's Oriole pair, or Yellow-bellied/Red-naped Sapsucker pair are different species. Others, like the Winter Wren, Brewer's Sparrow and Warbling Vireo, simply look or sound different in one part of Alberta versus another. In the future, some of these forms will be recognized as separate species, others will remain as interesting geographic variants within a species. We have to realize, however, that by virtue of our alterations to habitat we are changing the dynamics of the relationships between these species pairs or geographic variants. Despite the millions of hours spent watching birds, we actually know very little about the habitat requirements of many species and virtually nothing about the different needs of distinct populations. This is fertile ground for any birder to make a serious contribution to ornithology and wildlife management.

What is this book about?

Most biology comes back eventually to identification. If you do not know what you are looking at, how can you study it? There are many field guides on North American and Canadian birds but, despite these, beginning birders are overwhelmed by the diversity of birds and the difficulty in telling them apart. Our guide is written to help reduce the uncertainty about a bird's identification by giving you a sense of what key features separate this species from all others in Alberta. We provide the critical information about the birds you are likely to see. We do not worry about a similar species that lives in Florida or about distinguishing among juvenile plumages of sparrows, which are impossible to separate in the field. For many species, this means a focus only on the males. Yes, there are females, but your chances of seeing some of them away from their mates are remote, and females rarely vocalize. Although we use the term "birdwatching," for most of us birdlistening is closer to the truth. Learning the songs and calls of at least two thirds of our species is the best way to tell them apart.

Context is often a tremendous aid for identification. Our guide provides clues for context, not just where in the province you might see a species but in what habitat. We rate habitat as an identifier because sometimes it is extremely helpful to know that a species is found only in a certain kind of habitat. Through a combination of context, visual, vocal and behavioral characteristics, we try to narrow your choices down to a few species. From then on, it is up to you.

Do you need other guides?

Yes, books such as *The Birds of Canada*, by Earl Godfrey (1986), and *The Atlas of Breeding Birds of Alberta*, edited by Glen Semenchuk (1992), contain far more information about the biology of each species and, especially in Godfrey's book, details on female, juvenile and fall plumages. It is still the best reference guide about the birds of Canada to have in your home. Our guide focusses on Alberta and consequently will not help you on your trip to Arizona. You will need one of the many North American field guides on your travels in the United States. Using our approach of a hierarchical Field Checklist, though, will help you identify birds anywhere.

What does "common" or "rare" really mean?

With the exception of a game species or some rare birds, estimates of the abundance, even the status of a species, is an educated guess. There are far too few places in North America where data on bird numbers have been gathered consistently for long enough to allow definitive statements to be made. The cost of determining wildlife population status is simply too high to be undertaken on any but a few key "indicator" species. Governments do not have the resources.

Five years of surveying for breeding birds in Alberta in the late 1980s produced some marvellous information but also produced many questions. The highest densities and diversity of birds were seen near urban centres. This may not say anything about cities except that they contain lots of birdwatchers. Birds that were rare tended to be boreal forest specialists and ones that tended to be secretive. Are they rare, or just hard to census? The Atlas showed, however, that volunteers can produce meaningful data and convinced many wildlife officials that partnering with the public was the only means to truly monitor bird populations. These partnerships are just being developed but all of them depend on the public's willingness to document what they see.

For birders, estimates of a species' abundance can be translated into detectability, which is a measure of how likely you are to see this species if you visit the right habitat at the right time of year. Part of detectability is absolute numbers but part of it is a function of the behavior of the species. Remember, too, that statements about bird abundance reflect provincial estimates. A species might be uncommon overall but locally abundant. What is of interest is changing abundances; information from a number of local sources helps create a provincial picture. Documenting your observations over time can contribute to provincial status databases.

What is documentation?

Documentation means providing confirmatory details of an observation, not just where and when but how did you know what you were looking at? Photographs of birds or nests with eggs, recordings of songs, even detailed descriptions are the keys to documentation. With the quality of video recorders for both image and sound capture and the low price of

GPS (Global Positioning System) units, you have all the tools you need to provide first-rate documentation of any unusual observation.

The best documentation involves a physical specimen stored in a museum. It is the best because the identity can be verified or re-examined and compared, in the light of changing taxonomies and techniques. DNA-sequencing is being undertaken on many museum specimens that are tens, hundreds, even thousands of years old. Who knows how these specimens will be used ten years from now. Museum specimens are obtained in a variety of ways including delivery of dead birds to the Provincial Museum by concerned citizens. These have provided valuable clues to bird distribution and migration patterns. If you encounter a recently killed bird, put it in a plastic bag with a piece of paper that has your name, date when the bird was found and location where it was found, and freeze it as soon as possible. If you are near Edmonton, bring it to the Provincial Museum. If you live outside Edmonton, take it to your local Fish and Wildlife Office and say you would like this specimen to go to the Provincial Museum to be part of the province's Biodiversity Collection. You will be making a major contribution to our understanding of birds in Alberta.

What do you need to begin birding?

In addition to this guide, you will need binoculars and some instruction, and practice using them. Binoculars are small to large and cheap to unbelievably expensive. Two numbers describe a binocular's optics. The first is the level of magnification, the second is the diameter of the objective lens (the bigger one). The larger the lens the more light is captured and the better the binoculars are in dim light. Binoculars with combinations of high magnification (>7) and small objective lenses (<35) have small "fields of view" making the spotting of small birds difficult. Small binoculars are convenient, however, and 10x50s can be a pain on the neck. What should you start with? We recommend 7 power and relatively small glasses with 26 mm or 35 mm objective lenses, for example. For price, pay what you can afford, you do get what you pay for in binoculars. At the same time, birding can lead to bumping and dropping field glasses. So if you are rough with equipment, buy inexpensive binoculars.

Keeping detailed field notes of one's sightings can be very important in understanding birds. Recording things such as date, time of day, location, habitat and any interesting notes on behavior can prove to be invaluable. A diligent person's field notes eventually evolve into an important reference for identification, migration and breeding dates as well as ranges for the birds one has recorded.

Birdwatchers used to attract birds by making strange noises, sometimes referred to as "pishing." Many species have a distress call that sounds like "pishing" and will respond to the source of the "pish" by approaching. Ornithologists have long known that most songbirds respond aggressively to playback of their song. Males, of course, use their song to define their territory and protect their genetic investment in the next generation. They do not like intruding males. CD-ROMs with bird calls and portable CD players have put these tools in the hands of anyone who wants to use them. Without doubt these are invaluable tools which can help all beginners learn songs and catch a good look at a normally secretive species. The question is, what does this do to the birds? The answer is, nobody knows. If used infrequently on an individual, the effect is probably negligible. If used to the point of harassment then abandonment of the territory is a distinct possibility. Our recommendation is to use recordings of song primarily to compare to something you are hearing, not to aggravate males on their territories. Use discretion.

SPECIES NAMES AND STATUS

Notes on the AOU Changes

The taxonomic order and nomenclature that is used in this book is derived from the most recent, authoritative information. The common and scientific names follow the guidelines put forth by the American Ornithologists' Union's Check-list of North American Birds (7th edition, 1998) and the Forty-First Supplement to the Check-list (July, 1997, *Auk* Vol.114, #3). The order of the species list also follows the A.O.U. Check-list (7th edition).

Status

Status describes the biological well-being of a species' population within a defined area. In 1996, the Wildlife Management Division of Alberta's Natural Resources Service published the *Status of Alberta Wildlife* noting the stability of 479 mammals, reptiles, amphibians and birds occurring in the province. Each species' status was evaluated considering its abundance, breeding distribution, habitat integrity, population trends and its national/international status. Based on this information, each species was designated Red, Blue, Yellow A, Yellow B or Green status within the province.

- Red list species are those currently at risk, meaning their populations are in decline.

- Blue list indicates the species is believed to be at risk although more study must be done to determine its true status.

- Yellow A indicates the species has been experiencing a long-term decline in population and may be at risk.

- Species listed as Yellow B are currently not at risk but due to factors such as low natural populations, limited distributions or vulnerability to human-related change require attention so the populations will remain healthy.

- Species listed as Green are stable populations in secure habitats and therefore not considered at risk.

Due to lack of information or research, some species who are not thought to be at risk are considered Status Unknown. In the 1996 report, 4 bird species were listed as Red, 9 Blue, 67 Yellow and 280 as Green. There was also one bird listed as extirpated, and 9 as status undetermined.

For a copy of this report, contact:

Information   Centre-Publications
Alberta   Environmental   Protection
Natural Resources Service
Main Floor, Bramalea Building
9920-108 Street
Edmonton, Alberta
T5K 2M4
Ph: (403) 422-2079

THE NATURAL REGIONS OF ALBERTA

The Natural Regions of Alberta have most recently been defined in the 1994 Alberta Environmental Protection document *Natural Regions and Subregions of Alberta* (ISBN 0-7732-1303-1). This document divides the province into six major regions based on vegetation, soils, land forms and climate. The map on the opposite page illustrates these regions as defined below.

1 Boreal Forest Natural Region - The Boreal Forest Natural Region is the largest Natural Region in Alberta. It consists of broad lowland plains and isolated hill systems. This is the wettest Natural Region in the province with many bogs, fens and swamps. Vegetation consists of both mixed and coniferous forests.

2 Rocky Mountain Natural Region - The Rocky Mountain Natural Region is defined by the mountain range itself. As is to be expected from such a topographically diverse region, habitats too are highly varied with grasslands, deciduous, mixed and coniferous forests and alpine tundra. Many of the province's river systems start in this Natural Region and water courses tend to be steep, fast and cold.

3 Foothills Natural Region - The Foothills Natural Region is primarily a transitional zone between the Boreal Forest and the Rocky Mountains with some northern outliers consisting of flat-topped hills surrounded by mixed wood forests. The Foothills are forested largely with Lodgepole Pine but White Spruce and Aspen Poplar occur along the borders with the Boreal Forest Natural Region.

4 Canadian Shield Natural Region - The Canadian Shield Natural Region is found in the far northeastern of the province. Part of this region is characterized by exposed bedrock with Jack Pine woodlands, rock barrens and Black Spruce bogs in depressions. The other area has extensive sand plains, dune complexes and kame moraines. Lakes are common in both areas.

5 Parkland Natural Region - The Parkland Natural Region is largely a transitional zone between the grasslands and the coniferous forests. With the exception of the Peace River Parkland outlier, the region has more relief and is wetter than the Grassland Natural Region with many more permanent streams, lakes and wetlands. Aspen and Balsam poplar woodlands and Rough Fescue grasslands dominate this region.

6 Grassland Natural Region - The Grassland Natural Region occupies southern Alberta west of the Rocky Mountains. It is a flat or gently rolling plain with valley systems containing many coulees, ravines and intermittent water courses. Valleys often contain extensive badlands. Riparian habitats along the few permanent water courses commonly have cottonwoods and a variety of tall and low shrubs.

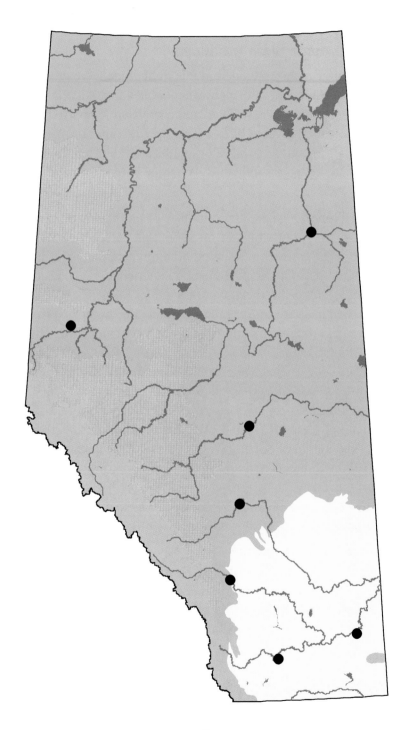

Species Range Maps

How the maps were produced

The range maps contained in this field guide were created using the most recent information available about Alberta birds. This information was calculated and correlated to approximate regions in Alberta where birds would breed, winter or reside year-round. In addition, migratory paths are indicated in the maps where they are applicable. The three vital information sources were:

Core References - There are a number of previously published references for Alberta birders. In 1976, Salt and Salt wrote *Birds of Alberta* which was based both on historical records and the authors' personal knowledge and experience. Another long-standing reference has been Godfrey's *The Birds of Canada* republished in 1986. More recently, Pinel et al. published their record of significant bird sightings in their Provincial Museum of Alberta Occasional Paper, *Alberta Birds, 1971-1980*, Vols. 1 & 2. These documents have formed the core set of references for both professional and amateur birders in province. *The Atlas of Breeding Birds of Alberta* was produced from the data gathered between 1987 and 1991. This project was undertaken by the Federation of Alberta Naturalists with the assistance of over 1000 volunteers and with the cooperation of both federal and provincial agencies. The data contained within the Atlas is the most current and extensive survey of the distribution of Alberta birds.

Key Databases - In addition to the Alberta Bird Atlas project, there have been a number of longer-running bird surveys in the province that have been providing an excellent source of information. Since the 1970s, Christmas Bird Counts have been held in a variety of locations in Alberta. The counts have been undertaken for much longer in the major centres, dating back to the first decade of this century. The Breeding Bird Survey project is a systematic survey of birds, not only in Alberta but all across North America, and this provides another vital body of information. In 1994 FAN began promoting a province-wide bird checklist program called the Alberta Birdlist Program. This program is currently being updated to encourage even greater participation.

Other Records - Every year the Calgary Field Naturalists publish Alberta bird records in their quarterly publication, *The Pica.* This document provides yet another source of birding information, particularly as it pertains to unusual sightings. In addition, as part of the Alberta Birdlist Program, FAN has helped to establish, with the assistance of the Provincial Museum of Alberta, an Alberta Rare Bird Records Committee consisting of selected birding experts from across the province. This committee has been initiated to evaluate unusual records that may involve extending traditional species ranges in the province.

How to use the species range maps

The species ranges have been overlaid onto a base map with certain rivers, lakes and towns in Alberta for reference. A labelled version of this base map is found inside the front cover of this guide. The maps portray the following information:

- Areas of year-round residence for the species are shaded green. Species movement within these regions will be dealt with in the text of the species account.

- Areas of summer/breeding-season residence are shaded yellow.

- Areas of winter residence are shaded blue.

- Migration paths are indicated using a colored arrow. The arrow is placed over the general area of the migration route and colored to indicate whether it is a migration towards the breeding range (yellow) or wintering range (blue) of the species.

When checking the range of the species, it is vital to take into account the scale, and thus accuracy, of the maps. If an observer finds the species close to, but outside, the documented ranges in the correct habitat type and at the right time of year, it is likely a valid sighting. However, if the species is observed far from its documented range, this could represent a range extension or an isolated extralimital occurrence. In either case it is vital to record further detailed information so that this important bird sighting can be reported to the Provincial Rare Bird Records Committee. Please refer to the earlier section on documentation for further information on what you should record in these instances.

Species Time Charts

The time charts contained in this field guide were created using information from several recognized sources that were used to create the bird range maps. For many species the details of their schedules, especially the end times of their breeding seasons, are largely unknown. In addition, birds are strongly influenced by climatic conditions, and thus time periods can easily vary by as much as one month from one season to the next, depending on the onset and severity of the winter weather. The species time charts thus provide a guideline as to when a species will be found within the shaded regions or along their migration routes.

The colors used are designed to match the shading of the range map. Therefore:

• Time periods for spring migration or breeding are indicated with a yellow shading. For birds that are year-round residents, the start of the breeding season is indicated by a yellow line.

• Time periods for fall migration or wintering are indicated with a blue shading.

• Year-round residency is indicated by green.

ALBERTA BIRDLIST PROGRAM

From 1986 - 1991 the Federation of Alberta Naturalists under-took the Alberta Bird Atlas Project. During this project over 1000 volunteers surveyed designated land areas for breeding birds. After the successful publication of the results in *The Atlas of Breeding Birds of Alberta*, many volunteers wanted to continue to gather information to contribute to the knowledge of birds in the province. In 1994 FAN initiated the Alberta Birdlist Program which is a provincial bird checklist program that adheres to North American guidelines for such projects to allow integration of data. These records are being entered into a province-wide database of bird records.

The Birdlist program is designed as part of a national strategy to gain valuable scientific data from birders' checklists. Two major values of this type of program are:

Birding Software

In 1995 FAN began distributing free DOS-based software for individual birders to record their own records and be able to submit them electronically. Currently, FAN is redeveloping this program to run in a Microsoft Windows 95 or Microsoft Windows NT 4.0 environment.

Provincial Checklists

For individuals who would like to contribute to the provincial bird database but don't wish to use a computer, FAN distributes copies of the provincial bird checklists free of charge. A checklist is also reprinted in the back of this book which can be photocopied for personal use. For further information on these programs contact:

Federation of Alberta Naturalists
Box 1472
Edmonton, Alberta
T5J 2N5
Phone: 403-453-8629
Fax: 403-453-8553
E-mail: fan@connect.ab.ca

KEY TO SPECIES PAGES

1 Common Name: This is the accepted English name for the bird, as determined by the American Ornithologists' Union.

2 Scientific Name: A two-part name consisting of the bird's genus and species names.

3 Sizes and weights: Indicates the average length and weight of Alberta specimens of the bird as well as the length and width of the egg.

4 Etymology: This is a deconstruction of the scientific name into the individual parts and their meanings. The language from which the name is derived is also indicated.

5 Status and Distribution: These are notes on the species' abundance and well-being in the province as well as where it can be located in the province.

6 Bird Photograph: The photo is included to complement the descriptors provided in the text. In some cases, there is an inset picture illustrating an important characteristic of the bird.

7 Photograph of the Egg: This photo shows the general shape, pattern and color of the eggs.

8 Field Checklist: The field checklist is used to identify the bird. This section contains four parts: Habitat, Sight, Sound and Behavior. They describe characteristics of the bird in question. In many cases, some characters may outweigh others in positively identifying the bird. To illustrate this, check-marks are used to "grade" the characteristics. The more check-marks the characteristic has, the more valuable it is for identification. If a characteristic has no check-marks, it is a poor attribute to use for ID.

9 Habitat: Describes the specific qualities of a habitat that the bird frequents or prefers.

10 Sight: This is a physical description of the bird. It emphasizes the important field marks used for identification as well as differences between males and females, adults and juveniles, as well as seasonal variation.

11 Sound: This is a description of the vocalizations or noises the bird may make.

12 Behavior: This describes behavior which may be specific to the bird and therefore useful in identification.

13 Similar Species: Species that are similar in appearance or behavior are listed and the differences between them are highlighted.

14 Remarks: The remarks section contains additional information that may be of interest or identification tips.

15 Species Range Map: This map illustrates the distribution of the species throughout the province (see page 10 for details).

16 Time Chart: The colored area on the bar indicates the period when the bird is in the province and is directly related to the similar by colored area on the map. In cases where the bird may move seasonally within the province, the multiple colors of the bar correspond with the multi-colored map.

17 Four Letter Code: This is the code for the species used by the Alberta Birdlist Project. A check-box and a date line are provided to record sightings of the species.

❶ *SORA*

❷ *Porzana carolina*

❸ *L: 210 mm W: 77 g Egg: 31 x 22 mm*

❹ **Etymology:** *Porzana* (L.) - "the crake;" *carolina* (ML.) - "of Carolina."

❺ **Status and Distribution:** The Sora is the most common rail in Alberta. The population in the province is stable. It is found in all regions of the province where suitable wetlands exist.

● ●

❽ Field Checklist

❾ ✓✓**Habitat:** The Sora has adapted to a variety of wetland habitats. It breeds in freshwater ponds, meandering streams, marshes, sloughs, or wet meadows, with at least a partial margin of extensive sedges, rushes or cattails. Flooded willow swamps are less popular.

❿ ✓✓✓**Sight:** This rail is chunky and has a short yellowish bill. The upperparts are olive brown, the breast is gray and the throat and front of the face are black.

⓫ ✓✓✓**Sound:** A sharp upslurred whistle and a descending series of loud notes, often described as a whinny or maniacal laugh.

⓬ ✓**Behavior:** In common with other rails, the Sora is reluctant to take flight when disturbed and prefers to use its laterally compressed body to slip quietly into the tangled vegetation.

● ●

⓭ **Similar species:** Yellow Rail.

⓮ **Remarks:** It is larger than the Yellow Rail and lacks the white patch on the wing. It has more olive on its back as opposed to the brown of the Yellow Rail. This is the most common and least secretive of the rails in the province. The Sora will usually build its nest in deeper water than other rails, where it is anchored to a tuft of rushes. In the fall, they are less secretive.

⓯ Jan	Feb	Mar	Apr	May	Jun	Jul	Aug	Sep	Oct	Nov	Dec

⓱ SORA ❑ Date: _____

RED-THROATED LOON

Gavia stellata

L: 620 mm   W: 2900 g   Egg: 74 x 45 mm

Etymology: *Gavia* (L.) - "Gull;" *stellata* (L.) - "starred," in reference to spots on the back of the bird in winter.

Status and Distribution: A rare breeder in Alberta. Only recorded breeding is at Margaret Lake in the Caribou Mountains. It has been recorded regularly on migration through the province as far south as Waterton Lakes National Park, with more records in the fall, than in the spring.

• •

Field Checklist

Habitat: This loon frequents fresh water ponds and lakes in sub-arctic forested areas, which are shallower and smaller than those chosen by other loons. Nesting is in a dry area along the shoreline.

✓✓✓**Sight:** This small loon has a triangular chestnut-red throat patch, gray head with pronounced striping on the hind neck, a plain uncheckered back and slender up-turned bill. Upperparts are blackish-brown with a green gloss. Underparts are mainly white.

✓✓**Sound:** Vocal mainly during the breeding season, the call is a harsh, repetitive cooing. A secondary call is a rapid "kwuk-kwuk-kwuk-kwuk."

✓**Behavior:** Dives of this species are shallower and shorter, and take-offs are quicker than in other loons.

• •

Similar species: Common Loon and Arctic Loon.

Remarks: It is separated from the Common Loon by its smaller size and upturned bill and the speckled rather than black back. It differs from the Arctic Loon by the upturned bill and checkered back. Unique to its family, this loon does not require a food supply in the nesting pond, but will make foraging flights of several kilometres to sources of prey fish. There are few overwintering records for this species in Alberta.

Jan	Feb	Mar	Apr	May	Jun	Jul	Aug	Sep	Oct	Nov	Dec

RTLO ❑   Date: _____

PACIFIC LOON

Gavia pacifica

L: 630 mm   W: 2950 g   Egg: 79 x 48 mm

Etymology: *Gavia* (L.) - "Gull;"
pacifica - refers to the wintering area.

Status and Distribution: This is a rare
breeder in Alberta as the province is at
the southern edge of its breeding
range. The only recorded breeding in
the province was in the extreme northeast corner of Alberta in the Canadian

Shield. Elsewhere in the province, it is a rare spring and fall migrant.

● ●

Field Checklist

✓**Habitat:** It breeds on deep, large lakes in tundra and boreal
forest areas. The nest is on the ground near water.

✓✓✓**Sight:** This medium-sized loon has a
silvery gray crown, forehead and back of
neck. The back is extensively spotted with
white patterning, including two large areas of
white on the wings and two smaller white
areas on the upper back. It has a black throat
and neck and white, streaked breast.

✓✓**Sound:** Calls include long, pulsed, raven-
like croaks, a prolonged mournful cat-like
"meow" (morning and dusk) and a dog-like yelp
given just before it dives.

Behavior: It is highly territorial during the breeding
season. Prey is captured during long sustained dives.

● ●

Similar species: Red-throated Loon and Common Loon.

Remarks: It is distinguished from the Red-throated by its straight rather
than curved bill and lighter-colored head. It is smaller than the Common
Loon and has a gray crown and back of neck, rather than black. This species
was previously considered a variant of the Arctic Loon but was accorded
full species status in 1985.

Jan	Feb	Mar	Apr	May	Jun	Jul	Aug	Sep	Oct	Nov	Dec

PALO ☐   Date: _____

COMMON LOON
Gavia immer

L: 740 mm   W: 3461 g   Egg: 89 x 57 mm

Etymology: *Gavia* (L.) - "Gull;" *immer* (L.) - "diver," or "to plunge into."

Status and Distribution: This species is common throughout the province except in the grassland area where it is an uncommon breeder.

• •

Field Checklist

✓**Habitat:** It prefers clear, open lakes with minimal shoreline development, little recreational activity and an abundance of small fish.

✓✓**Sight:** The head, upper throat and bill are all black. There is a patch of vertical white lines on the lower throat and white spots forming bars across the black back.

✓✓✓**Sound:** A lonely echoing call that is readily associated with loons and symbolic of northern wilderness.

✓**Behavior:** Solitary nester, very attentive at the nest. It stays under water for up to a minute when feeding.

• •

Similar species: Red-throated Loon.

Remarks: The differences between these species are outlined in the species description of the Red-throated Loon. It has disappeared from much of its southeastern Canadian range because of loss of nesting habitat to campers and cottagers and its sensitivity to human disturbance. It is especially sensitive to disturbance from motor boats on its breeding lakes. The Common Loon can take flight only from water. It requires a long bout of running and flapping across the surface to get airborne. It has been recorded in Alberta in winter where open water is available.

Jan	Feb	Mar	Apr	May	Jun	Jul	Aug	Sep	Oct	Nov	Dec

COLO ❏   Date: _____

PIED-BILLED GREBE

Podilymbus podiceps

Photo: G.Beyersbergen

L: 288 mm W: 245 g Egg: 43 x 30 mm

Etymology: *Podiceps* (L.) - "rump foot," in reference to the posterior position of the feet; and part of *Colymbus* (Gr.) from *Kolumbos*, "a diving bird."

Status and Distribution: The most common grebe in North America, the Pied-billed Grebe is found in wetland habitats throughout Alberta.

• •

Field Checklist

✓**Habitat:** It prefers ponds, lakes or sloughs with dense emergent growth along the shoreline or around islands.

✓✓✓**Sight:** This is a small, shy grebe. It is brownish black or grayish black with a black throat patch, brown eyes and a stubby whitish bill with a black ring.

✓**Sound:** Loud voice heard as "kuck-kuck-kuck-gulip-gulip-gulip" with notes rising in pitch and a pause before the "gulips."

✓✓**Behavior:** Rarely seen in the open, the Pied-billed Grebe may submerge when disturbed with only its bill showing.

• •

Similar species: None (visually), American Coot (vocally).

Remarks: Very difficult to observe but distinguished from other grebes by the lack of a crest or ruff. This grebe is solitary during the breeding season and in the fall, birds congregate in flocks on larger lakes. Grebes appear to migrate at night. Pied-billed Grebes have been recorded overwintering in the province. Sloughs are wonderful places to listen for birds. The Pied-billed Grebe and the American Coot share hoots and clucks that are reminiscent of Chimpanzees.

Jan	Feb	Mar	Apr	May	Jun	Jul	Aug	Sep	Oct	Nov	Dec

PBGR ☐   **Date:** _____

Order: Podicipediformes - Family: Podicipedidae

HORNED GREBE
Podiceps auritus

L: 335 mm   W: 420 g   Egg: 43.2 x 29 mm

Etymology: *Podiceps* (L.) - "rump foot," in reference to the posterior position of the feet; *auritus* (L.) - "eared."

Status and Distribution: This grebe has the lowest population densities in Alberta but is found throughout the province. Alberta has placed it on its Yellow List indicating a concern over long-term declines in numbers.

• •

Field Checklist

✓**Habitat:** This grebe nests in open and forested areas in ponds and lakes with extensive marshy vegetation.

✓✓✓**Sight:** It is easily identified by its buffy ear tufts or "horns," glossy black crown and neck ruff, and chestnut neck and sides. The upperparts of the body are black and the underparts are white.

✓✓**Sound:** Usually silent but occasionally it will utter a high pitched, pig-like squeal followed by a loud "ka-rac."

✓**Behavior:** It is considered the least wary of the grebes, but is highly protective of its nest. Courtship is an elaborate dance with both birds rising out of the water side by side.

• •

Similar species: Similar in size to the Pied-billed and Eared Grebes

Remarks: The "horns" are distinctive and it has a narrow pointed bill rather than the stubby one of the Pied-billed. Look for the reddish neck, not a black one like the Eared Grebe. It is a weak flier and rarely leaves the water, except for migration. Young brood on their parents' back and will sometimes be carried underwater when the parent dives. Horned Grebes have been observed overwintering at Lethbridge, Wabamum Lake and Waterton Lake.

Jan	Feb	Mar	Apr	May	Jun	Jul	Aug	Sep	Oct	Nov	Dec

HOGR ☐   Date: _____

RED-NECKED GREBE

Podiceps grisegena

L: 500 mm W: 1121 g Egg: 60 x 32 mm

Etymology: *Podiceps* (L.) - "rump foot," in reference to the posterior position of the feet; *grisegena* (L.) - *griseus,* "gray;" *gena,* "cheek."

Status and Distribution: In Alberta there is a concern for declining numbers of this species. It nests throughout the province and is a fairly common nester in the central part of Alberta. It is less common in the mountains, foothills and prairie areas of the province.

• •

Field Checklist

✓**Habitat:** It is found on small, shallow lakes or in shallow protected areas and bays of larger lakes with extensive emergent and submergent vegetation.

✓✓✓**Sight:** This large grebe has a broad, black crown, white cheek patches, and a chestnut neck. In flight two white patches are visible on the leading edges of the wings. The feet as pictured above are lobed to aid in diving but they render grebes awkward on land.

✓✓**Sound:** Loud, raucous "kraagh" and a wailing call are given during courtship.

✓**Behavior:** This species shows little hostility to intruders and if disturbed quietly retires. Young ride on their parents' backs.

• •

Similar species: Other members of the grebe family.

Remarks: This grebe is easily recognized by its larger size and distinctive coloration. Increased recreational activity and cottage development has contributed to a major decline on some Alberta lakes. In the fall they flock in considerable numbers on larger lakes, often with other grebes and loons. Overwintering has been previously recorded in Alberta. The call of the Red-necked is not as dramatic as that of a Common Loon but they are often heard together.

Jan	Feb	Mar	Apr	May	Jun	Jul	Aug	Sep	Oct	Nov	Dec

RNGR ☐ Date: _____

Grebes

CLARK'S GREBE

Aechmophorus clarkii

Photo: D.R. Franz/Cornell

L: 629 mm W: 1245 g Egg: 61 x 39 mm

Etymology: *Aechmophorus* (Gr.) - *aichme*, "spear" and *phoreus*, "bearer;" *clarkii* - for J. H. Clark, a 19th century collector.

Status and Distribution: Population status is unknown. It is a rare breeder in Alberta, nesting only in the extreme south of province, which is the northern periphery of its range.

• •

Field Checklist

✓**Habitat:** It is found on larger lakes with abundant fish populations and lakeside emergent vegetation.

✓✓✓**Sight:** This is a large grebe with a graceful, long neck, orange-yellow bill, black on the crown and down the back of the neck to the upper body. The white of the face, throat and neck continue onto the underparts. Black and white are in sharp contrast on the long, slender neck. The black on the crown does not extend down to the eye.

Sound: Same call as the Western Grebe.

✓**Behavior:** Similar courtship display to the Western Grebe.

• •

Similar species: Western Grebe.

Remarks: The distinction between these two species is the lack of black around the eye in the Clark's Grebe and its bright orange-yellow bill rather than the darker greenish-yellow of the Western Grebe. Unique to both of these species is the male's habit of feeding the female before nesting. It tends to forage in deeper water and uses a "spring" dive more often to reach its food. This former "light phase" of the Western Grebe was accorded full species status in 1985.

Jan	Feb	Mar	Apr	May	Jun	Jul	Aug	Sep	Oct	Nov	Dec

CLGR ☐   Date: _____

Order: Pelecaniformes - Family: Pelecanidae   **Pelicans**

AMERICAN
WHITE PELICAN
Pelecanus erythrorhynchos

Photo: J.Kristensen

L: 1446 mm   W: 5047 g   Egg: 87 x 56 mm

Etymology: *Pelecanus* (L.) - "wood-pecker," which refers to the birds pecking habits; *erythrorhynchos* (Gr.) - *erythros,* "red," and *rhyncos,* "beak."

Status and Distribution: The size of the population in Alberta seems to be increasing but the number of colonies is decreasing. Nesting colonies are found in the eastern part of the province from the American border to the Northwest Territories.

● ●

Field Checklist

✓**Habitat:** It nests and feeds in remote lakes with extensive shallows near shore and good fish populations.

✓✓✓**Sight:** This is among the world's largest birds, with a weight of 5 - 8 kg and a wing-span of over 2 m. It is pure white with black wings. Its yellow pouch, or gular sac, can hold 13 litres of fish and water.

Sound: It has no distinctive vocalization, but in colonies it may utter a low grunting noise.

✓**Behavior:** The Pelican feeds from the surface by plunging its head into water and scooping up fish. In flight pelicans travel in long lines or a "V" formation. They fly with a slow wingbeat seemingly flapping in sequence down the line of birds.

● ●

Similar species: None.

Remarks: Pelicans are sensitive to human disturbance; untimely visits in or near a colony can result in heavy predation or the total abandonment of a nesting island. Several colonies have been designated as Seasonal Wildlife Sanctuaries, wherein all public access is prohibited within 1 km of the nesting island between April 15 and September 15. Many non-breeding pelicans are seen "loafing" on parkland or boreal forest lakes.

Jan	Feb	Mar	Apr	May	Jun	Jul	Aug	Sep	Oct	Nov	Dec

25

AWPE ☐   Date: _____

Order: Pelecaniformes - Family: Phalacrocoracidae

DOUBLE-CRESTED CORMORANT

Phalacrocorax auritus

L: 805 mm   W: 2231 g   Egg: 51 x 38 mm

Etymology: *Phalacrocorax* (L.) -
"cormorant" or *phalakros* (Gr.) - "bald"
and *korax* (Gr.) - "crow or raven;"
auritus (L.) - "eared."

Status and Distribution: The size of the population in Alberta is increasing but continued protection of colonies is required. Breeding colonies are found in the central and southern parts of the province east of the foothills.

• •

Field Checklist

✓**Habitat:** The Cormorant breeds on larger lakes and reservoirs with good fish populations and undisturbed low-lying islands for nesting.

✓✓✓**Sight:** The Double-Crested Cormorant is jet-black with a bronze sheen and has a long sinuous neck with yellow-orange throat patches. In spring they have long fine feathers behind each eye, forming the double crests.

Sound: They do not vocalize with the exception of grunts emitted in the colony.

✓✓**Behavior:** After hunting for fish, the birds perch and hold their wings extended to dry.

• •

Similar species: None.

Remarks: In Alberta, this species is distinctive. Its tendency to nest on islands leaves colonies highly susceptible to water-level fluctuations particularly on reservoirs. Several colonies established in the last 20 years have taken to building nests in trees on wooded islands. Overwintering has been recorded at Wabamun Lake and in southern Alberta. Historically, Cormorants were persecuted as "competitors" with commercial fishing. Studies showed that the birds had been unjustly accused.

Jan	Feb	Mar	Apr	May	Jun	Jul	Aug	Sep	Oct	Nov	Dec

DCCO ❏   Date: _____

Order: Ciconiiformes - Family: Ardeidae

AMERICAN BITTERN

Botaurus lentiginosus

Photo: J.Kristensen

L: 624 mm   W: 837 g   Egg: 49 x 37 mm

Etymology: *Botaurus* (ML.) - "a bittern;" *lentiginosus* (L.) - "freckled."

Status and Distribution: The status is unknown at present but a decline is suspected. It breeds in suitable marshy habitat throughout the province with a few records in the Rocky Mountains. It is most common in the central parkland.

• •

Field Checklist

✓✓**Habitat:** The Bittern breeds in marshes, swamps, moist meadows, or wet alder and willow thickets where there is a dense growth of emergent vegetation or tall grasses.

✓**Sight:** This heron-like bird has short legs and a thick neck. The upper parts are a pale dark brown with fine streaking. The under-parts are a yellowish-buff with broad brown streaks. The yellow beak has a black stripe which extends backwards under the eye.

✓✓✓**Sound:** A repeated "pump-r-lunk" sound like a dry suction pump is the common call.

✓**Behavior:** When alarmed it is a master of concealment, drawing in its plumage, pointing its bill straight in the air and remaining motionless for long intervals.

• •

Similar species: Juvenile Black-crowned Night-Heron.

Remarks: In flight, at a distance, its outline is similar to that of a heron. The juvenile heron has no pattern on its back and does not have the yellowish coloration. The Bittern prefers secluded bogs and swamps where it can lead its solitary existence. Drainage, and cultivation of marshes is a continuing threat to the American Bittern.

Jan	Feb	Mar	Apr	May	Jun	Jul	Aug	Sep	Oct	Nov	Dec

27   AMBI ☐   Date: _____

Herons and Egrets

GREAT BLUE HERON

Ardea herodias

Photo: J.Kristensen

L: 1085 mm   W: 1589 g   Egg: 64 x 45 mm

Etymology: *Ardea* (L.) - "heron;"
herodias (Gr.) - "a heron."

Status and Distribution: The
population is stable in the province
with about 1500 breeding pairs in 75
colonies. It nests mainly in central and
southern Alberta east of the foothills,
with some colonies farther north.

• •

Field Checklist

✓**Habitat:** The Great Blue Heron is found in open shallow
water at the edges of lakes, streams, rivers,
ponds and marshes.

✓✓✓**Sight:** This is the largest heron in
Canada. It has a white crown, a black stripe
through the eye that extends back onto large
plumes, with white below the eye. The long
bill is orange and the neck is grayish-brown.
The upper body is blue-gray and the underparts are light with dark streaks.

✓**Sound:** They utter an alarm call that is a loud
guttural "grak."

✓✓**Behavior:** The Great Blue Heron forages either
by standing still in the shallows or stalking in a slow,
deliberate pace and then, with a rapid stroke of its sharp bill, its
prey is caught.

• •

Similar species: Sandhill Crane.

Remarks: It has distinctive blue coloration and in flight, unlike cranes, the
neck is folded and the head is drawn back against the shoulders. The birds
are solitary outside of the breeding season. Protection of their colonies from
disturbance is essential. The northernmost Great Blue Heron colony in
Canada is on Lake Claire.

Jan	Feb	Mar	Apr	May	Jun	Jul	Aug	Sep	Oct	Nov	Dec

GBLH ☐   Date: _____

BLACK-CROWNED NIGHT-HERON

Nycticorax nycticorax

L: 610 mm   W: 854 g   Egg: 53 x 37 mm

Etymology: *Nycticorax* (Gr.) - *nyx, nyctos,* "night" and *corax,* "a crow."

Status and Distribution: The population in Alberta is increasing but this species is on the provincial Yellow List as it requires special management. It is found in southern and central Alberta, west of the foothills and, north to Lac la Biche.

Photo: B. Carroll

Field Checklist

✓**Habitat:** The Black-crowned Night-Heron tends to colonize relatively large bodies of water with dense emergent vegetation. In southern Alberta it uses man-made impoundments.

✓✓✓**Sight:** It is a small stocky wader recognizable by its greenish-black crown and long, slender, white head plumes and large black bill. The upper parts are a pale bluish-gray and the throat is white, blending into a pale gray on the breast and underparts. Look for the red eye.

✓✓**Sound:** Its resounding "quawk" may be heard at dusk as the bird flies to its feeding ground.

Behavior: Similar to other herons, it is an excellent still fisherman and an active stalker.

Similar species: None similar to the adult bird.

Remarks: The young Night-Heron is striped like a Bittern but it does not have the yellowish color. It is active in night feeding at the marshy shallows of lakes, streams and irrigation ditches. In daylight hours, it is likely to be found roosting in nearby trees. It nests in trees in most parts of its range but also nests in dense emergent vegetation. Although a regular breeder now, it was first sighted in Alberta in 1958.

Jan	Feb	Mar	Apr	May	Jun	Jul	Aug	Sep	Oct	Nov	Dec

29

BCNH ☐   Date: _____

WHITE-FACED IBIS

Plegadis chihi

L: 584 mm   W: 750 g   Egg: 59 x 39 mm

Etymology: *Plegadis* (Gr.) - "a sickle or scythe;" *chihi* - a South American native name for the bird.

Status and Distribution: With less than 20 pairs in the province this species is on the Yellow List as it is an isolated breeder in Alberta, disjunct from populations in the south. They have been observed only in the extreme south of the province.

● ●

Field Checklist

✓Habitat: The Ibis prefers marshes of larger lakes for breeding and mud flats, flooded pastures and irrigated fields for foraging.

✓✓✓Sight: This is a medium-sized, storklike bird. It is dark chestnut with a purple and green gloss and a long down-curving bill. In breeding plumage it has a bare spot in front of the eye that is bordered with white feathers.

✓Sound: In flight it may utter a quacking sound.

Behavior: It likes to feed and travel in groups.

● ●

Similar species: None.

Remarks: Although previously reported in the province, this bird was first confirmed in Alberta in 1974 at Pakowki Lake where nesting was later established. This species is vulnerable to marsh drainage, human distur-bance and pesticide contamination. It will nest in colonies often with herons or other colonial birds. Ibis are primarily tropical birds and the White-faced is the lone western and northern straggler. It is virtually identical to the Glossy Ibis of the southeastern United States.

Jan	Feb	Mar	Apr	May	Jun	Jul	Aug	Sep	Oct	Nov	Dec

WFIB ❒   Date: _____

TURKEY VULTURE

Cathartes aura

L: 762 mm   W: 2100 g   Egg: 69 x 47 mm

Etymology: *Cathartes* (Gr.) - "a purifier;" *aura* - South American name for the bird.

Status and Distribution: There are thought to be less than 100 breeding pairs in the province. It is uncommon as it is at the northern limit of its range with records concentrated in the Cold Lake area south to the North Saskatchewan River and in the Red Deer River valley near Big Valley. Other areas with records include Wainwright, Cypress Hills and Chain Lakes.

● ●

Field Checklist

✓**Habitat:** These vultures like to roost in trees near a stable source of food and water. They nest in undisturbed areas, preferring rocky outcrops, caves and crevices in cliffs, or a scrape beneath a log in a mixed forest.

✓✓✓**Sight:** It is a large bird with a wing span up to 2 m. It has a dark coloration, a hooked beak and a naked, red upper neck and head. In flight, the body and fore-part of the wings appear dark and the flight feathers appear dark grey. The tail is long and rounded.

✓**Sound:** It is usually silent but may hiss when disturbed.

✓**Behavior:** Vultures are rarely seen on the ground except when feeding on carrion, and are most often observed circling on warm, rising air currents. When soaring, they hold their wings in a slight "V" unlike hawks whose wing profile is more horizontal.

● ●

Similar species: None in Alberta.

Remarks: This bird can be observed circling on thermals for hours with little visible evidence of wing movement. It feeds on carrion as its weak beak and feet are not suited to taking live prey.

Jan	Feb	Mar	Apr	May	Jun	Jul	Aug	Sep	Oct	Nov	Dec

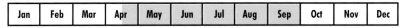

Order: Ciconiiformes - Family: Ardeidae

CATTLE EGRET
Bubulcus ibis

Photo: J.Kristensen

The first observations of this Old World species in North America were in 1940s and in Alberta in 1964, near Big Springs. There have been sporadic records, mainly in southern Alberta, since that time. Across North America it appears to be increasing in numbers, preferring open habitat such as pastures, fields and marshes where it may be found foraging in association with grazing animals.

This member of the heron family is small and stocky with a thick neck. It is white overall but in breeding plumage the crown, breast and mantle are buffy-orange. The short bill is yellow and the legs are a greenish-yellow. In immature birds the legs are dusky brown. It does not have a distinctive call but it will utter a series of croaking notes, most often when nesting.

It is a social species and prefers to nest in proximity to others, often in the same tree. This may take place near colonies of herons and there is some concern that these invaders will displace native species from limited nesting habitat.

• •

GREATER WHITE-FRONTED GOOSE

Anser albifrons

Photo: K.Morck

L: 714 mm   W: 2888 g   Egg: 76 x 52 mm

Etymology: *Anser* (L.) - "goose;" *albifrons* (L.) - *albus*, "white" and *frons*, "forehead."

Status and Distribution: This common spring and fall migrant uses the flyway in east-central Alberta, with staging taking place in the Hanna area, Beaverhill Lake and the Peace-Athabasca Delta.

• •

Field Checklist

✓**Habitat:** This goose is found on large bodies of water during migration with adjacent grassy or grain fields for feeding.

✓✓✓**Sight:** It is a medium-sized grayish-brown goose with no black on its head or neck and distinctive yellow legs. The white forehead and bill patch give this species its name. It has irregularly black-spotted underparts and a white rump.

✓✓**Sound:** Its high pitched "wah-wah" is distinct from the honking of the Canada Goose.

Behavior: When feeding and flying, they tend to be segregated from Canada and Snow geese, although they may be in proximity.

• •

Similar species: None

Remarks: This species is distinctive as it is the only Alberta gray goose without a black head. The White-front begins to migrate through Alberta in late March or early April on its way to its Arctic breeding grounds. Spring migration peaks in late April. Fall migration is more sporadic. The irregular black streaking on its breast gives this goose its common, local name, speckle-belly.

Jan	Feb	Mar	Apr	May	Jun	Jul	Aug	Sep	Oct	Nov	Dec

GWFG ❑   Date: _____

Ducks, Geese and Swans

Order: Anseriformes - Family: Anatidae

SNOW GOOSE

Chen caerulescens

L: 693 mm   W: 2130 g   Egg: 70 x 44.5 mm

Etymology: *Chen* (Gr.) - "goose;"
caerulescens (L.) - "bluish."

Status and Distribution: This common goose migrates through the province in both spring and fall. Its arrival at staging lakes in eastern Alberta can be predicted locally almost to the day.
Beaverhill Lake is one of the largest staging areas for the Snow Goose in Alberta and site of the Snow Goose Festival at the end of April.

• •

Field Checklist

Habitat: In Alberta it favors lakes, wet fields and grain fields during its migration and staging.

✓✓✓**Sight:** In the white phase, this goose is white with black wing tips, has a pinkish bill that is lined with a black "grin," and has purplish red legs. The blue phase has a predominantly slate-colored body with a white head and neck. In both phases, the head and upper neck can be rust-stained and the tails are grayish.

✓**Sound:** In flight and on the ground it utters a "kouk, kouk" chorus.

✓**Behavior:** They raft up in large flocks, away from shore on larger bodies of water and are extremely wary when choosing feeding grounds.

• •

Similar species: Ross's Goose

Remarks: The Snow Goose is larger than the Ross's Goose and has the grinning patch on its bill. It is noisy in flight while the Ross's Goose is usually silent. The local name "wavey" is derived from the Cree word "wa-wa," meaning wild goose. There are breeding records for Alberta but normally it is a high Arctic breeder.

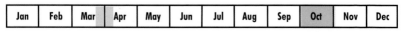

Jan	Feb	Mar	Apr	May	Jun	Jul	Aug	Sep	Oct	Nov	Dec

SNGO ☐   Date: _____

ROSS'S GOOSE
Chen rossii

Photo: R.Gehlert

L: 570 mm W: 1531 g Egg: 70 x 47 mm

Etymology: *Chen* (Gr.) - "goose;" *rossii* (ML.) - named after Bernard R. Ross, a chief factor of the Hudson's Bay Company.

Status and Distribution: This small goose is a regular migrant through eastern Alberta but is much less common than the Snow Goose.

• •

Field Checklist

Habitat: It visits shallow productive lakes in east-central Alberta during migration. Beaverhill Lake is an excellent location to view this bird during migration.

✓✓**Sight:** Ross's Goose is mainly white with black wing tips. The bill of this goose is dark at the base with numerous warty protuberances, which have provoked such attractive common names as "Scabby-nosed Wavey." The bill lacks the black patches, along the side, which gives the Snow Goose its "grin." The neck is relatively short compared to that of the Snow Goose.

✓✓**Sound:** It gives a rapid, shrill honking reminiscent of a Canada Goose.

✓**Behavior:** It is often flocked with Snow Geese but makes little noise while in flight. It eats grain and new growth in fields in Alberta to provide the energy to complete its migration.

• •

Similar species: Snow Goose, as noted above.

Remarks: On migration it arrives in Alberta earlier than the Snow Goose in both the spring and the fall, but both species can be observed at the same time at staging lakes. Almost all of the Ross's Goose population winters in central California and breeds in the high Arctic. Its breeding grounds were a mystery until the first nest was discovered in 1938.

Jan	Feb	Mar	Apr	May	Jun	Jul	Aug	Sep	Oct	Nov	Dec

ROGO ◻ Date: _____

Ducks, Geese and Swans

Order: Anseriformes - Family: Anatidae

CANADA GOOSE

Branta canadensis

Photo: B.Kulba

L: 870 mm   W: 3586 g   Egg: 87 x 59 mm

Etymology: *Branta* (ML.) - "to burn;" *canadensis* (ML.) - "Canadian," which refers to the bird's main summer range.

Status and Distribution: There are several distinct races of the Canada Goose in Canada. Some pass through as migrants, but only the large subspecies *B. c. moffitti* breeds here. Canada Geese breed throughout the province with concentrations in central and southern Alberta.

• •

Field Checklist

✓**Habitat:** Very adaptable, this goose usually congregates and nests near lakes, ponds, sloughs, rivers and irrigation reservoirs.

✓✓✓**Sight:** It varies in weight from 2 kg to 8 kg. This gray goose has a black head and neck with white cheek patches and sometimes a white collar at the base of the black neck. The underparts are usually lighter.

✓✓**Sound:** A sonorous honk.

✓**Behavior:** During nesting, the female incubates while the male stands guard nearby. Parents are very attentive to their young.

• •

Similar species: None.

Remarks: This is a distinctive species. Canada Geese exhibit strong pair and family bonds; the young fly south with the parents and return to the breeding grounds the following year. They are primary grazers eating the shoots of grasses and sedges. As their numbers increase, they are coming into conflict with people in areas such as golf courses. Overwintering has been recorded at several locations in the province where there is open water. Birders may choose different harbingers of spring, but for many the return of the Canada Goose in March is a much awaited event.

Jan	Feb	Mar	Apr	May	Jun	Jul	Aug	Sep	Oct	Nov	Dec

CAGO ☐   Date: _____

Order: Anseriformes - Family: Anatidae

TRUMPETER SWAN

Cygnus buccinator

L: 1465 mm   W: 7133 g   Egg: 111 x 72 mm

Etymology: *Cygnus* (Gr.) - *kyknos,* "swan;" *buccinator* (L.) - "trumpeter."

Status and Distribution: It is on Alberta's Blue List as a species that is considered endangered in the province with a breeding population of less than 100 pairs. The majority are found in the Peace River District near Grande Prairie. Smaller populations are found in the Whitecourt/Edson area, Elinor Lake, Fawcett Lake, Otter Lake, the Chinchaga River/Clear Hills area and Waterton Lakes and Elk Island National parks.

• •

Field Checklist

✓**Habitat:** This species is found on small-to-medium sized shallow, isolated lakes that have well established emergent and submergent vegetation.

✓✓**Sight:** The largest of North America's waterfowl, it has a wingspan over 2.4 m and can weigh up to 12 kg. It is completely white with a black bill.

✓✓✓**Sound:** The bird's long twisted windpipe acts as a resonating chamber to produce a loud bugle-like call.

✓**Behavior:** They are highly territorial in the spring so it is rare to see more than one pair on a lake.

• •

Similar species: Tundra Swan

Remarks: The Trumpeter Swan is larger than the Tundra Swan and its voice is considerably deeper and of a different quality. The Trumpeter never has a yellow or orange spot in front of the eye. Population numbers are limited by the lack of key wintering habitat in Idaho, Montana and Wyoming. Overwintering has occurred in mild winters in southern Alberta.

Jan	Feb	Mar	Apr	May	Jun	Jul	Aug	Sep	Oct	Nov	Dec

TPSW ❏   Date: _____

Ducks, Geese and Swans

GADWALL

Anas strepera

L: 496 mm   W: 913 g   Egg: 54 x 39 mm

Etymology: *Anas* (L.) - "a duck;" *strepera* (L.) - "noisy."

Status and Distribution: The Gadwall population is deemed to be stable in Alberta. It prefers the grassland and parkland and southern boreal regions of the province but is found in most areas.

Field Checklist

✓**Habitat:** The Gadwall is seen in marshes, sloughs and shallow lake margins with good cover and grassy margins extending far back from the shore. It prefers grassy islands for nesting and favors alkaline waters over fresh.

✓✓✓**Sight:** The back, sides and flanks of the male are grayish, finely vermiculated with buff. The upper wings are chestnut, chest is darker gray with buff crescent marks and the rump is black. The female has mottled brown upper parts and a white breast. Both have a distinctive white speculum bordered in black at the front.

✓✓**Sound:** The female has a high-pitched soft "quack" while the male has a low-pitched "raeh", followed by a whistled "cee, cee."

✓**Behavior:** The wingbeat is rapid and produces a low whistle.

Similar species: Female Mallard.

Remarks: Because the male lacks brilliant colors, it is one of the most misidentified species. The female differs from the female Mallard by the yellow sides on her gray bill, which is also shorter. The white wing patch is also distinctive in flight. Some of the highest nest densities in North America occur at Jessie Lake in Alberta. Overwintering is common.

Jan	Feb	Mar	Apr	May	Jun	Jul	Aug	Sep	Oct	Nov	Dec

GADW ☐   Date: _____

AMERICAN WIGEON

Anas americana

L: 480 mm   W: 735 g   Egg: 54 x 38

Etymology: *Anas* (L.) - "a duck;" *americana* (ML.)- "the American range."

Status and Distribution: The populations of this species are stable but the continued degradation of breeding habitat in agricultural areas is of concern. It breeds in all areas of the province with a preference for the parkland and southern boreal regions.

• •

Field Checklist

✓**Habitat:** It prefers larger sloughs and ponds and the marshy areas bordering large lakes. Nesting is in dry meadows adjacent to these water bodies.

✓✓✓**Sight:** The forehead and crown of the male are white, and there is a green face patch from the eye to the nape. The back, sides and upper breast are pinkish brown and the lower parts are white. The forewing has a large white patch and the speculum is green. The female is drab brown with gray streaks on the head and neck, the fore-wing has a less defined white patch and the belly is white.

✓**Sound:** The female gives a low "quack" and the male has a distinctive nasal whistle usually given in a series of three.

Behavior: It is known to take food directly from the mouths of American Coots and diving ducks such as the Canvasback and Redhead.

• •

Similar species: Eurasian Wigeon.

Remarks: The rare Eurasian has a brown face and cream-colored cap. The American Wigeon is distinctive with its white cap and green face patch. It is also known by the local name of baldpate. There are overwintering records for Lake Wabamun and southern Alberta.

Jan	Feb	Mar	Apr	May	Jun	Jul	Aug	Sep	Oct	Nov	Dec

AMWI ❑   Date: _____

Ducks, Geese and Swans

MALLARD
Anas platyrhynchos

L: 547 mm   W: 1092 g   Egg: 58 x 41 mm

Etymology: *Anas* (L.) - "a duck;" *platyrhynchos* (Gr.) - *platus,* "broad," and *rhynchos,* "bill."

Status and Distribution: This is the most widely distributed and abundant duck in Alberta. It breeds where suitable habitat is available.

Photo: D. Wood

• •

Field Checklist

✓**Habitat:** The presence of shallow-water feeding areas and availability of suitable nest sites are limiting factors for breeding. It uses marshes, ponds, the shallows of lakes, ditches and flooded land, foraging on both the water and land. The nest is on fairly dry ground where there is tall vegetation for cover.

✓✓✓**Sight:** The male in his breeding plumage has a brilliant green head and upper neck, a white collar and chestnut breast. The under-parts are a light gray. The female has a buff-colored head, brown back, buff breast streaked with darker brown and a purple wing patch bordered with white bars. In flight, the white on the tail is visible.

✓**Sound:** The female has a loud "quack, quack, quack" while the male's "quack" is softer and high-pitched.

Behavior: Mallards accumulate in large flocks in the fall, feeding on grain fields at dawn and dusk.

• •

Similar species: The female is similar to several other species.

Remarks: Several other female ducks have similar coloration but the purple speculum with the white borders is distinctive. The number of Mallards on the prairies is directly related to the number of ponds available for breeding. During dry conditions on the prairies, it will fly farther north into the boreal areas to nest. This is a common species on open water over winter and the ancestor of our domestic white duck.

Jan	Feb	Mar	Apr	May	Jun	Jul	Aug	Sep	Oct	Nov	Dec

MALL ☐   Date: _____

BLUE-WINGED TEAL

Anas discors

Photo: K.Morck

L: 377 mm   W: 372 g   Egg: 47 x 37 mm

Etymology: *Anas* (L.) - "a duck;" *discors* (Gr.) - *discoy* and *oris*, "disc about the mouth."

Status and Distribution: This is the common teal of the grassland and parkland regions. It is found in all areas of the province with suitable habitat, but is more common in the central and southern parts of Alberta.

●●●

Field Checklist

✓**Habitat:** It prefers marshes, sloughs, ponds and weedy edges of lakes and slow-moving water. It is found more along shore-lines than in open water. The nest is on dry ground but is seldom far from water.

✓✓✓**Sight:** The male of this small duck has a gray head with a large white crescent in front of the eye. The forewing is light blue with a white border. The light brown breast and flanks are spotted with black. The female has a uniformly brown head with a buffy mark just behind the bill and heavy brown streaking on the breast and flanks.

✓**Sound:** The male's call is a high-pitched "seef, seef, seef" while the female's call is a weak "quack."

Behavior: The Blue-wing is a dabbling duck and spends most of its time foraging on the surface or tipping (head-first plunges) in shallow water.

●●●

Similar species: Female Cinnamon Teal

Remarks: The females of these two species are too similar to separate in the field and can only be identified by seeing the accompanying male. To make it more challenging, these species are known to hybridize. Overwintering is not common, although it has been recorded at Calgary and Wabamun Lake.

Jan	Feb	Mar	Apr	May	Jun	Jul	Aug	Sep	Oct	Nov	Dec

BWTE ☐   Date: _____

Ducks, Geese and Swans

Order: Anseriformes - Family: Anatidae

CINNAMON TEAL

Anas cyanoptera

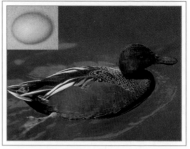

L: 396 mm   W: 384 g   Egg: 48 x 35 mm

Etymology: *Anas* (L.) - "a duck;" *cyanoptera* (Gr.) - *kuanos,* "dark blue" and *pteron,* "wing."

Status and Distribution: This duck has been recorded more frequently in Alberta in the last thirty years but is still considered an uncommon summer resident. It is found mainly in the grassland and parkland areas with records as far north as Ft. McMurray and Grande Prairie.

● ●

Field Checklist

✓**Habitat:** It prefers shallow lake margins, marshes, ponds and ditches with emergent vegetation and muddy shorelines.

✓✓✓**Sight:** The male is conspicuous with cinnamon red on the head, neck, shoulders, breast and flanks. The forewing is chalky-blue and the speculum is bright green with black borders. His summer plumage is similar to that of the female. She is heavily mottled, brown on the body and lighter on the head, with a blue patch on the forewing.

✓**Sound:** This teal is not very vocal. The drake has a rattling call while the female utters a weak "quack."

✓**Behavior:** Up and down movement of the head usually signals that this duck is about to take flight.

● ●

Similar species: Female Blue-winged Teal.

Remarks: So similar are females of these two species that it is almost impossible to differentiate between them without the presence of a mate. The Cinnamon Teal nest is often parasitized by the Redhead. There are few fall observations for this species, but this may be due to the lack of distinctive plumage at this time. No overwintering has been recorded. The spring male Cinnamon Teal is a spectacular bird. See if you can spot his red eye against the brilliant cinnamon plumage.

Jan	Feb	Mar	Apr	May	Jun	Jul	Aug	Sep	Oct	Nov	Dec

CITE ☐   Date: _____

NORTHERN SHOVELER

Anas clypeata

L: 472 mm   W: 576 g   Egg: 52 x 37 mm

Etymology: *Anas* (L.) - "a duck;" *clypeata* (L.) - "furnished with a shield," referring to the large bill.

Status and Distribution: Breeding populations of the Shoveler are stable. It nests across the province with the preferred areas being the parkland and grasslands.

Field Checklist

✓**Habitat:** It uses marshy areas with shallow waterways, muddy lakes, sloughs and bogs. It prefers those which contain abundant aquatic vegetation. Nests are on the ground in dry sites, close to water and sheltered by vegetation.

✓✓✓**Sight:** The bill is long and narrow at the base becoming wider at the tip. The breeding male has a green head, dull black throat, white breast, shoulders, patch in front of the tail, and a blue forewing. The female is buff and brown except for the blue forewing.

✓**Sound:** Not very vocal but the male utters a guttural "wook, wook, wook" while the female gives a weak "quack."

✓**Behavior:** To feed, it paddles slowly, moving its head from side to side filtering surface water through the lamellae of the bill to obtain small animals and plants.

Similar species: Female Mallard

Remarks: The male is quite distinctive; however, the female is primarily distinguished from the female Mallard by the spoon-shaped bill and the lack of a blue speculum. The uniquely shaped bill leads to the local name of "spoonbill." It is distinctive enough to be obvious in flight. Some overwintering has occurred at Lake Wabamun.

Jan	Feb	Mar	Apr	May	Jun	Jul	Aug	Sep	Oct	Nov	Dec

45   NOSV ❐   Date: _____

Ducks, Geese and Swans

Order: Anseriformes - Family: Anatidae

NORTHERN PINTAIL

Anas acuta

L: 595 mm   W: 834 g   Egg: 54 x 37 mm

Etymology: *Anas* (L.) - "a duck;" *acuta* (L.) - "sharp," referring to the bird's tail.

Status and Distribution: Although it showed drastic decreases in the past, its population has shown a recent recovery. The Pintail breeds throughout the province, but is most common in central and southern areas.

Field Checklist

Habitat: It favors open terrain with shallow ponds, marshes and reedy shallow lakes, usually with drier margins. Nesting is on the ground in areas with low or sparse vegetation.

✓✓✓**Sight:** It has a slim body and high neck profile. The male has a brown head and neck, white throat with a white line extending up either side of the neck to the ear. The back and sides are grayish and the two central tail feathers are long and black. The female has a brown and black streaked head and neck, the upper back is dark brown with "u"-shaped lighter markings, the speculum is bronze bordered with brown and white. The male resembles the female during the summer until early fall.

✓**Sound:** The male infrequently uses a high-pitched whistle while the female has a low-pitched "quack."

✓**Behavior:** This wary bird builds its nest farther from water than do other duck species.

Similar species: The female is similar to the female Mallard.

Remarks: She can be distinguished from the female Mallard by the lack of a purple speculum. Her speculum is bronze bordered by a reddish brown line in front and a thin white line behind. This species frequently overwinters where open water is available.

Jan	Feb	Mar	Apr	May	Jun	Jul	Aug	Sep	Oct	Nov	Dec

46

NOPI ❑   Date: _____

GREEN-WINGED TEAL

Anas crecca

Photo: D. Wood

L: 370 mm W: 325 g Egg: 46 x 32 mm

Etymology: *Anas* (L.) - "a duck;" *crecca* (Gr.) - *kreko,* "cause a string to sound by striking it."

Status and Distribution: The population of this duck is relatively stable in the province. The Green-winged Teal breeds in suitable habitat in all parts of the province.

• •

Field Checklist

✓**Habitat:** They prefer shallows of lakes, wooded ponds, and streams in parkland and boreal areas. Nesting is in upland areas with dense grass or brush. In prairie habitat, they normally nest on low ground near sloughs.

✓✓✓**Sight:** The breeding male of Alberta's smallest duck is grayish with a chestnut head and green face patch, a vertical white bar on the side of the body in front of the wing and a bright green wing patch (speculum). The female is dusky brown with a white throat, a dusky stripe through the eye and a small green wing patch.

✓**Sound:** The male's call is a whistling "dweep" and that of the female is a low soft quack.

✓**Behavior:** It is known to fly over 70 km per hour marking it as one of the fastest-flying ducks. The female will vigorously defend her young with a distraction display.

• •

Similar species: Blue-winged Teal and Cinnamon Teal.

Remarks: Although similar in size to the other two teal species, it can be distinguished from these teal by the lack of blue on the fore-wing. The Green-winged Teal overwinters in the province on a regular basis.

Jan	Feb	Mar	Apr	May	Jun	Jul	Aug	Sep	Oct	Nov	Dec

GWTE ☐ Date: _____

Ducks, Geese and Swans

CANVASBACK
Aythya valisineria

L: *525 mm* W: *1084 g* Egg: *61 x 43 mm*

Etymology: *Aythya* (Gr.) - "a kind of water bird;" *valisineria* (L.) - referring to a plant, the wild celery, eaten by this duck.

Status and Distribution: This is the least abundant of the major game duck species in North America. It is locally common in the parkland and southern boreal regions of the province. It is also found in the grassland region and nests in the Peace-Athabasca Delta. Beaverhill and Utikuma lakes are major resting lakes for moulting.

• •

Field Checklist

Habitat: The Canvasback prefers lakes and ponds with emergent vegetation including sedges, stands of bulrushes. In treed areas, it uses open marshes. Canvasbacks prefer to nest in cattail cover.

✓✓✓**Sight:** The male is distinguished by its long bill, sloping forehead, chestnut head and neck, and canvas-colored (white) back. The female has the same distinctive profile and has a light brown breast and grayish sides.

Sound: The male is usually silent but will use a cooing sound during courtship.

Behavior: The Canvasback nest is frequently parasitized by both the Redhead and the Ruddy Duck.

• •

Similar species: Redhead.

Remarks: The male Canvasback has the red of the head and neck extending to the shoulders and not ending at mid-neck as in the Redhead. The females of the two species are almost identically colored with the Canvasback being somewhat lighter. There are records of overwintering in Alberta.

Jan	Feb	Mar	Apr	May	Jun	Jul	Aug	Sep	Oct	Nov	Dec

CANV ❏ Date: _____

Order: Anseriformes - Family: Anatidae

REDHEAD

Aythya americana

L: 493 mm   W: 984 g   Egg: 58 x 41 mm

Photo: W. Burgess

Etymology: *Aythya* (Gr.) - "a kind of water bird;" *americana* (ML.) - referring to the American range.

Status and Distribution: Its population is not abundant but locally it is common. The Redhead is found in all parts of the province but only rarely in the mountain and foothills areas. It prefers the central part of Alberta. In the northeast, breeding records are scarce although it is seen during migration.

●●●●●●●●●●●●●●●●●●●●●●●●●●●●●●●●●●●●●●●

Field Checklist

✓**Habitat:** The Redhead prefers deeper lakes and ponds that provide fairly dense emergent vegetation for nesting cover.

✓✓✓**Sight:** The adult male has a bright coppery head and upper neck with a gray back and side. It has a bluish bill with a black tip. The female is uniformly brownish, slightly darker on the crown with a whitish chin and faint pale streak behind the eye.

✓**Sound:** In courtship the male utters a catlike "meow" and the female infrequently uses a "kurr, kurr, kurr".

✓**Behavior:** It exhibits the greatest tendency of all ducks towards nest parasitism - the laying of eggs in the nest of another bird. The Redhead female is a poor parent, often deserting her brood at an early stage.

●●●●●●●●●●●●●●●●●●●●●●●●●●●●●●●●●●●●●●●

Similar species: Canvasback

Remarks: It has a different head profile than the Canvasback with a more vertical forehead as opposed to the long sloping forehead of the Canvasback. The red of the head stops at mid-neck instead of continuing to the shoulders as in the Canvasback. The females are quite similar although the female Redhead is a bit darker. It will overwinter in areas of open water.

Jan	Feb	Mar	Apr	May	Jun	Jul	Aug	Sep	Oct	Nov	Dec

REDH ☐   Date: _____

Ducks, Geese and Swans

Order: Anseriformes - Family: Anatidae

RING-NECKED DUCK

Aythya collaris

Photo: G.Beyersbergen

L: 410 mm   W: 650 g   Egg: 58 x 41 mm

Etymology: *Aythya* (Gr.) - "a kind of water bird;" *collaris* (L.) - "collared."

Status and Distribution: The breeding population is stable. It breeds in northern and central Alberta south to Red Deer, with breeding localized in the southwest and the Cypress Hills.

• •

Field Checklist

Habitat: These divers prefer sloughs, marshes, swamps, beaver impoundments and bogs, and are usually not found far from shore on large expanses of open water.

✓✓✓**Sight:** The male has a black head and neck glossed with purple, a black back and breast, gray sides and a white band extending upward in front of the folded wing. Its bill is gray-blue with a white ring near the black tip and a white line at the base. It has an inconspicuous chestnut ring at the base of the neck. The female is grayish-brown with an white eye ring and a white ring near the tip of the bill.

Sound: Usually silent but during courtship it will use a high-pitched whistle while the female utters a low growl.

Behavior: It feeds in shallower water than most diving ducks.

• •

Similar species: Lesser Scaup.

Remarks: The male is separated from the Lesser Scaup by the completely black back, the white line at the base of the bill and the light ring near the tip of the bill. Both sexes have a gray speculum whereas the scaup's is white. It has been recorded overwintering at Lake Wabamun and in Edmonton.

Jan	Feb	Mar	Apr	May	Jun	Jul	Aug	Sep	Oct	Nov	Dec

RNDU ☐   Date: _____

Ducks, Geese and Swans

GREATER SCAUP

Aythya marila

L: 460 mm   W: 900 g   Egg: 63.5 x 43 mm

Etymology: *Aythya* (Gr.) - "a kind of water bird;" *marila* (Gr.) - *marile*, "charcoal."

Status and Distribution: This is an uncommon migrant in the province and its breeding status is uncertain as northern Alberta is the southern limit of its breeding range. Reports of possible breeding activity come from the Caribou Mountains, north of Ft. Vermilion.

● ●

Field Checklist

✓**Habitat:** The Greater Scaup prefers larger bodies of water including lakes, ponds and slow reaches of rivers, nesting on the ground with little cover, in proximity to water.

✓✓✓**Sight:** The male is black on the head, neck, front part of the body and the tail. The head and neck have a green gloss over the black. The middle back is barred black and white and the abdomen is white. The wing is dark with a white speculum. The female has a dark brown head with a white area at the base of the bill. The upper parts of the body are dark brown with a white speculum and the lower parts are brown.

✓**Sound:** Similar to the Lesser Scaup. The male is usually quiet but uses a soft cooing during courtship; the female gives a low "carrr."

Behavior: It is more often associated with open and larger water bodies than is the Lesser Scaup.

● ●

Similar species: Lesser Scaup.

Remarks: It is distinguished from the Lesser Scaup by the green, not purple, gloss over its black head and neck, the distinctive and longer white wing bar and the whiter sides and flanks. It is recorded earlier in the spring in Alberta than is the Lesser Scaup.

Jan	Feb	Mar	Apr	May	Jun	Jul	Aug	Sep	Oct	Nov	Dec

GRSC ☐   Date: _____

Ducks, Geese and Swans

Order: Anseriformes - Family: Anatidae

LESSER SCAUP

Aythya affinis

L: 414 mm   W: 702 g   Egg: 57 x 39 mm

Photo: G.Beyersbergen

Etymology: *Aythya* (Gr.) - "a kind of water bird;" *affinis* (L.) - "related," to the Greater Scaup.

Status and Distribution: This species is relatively abundant in the province. It is found in all regions with suitable habitat, but is less common in the mountain areas. In the grassland it is locally common where suitable water bodies exist.

● ●

Field Checklist

✓**Habitat:** The Lesser Scaup prefers permanent water bodies with dense emergent vegetation along the margins. It nests in uplands with tall and dense herbaceous vegetation in proximity to the water. Islands are favored nesting sites.

✓✓**Sight:** The male is black on the front half of its body with a purple sheen to the dark head. The back is gray while the sides and flanks are white vermiculated with gray, and the tail is dark. The female has dark brown upper parts and is buffy brown below, with a distinctive white facial mark between the bill and the eye.

✓**Sound:** The male is vocal only in courtship using a cooing sound, while the female sounds a low "carrr".

Behavior: This scaup nests later than any other duck in Alberta.

● ●

Similar species: Greater Scaup and Ring-necked Duck.

Remarks: It has a purplish sheen to the head and not green as seen on the Greater Scaup. The white wing stripe is shorter and there is more gray on the sides compared to its larger relative. Its back is gray, not black like the Ring-necked Duck and the white stripe on the wing, which is visible in flight, is not present on the Ring-necked. It is a late fall migrant and overwintering records exist for areas of open water.

Jan	Feb	Mar	Apr	May	Jun	Jul	Aug	Sep	Oct	Nov	Dec

LESC ☐   Date: _____

Order: Anseriformes - Family: Anatidae

Ducks, Geese and Swans

HARLEQUIN DUCK

Histrionicus histrionicus

L: 407 mm W: 552 g Egg: 58 x 42 mm

Photo: T.Thormin

Etymology: *Histrionicus* (L.) - *histrio,* "stage player," referring to the plumage.

Status and Distribution: This species is on the Yellow List due to concerns over a long term decline and their restricted distribution. Alberta is the eastern limit of the Pacific population. Breeding records are restricted to the mountains and foothills; however, there are observations of this duck well to the east of the mountains.

• •

Field Checklist

✓✓**Habitat:** It chooses pristine breeding habitat away from disturbance, favoring fast-flowing mountain streams that provide suitable food and sheltered nest sites. The streams are usually surrounded by forest or patches of willow and alder.

✓✓✓**Sight:** The male is slate blue with bright chestnut sides and flanks while the female is dull brown. Both sexes have grayish-white areas on the cheeks, white between the eye and the forehead, and a rounded white spot between the eye and the back of the neck.

✓**Sound:** Males are usually quiet but will give a low whistling sound; females utter a low croak.

Behavior: The male leaves the breeding area and returns to the coast shortly after incubation begins.

• •

Similar species: Female Bufflehead and female Ruddy Duck

Remarks: The female Harlequin is larger and darker than the Bufflehead, and has three white spots instead of one on the face. She has a narrower bill than the Ruddy and she is sooty brown without the reddish tinge. Although this duck is on the Yellow list, governments continue to approve commercial activities that are deleterious to this species.

Jan	Feb	Mar	Apr	May	Jun	Jul	Aug	Sep	Oct	Nov	Dec

HADU ❐ Date: _____

Ducks, Geese and Swans

SURF SCOTER

Melanitta perspicillata

L: 475 mm W: 958 g Egg: 61 x 43 mm

Etymology: *Melanitta* (Gr.) - *mellas,* "black" and *nitta,* "duck;" *perspicillata* (L.) - "conspicuous."

Status and Distribution: This is a rare breeder in the province, with nesting records widespread throughout central and northern Alberta. Alberta is the southern limit of its continental breeding range. They are more common on migration.

• •

Field Checklist

✓**Habitat:** It favors lakes, ponds, bogs or streams with adjacent shrubby cover or wooded areas. The nest is away from water and sheltered by low branches and shrubs.

✓✓✓**Sight:** The adult male is thickset, black with a white triangle on the forehead and another on the nape, a white eye and a black patch on the sides of the bill. The bill is heavy at the base and marked with red, orange, black and white. The female has a brownish-black head with white cheek, ear and nape markings. The upper body is dark brown, paling somewhat in the lower parts.

✓**Sound:** Usually quiet, but it can utter a croaking sound. In flight, the wings produce a loud whistle.

✓**Behavior:** As this duck dives, it springs clear of the water and lunges forward and down in a high arc. It opens its wings as it dives and uses them for propulsion under water.

• •

Similar species: White-winged Scoter

Remarks: Both sexes lack the white on the wings, which is a distinctive feature on the White-winged Scoter.

Jan	Feb	Mar	Apr	May	Jun	Jul	Aug	Sep	Oct	Nov	Dec

SUSC ☐ Date: _____

WHITE-WINGED SCOTER

Melanitta fusca

Photo: G. Beyersbergen

L: 520 mm   W: 1579 g   Egg: 71 x 48 mm

Etymology: *Melanitta* (Gr.) - *mellas* "black" and *nitta* "duck;" *fusca* (L.) - "dark, dusky."

Status and Distribution: The most common breeding scoter in the province, it is not abundant anywhere in its range. The small breeding population is widespread and found in every region except the mountains. In spring and fall migration, this duck can be seen anywhere.

• •

Field Checklist

✓**Habitat:** It breeds near ponds, lakes, oxbows and sluggish streams in open country where there is low dense ground cover for nesting. Undisturbed islands are readily utilized. The nest is usually in a patch of brush or herbaceous growth.

✓✓✓**Sight:** The male is black with a large crescent-shaped marking below the eye and a small one above the eye. The female is sooty, olive-brown overall with small white cheek and ear patches. Both have prominent white wing patches in flight, a thick neck and a swollen region at the base of the bill.

✓**Sound:** A croaking voice is the best they can do.

✓**Behavior:** They have unusual endurance underwater with dives commonly exceeding one minute. Except when the female is nesting, these ducks do not come to shore.

• •

Similar species: Surf Scoter

Remarks: The male White-winged Scoter does not have the white triangle on his nape and forehead that the Surf Scoter does and both sexes display the white wing patch. They are most commonly seen in rafts of various sizes or in low flight over the water.

Jan	Feb	Mar	Apr	May	Jun	Jul	Aug	Sep	Oct	Nov	Dec

WWSC ❐   Date: _____

Ducs, Geese and Swans

Order: Anseriformes - Family: Anatidae

BUFFLEHEAD
Bucephala albeola

Photo: T. Thormin

L: 364 mm   W: 411 g   Egg: 51 x 37 mm

Etymology: *Bucephala* (Gr.) - *bous*, "ox or bull" and *kephale*, "head;" *albeola* (L.) -*albus*, "white" and *olus*, diminutive suffix; "little white head."

Status and Distribution: The Bufflehead population is stable with breeding recorded in all regions. The highest concentrations are in central Alberta. They are scattered in northern Alberta and relatively uncommon in the south.

Field Checklist

✓**Habitat:** It prefers small lakes with vegetated margins and extensive open water, and areas where poplar communities dominate. The nest is in a tree cavity close to water.

✓✓✓**Sight:** The male of this small diving duck has a disproportionately large, dark head with a conspicuous broad white area extending back from the eyes. The body is mostly white and the centre of the back is black. The female is dark brown, white below and has a small white cheek and wing patch.

✓**Sound:** The female's call is a low hoarse quack while the male uses a squeaky whistling call.

Behavior: They are paired when they reach their breeding areas and start nesting soon after arrival.

Similar species: Female scaup and female Harlequin Duck.

Remarks: The female Bufflehead is smaller than the scaups and has the white cheek patch rather than the white patch at the base of the bill. It differs from the female Harlequin by its solid white underparts and one rather than two cheek patches. The continued clearing of poplar for agriculture and forestry is reducing the breeding habitat of this duck. There are several overwintering records from areas of open water.

Jan	Feb	Mar	Apr	May	Jun	Jul	Aug	Sep	Oct	Nov	Dec

56

BUFF ❒   Date: _____

COMMON GOLDENEYE
Bucephala clangula

L: 448 mm W: 793 g Egg: 60 x 43 mm

Etymology: *Bucephala* (Gr.) - *bous,* "ox or bull" and *kephale,* "head;" *clangula* (ML.) - "noise," referring to the whistle of the wings.

Status and Distribution: It is a common breeder in the central part of Alberta, uncommon in the south and is widely distributed in the northern parts of the province.

• •

Field Checklist

✓✓**Habitat:** Preference is for woodland lakes, shallows of rivers and muskeg ponds with marshy shores and adjacent stands of deciduous trees for nest sites. It nests in natural cavities, abandoned holes of large woodpeckers or nest boxes.

✓✓✓**Sight:** The male is mostly white-bodied with a black back, iridescent green head, and an oval white mark between the bill and the eye. The female has a gray and white body, brown head and narrow white collar.

✓**Sound:** The male's call is a high "jeee-at" and the female uses a low "grack." In flight the rapid wingbeats produce a whistling sound.

✓**Behavior:** The hatchlings climb to the entrance of the nest and jump to the ground with small wings outstretched to break their fall and then hike to find water.

• •

Similar species: Barrow's Goldeneye.

Remarks: This goldeneye has a greenish sheen to the head and an oval white patch between eye and bill, whereas the Barrow's has a purplish sheen and a distinctive crescent-shaped white patch between eye and bill. The females are so similar that only their association with the male will separate them. It is a wondrous sight to see this duck circling and then landing in a boreal forest spruce tree.

Jan	Feb	Mar	Apr	May	Jun	Jul	Aug	Sep	Oct	Nov	Dec

COGO ❏ Date: _____

Ducks, Geese and Swans

Order: Anseriformes - Family: Anatidae

BARROW'S GOLDENEYE

Bucephala islandica

L: 479 mm W: 1075 g Egg: 62 x 45 mm

Etymology: *Bucephala* (Gr.) - *bous*, "ox or bull" and *kephale*, "head;" *islandica* (ML.) - "of Iceland."

Status and Distribution: The eastern limit of the western Canadian population is in southwestern Alberta. The majority of the breeding is in the mountains and foothills. There are migration records from Wood Buffalo National Park and the Cypress Hills.

● ●

Field Checklist

✓**Habitat:** They prefer alkaline lakes, beaver ponds and stream-side sloughs, with a dense growth of submerged vegetation. The nest is in abandoned woodpecker or flicker holes enlarged by natural decay. It is normally over or near water.

✓✓✓**Sight:** Barrow's is a white duck with a black head and back. There is a purplish sheen to the head and a crescent-shaped white patch between the bill and the eyes. The white wing patch is divided horizontally by a black bar. The female is gray and white with a brown head and white collar.

Sound: Usually quiet, but the male may use a whistling call during courtship.

Behavior: Females with broods are very aggressive towards other females with broods.

● ●

Similar species: Common Goldeneye

Remarks: This goldeneye has a purple sheen to the head and a distinctive crescent-shaped white patch compared to the green sheen and oval-shaped patch of the Common Goldeneye. The females are similar and can only be differentiated by their association with the male. Hybridization between the two goldeneye species has been reported. Overwintering occurs in Alberta.

Jan	Feb	Mar	Apr	May	Jun	Jul	Aug	Sep	Oct	Nov	Dec

BOGO ☐   Date: _____

HOODED MERGANSER

Lophodytes cucullatus

L: 422 mm W: 640 g Egg: 54 x 45 mm

Etymology: *Lophodytes* (Gr.) - *lophos,* "a crest" and *dytes,* "diver;" *cucullatus* (L.) - "hooded."

Status and Distribution: It is uncommon in the province and has been reported breeding intermittently at

several locations including the three mountain national parks, the Crowsnest Pass, Longview, Barrhead, Fort Mackay, Camrose and near Taber.

● ●

Field Checklist

✓**Habitat:** This merganser breeds in ponds, lakes and rivers that have a margin of emergent vegetation, fish available for food, and a woodland border to provide nest sites.

✓✓✓**Sight:** The male has a black head, neck and back, reddish brown sides, and white underparts with two black bands across the breast. A large white triangular patch on the back of the head forms part of a large and expandable crest. The female has a grayish-brown head and throat, dark brown upper parts with a white wing patch, pale grayish-brown underparts and a white belly. She often holds her crest raised.

Sound: Usually quiet, but the male may give a croaking call.

✓**Behavior:** While tending the brood, the female uses a distraction display to draw away intruders while the young dive and swim away to hide in shoreline vegetation.

● ●

Similar species: None

Remarks: It is one of the fastest-flying ducks but its body shape makes it awkward on land, and it requires long takeoffs from water. It has been recorded overwintering at Lake Wabamun and Calgary.

Jan	Feb	Mar	Apr	May	Jun	Jul	Aug	Sep	Oct	Nov	Dec

59

Ducks, Geese and Swans

Order: Anseriformes - Family: Anatidae

RED-BREASTED MERGANSER

Mergus serrator

Photo: G.Beyersbergen

L: 550 mm W: 993 g Egg: 64 x 43 mm

Etymology: *Mergus* (L.) - "a diver;" *serrator* (L.) - "one who saws."

Status and Distribution: The status is not known but it is an uncommon breeder. The breeding range is north of Lesser Slave Lake, with extralimital records to Red Deer and Rocky Mountain House.

● ●

Field Checklist

✓✓**Habitat:** They prefer the bays, lagoons and estuaries of larger lakes and rivers, using more open, deeper water than the Common Merganser. Their nests are on the ground usually within 10 m of water and sheltered by low vegetation.

✓✓✓**Sight:** The male has a glossy, dark green head and upper neck, a black back, white underparts, red legs and bill. It has a double pointed crest, mottled sides and a reddish band across the breast. The female has a pale reddish-cinnamon head that blends gradually into the gray neck. Upper body is gray, sides brownish-gray and lower parts are white.

✓✓**Sound:** The male's vocalization is a "yeow, yeow" while the female has a harsh "karr, karr".

✓**Behavior:** It hunts with its head submerged as it looks for prey.

● ●

Similar species: Common Merganser.

Remarks: The double pointed crest and the reddish band distinguish this male from the male Common Merganser. The females of the two species are more similar with the female Red-breasted lacking the sharply contrasting definition on the throat. There are more records for spring migration than for the fall, and overwintering has been recorded in the province.

Jan	Feb	Mar	Apr	May	Jun	Jul	Aug	Sep	Oct	Nov	Dec

RBME ☐   Date: _____

Order: Anseriformes - Family: Anatidae

Photo: G.Beyersbergen

Ducks, Geese and Swans

COMMON MERGANSER

Mergus merganser

L: 606 mm W: 1416 g Egg: 66 x 46 mm

Etymology: *Mergus* (L.) - "a diver;" *anser* (L.) - "goose."

Status and Distribution: This merganser is not deemed to be at risk because its population is stable. Common in the mountains, foothills and boreal areas where habitat is available. It is uncommon in the south.

• •

Field Checklist

✓**Habitat:** As with other mergansers, it prefers lakes and rivers with clear water and wooded shores that provide nesting areas. They commonly nest in a tree cavity or in a nest box, but have been known to nest on the ground.

✓✓✓**Sight:** The male has a black head and upper neck that are darkly glossed over in green, black back, and a gray rump. The sides, breast and belly are white with a salmon tinge. The female has a conspicuous head crest, head and upper neck are brown with a sharp line where it meets the gray lower neck. The upper throat has a white patch. Both sexes have the red bill, iris and legs characteristic of mergansers.

✓**Sound:** The female utters a harsh "karr, karr" while the male uses a twangy note.

✓**Behavior:** They will cooperatively cut off a school of fish and drive it into the shallows, engulfing the prey as it becomes trapped.

• •

Similar species: Red-breasted Merganser

Remarks: The male Common Merganser is larger, has white sides and lacks the crest and reddish breast band of the Red-breasted Merganser. The female Common shows a sharper delineation between her red neck and white breast. There are several overwintering records for the province.

Jan	Feb	Mar	Apr	May	Jun	Jul	Aug	Sep	Oct	Nov	Dec

61

COME ☐   Date: _____

Ducks, Geese and Swans

Order: Anseriformes - Family: Anatidae

RUDDY DUCK

Oxyura jamaicensis

Photo: D. Wood

L: 388 mm   W: 622 g   Egg: 64 x 42 mm

Etymology: *Oxyura* (Gr.) - *oxys*, "sharp" and *ura*, "tail;" *jamaicensis* (ML.) - "of Jamaica."

Status and Distribution: It breeds across the province. It is common in the central part of the province, less common in the south and rare in mountains and foothills.

• •

Field Checklist

✓**Habitat:** The Ruddy Duck prefers permanent water bodies with emergent vegetation and stable water levels. Nesting habitat must have open water close to nesting cover, including emergent plants providing adequate cover density.

✓✓✓**Sight:** The small male has a reddish body plumage, a black cap on the head, white cheeks and a bright blue bill. The female is dark brown above, lighter below, and has a gray bill and a white cheek that is divided horizontally by a brown bar. Both sexes have broad flattened bills and long tails that are usually held cocked above the body.

Sound: During the breeding season the male will give a croaking call "chi, chi, chi, chi, queer."

Behavior: If disturbed, it will dive rather than fly.

• •

Similar species: Female Bufflehead and female Harlequin Duck

Remarks: The female Ruddy Duck does not have a white wing spot, is not as white below as the female Bufflehead and has different facial markings from both the female Bufflehead and Harlequin. This duck is quite grebe-like with large feet and hind limbs positioned far back on the body. Unlike most ducks, the male will stay on the nesting grounds and accompany the brood through the breeding season. The erect tail gives them their group name "stiff-tailed ducks." Overwintering has been recorded in the province.

Jan	Feb	Mar	Apr	May	Jun	Jul	Aug	Sep	Oct	Nov	Dec

RUDU ☐   Date: _____

EURASIAN WIGEON

Anas penelope

Photo: T. Thormin

This Old World species has reached North America from both the east and west and is likely nesting on this continent. In Alberta it is a scarce transient, recorded more often in the spring than fall. Seen locally only as males or pairs, they mainly occur in the grasslands areas. It is often seen in the presence of the American Wigeon. It prefers marshes and margins of shallow waterbodies with open fields nearby.

It is similarly patterned to the American Wigeon but the male has a rusty red head and neck, and the forehead and crown are a creamy buff. The females of the two species are very difficult to separate in the field. Although the female Eurasian may have some rusty coloration on the head, the main feature separating the two is the grayish axillars in the Eurasian wigeon and the white axillars in the American.

● ●

AMERICAN BLACK DUCK

Anas rubripes

This duck, commonly called the Black Mallard, is very common in eastern Canada but only a sporadic visitor to Alberta. Scattered breeding records over the last fifty years occur mainly in the central part of the province. There have also been reports of interbreeding between this species and Mallards in the Calgary area. Records for the province have been of single birds or pairs. It is very difficult to differentiate this species from female Mallards.

It is similar to the Mallard in its preferred choice of a wide variety of aquatic habitats for breeding and feeding and grain fields for foraging in the fall. The call, a series of quacks, is again similar to the Mallard. It resembles a very dark female Mallard. The upperparts are a dark brown, with the face, chin and throat somewhat lighter. The face is slightly streaked. The wing patch is purple, bordered in black rather than white as in the Mallard. The underwings are a silvery-white. The bill of the male is greenish-yellow and that of the female a pale drab green.

OLDSQUAW

Clangula hyemalis

The Oldsquaw, an abundant species in North America, is a regular migrant in northern Alberta and the mountains with a few records from southern areas of the province. It is recorded most often in the spring, though only in small numbers. Fall records are fewer and are mainly from southern Alberta.

This duck has three distinctive seasonal color changes. In the late spring when it is most likely to be observed in the province, the male has a dark brown head, neck, breast and back with white underparts. The sides of the head have a mask-like gray patch and there is a small white patch near the eye. Very conspicuous are the long, narrow, central tail feathers. The female has dark brown upper parts, the feathers edged lighter; the lower parts are white with a dull brown breast band. There is a dark crown patch on the head extending down the back of the neck and dark patches on the cheek and ear, with a white eye ring extending back from the eye.

This is a vocal duck with a variety of musical, somewhat yodelling calls characterized as "ow-ow-owlla."

OSPREY

Pandion haliaetus

L: 578 mm W: 1610 g Egg: 61 x 46 mm

Etymology: *Pandion* (Gr.) - *pan*, "all" and *dio* "God;" *haliaetus* (Gr.) - *halos* "the sea" and *aetos*, "eagle."

Status and Distribution: The status of the Osprey in Alberta is unknown although it is believed to be in decline in Western Canada. It is found throughout Alberta; in the arid southeastern portions it is rare.

Field Checklist

✓✓**Habitat:** It is found in the vicinity of permanent lakes and rivers with an adequate supply of fish and nesting sites.

✓✓✓**Sight:** A large narrow-winged raptor that has dark brown upperparts and white underparts sometimes with a faint band of light brown spots on the breast. The head has a white throat, black ear-bars, a crest of white, dark-tipped feathers and a black beak. The tail is barred with pale brown.

✓**Sound:** A high-pitched whistling "kayu, kayu, kayu," usually consisting of 10 - 14 calls.

✓✓**Behavior:** The birds hunt high over shallow waters, diving on prey, hitting the water feet first with wings raised above its back.

Similar species: None

Remarks: Its presence near water and its hunting methods make it distinctive. It builds enormous nests of large sticks and branches in isolated tree tops or a man-made structure. The nests are reused and augmented each year. Although its prey is entirely fish, studies have shown that the majority of its food is fish of low economic importance. It is critical that its nest sites be protected. Bald Eagles are known to harass Osprey carrying fish, in an attempt to rob them of their catch. There have been records of overwintering in the southern part of the province.

Jan	Feb	Mar	Apr	May	Jun	Jul	Aug	Sep	Oct	Nov	Dec

OSPR ❏   Date: _____

Hawks and Eagles

BALD EAGLE

Haliaeetus leucocephalus

L: 830 mm   W: 4639 g   Egg: 71 x 54 mm

Etymology: *Haliaetus* (Gr.) - *halos,* "the sea" and *aetos,* "eagle;" *leucocephalus* (Gr.) - *leukos,* "white" and *cephalos,* "head."

Status and Distribution: In Alberta, the Bald Eagle has a low density over most of its range. It is most common in the northern half of the province and the western foothills and mountains. It is uncommon in the southeastern part of Alberta

• •

Field Checklist

✓✓**Habitat:** Its primary nesting requirements are proximity to a large body of water with suitable tall trees near shore for nesting and roosting, and a good fish population.

✓✓✓**Sight:** A large dark brown eagle (2 m wingspan) with a white head, neck and tail in adult birds. Juvenile birds have a darker buffy brown head that lightens in successive years, reaching the white stage in the fourth or fifth year.

✓**Sound:** A weak high-pitched scream.

✓**Behavior:** They are opportunistic feeders with scavenged and live fish forming the bulk of their diet but they also take grounded or injured waterfowl. They are well known for their piracy of prey from other eagles, hawks and mergansers.

• •

Similar species: Juveniles similar to Golden Eagle, the Bald having a larger beak and unfeathered lower legs.

Remarks: In adult plumage, this eagle is unmistakable. Bald Eagles are normally solitary nesters but sometimes several pairs will nest close to one another. There are several overwintering records mainly in southern Alberta, but it has been recorded north to Edmonton and Wabamun Lake.

Jan	Feb	Mar	Apr	May	Jun	Jul	Aug	Sep	Oct	Nov	Dec

BAEA ☐   Date: _____

NORTHERN HARRIER

Circus cyaneus

L: *498 mm* W: *371 g* Egg: *47 x 36 mm*

Etymology: *Circus* (Gr.) - *kirkos,* "a kind of hawk;" *cyaneus* (Gr.) - *kyaneous,* "dark blue."

Status and Distribution: At present in Alberta there is a concern over the

declining southern breeding populations. It is found throughout the province but is most common in central and southern areas.

●●

Field Checklist

✓**Habitat:** It is a bird of open country where it hunts over marshes, meadows and cultivated fields.

✓✓✓**Sight:** This medium-sized hawk has a long slender profile. The male bird is light gray above, white below and has black wing tips. The female (pictured above) is reddish-brown above and white below. Both have a distinctive white rump patch on the upper tail. It has a partial facial disc, a ruff of feathers that allows it to focus sound.

Sound: Vocalizes infrequently but may issue a chattering noise near the nest.

✓✓**Behavior:** It has a spectacular aerial courtship ritual which has been described as "skydancing." It also has a distinctive hunting style which is a slow sail over open terrain, often less than 3 metres above the ground. When prey is sighted, it drops to the ground to seize it. When soaring, its wings are held above horizontal, which is different from most hawks.

●●●●●●●●●●●●●●●●●●●●●●●●●●●●●●●●●●●●●●

Similar species: None, as this is North America's only harrier.

Remarks: Management agencies are concerned that the Northern Harrier's breeding and foraging habitats are deteriorating with the elimination of large wetlands in the prairie-parkland areas of the province. There are winter records for this bird in the Lethbridge, Medicine Hat and High River areas.

Jan	Feb	Mar	Apr	May	Jun	Jul	Aug	Sep	Oct	Nov	Dec

NOHA ❏   **Date:** _____

SHARP-SHINNED HAWK

Accipiter striatus

L: 335 mm   W: 151 g   Egg: 38 x 40 mm

Etymology: *Accipiter* (L.) - "hawk;" *striatus* (L.) - "striped," referring to streaks on breast.

Status and Distribution: Although its status is still rated as unknown, it is not considered at risk. This hawk is found throughout the forested areas of the province.

• •

Field Checklist

✓**Habitat:** The Sharp-shinned Hawk prefers thick deciduous and mixedwood forests to heavy conifer growth.

✓✓✓**Sight:** The smallest of Alberta's accipiters, it has a square, notched tail. It is grayish blue above including the head, has a white throat and the lowerparts are transversely barred with reddish brown and white.

✓**Sound:** Usually only vocal only near the nest, the call is a high-pitched "ke, ke, ke, ke."

✓**Behavior:** The flight is a swift and irregular series of alternating strokes and short glides. They rarely hunt in the open, preferring to sit and wait for prey to move before attacking. Birds are rarely seen above the forest canopy except in display.

• •

Similar species: Cooper's Hawk and Merlin.

Remarks: This hawk is very similar to Cooper's Hawk but is smaller, has relatively longer legs and a square as opposed to a round tail. It can be separated from the Merlin by its shorter, rounder wings and lack of a tooth-like projection on the upper beak. Its main food is the smaller species of passerines such as sparrows. Overwintering birds have been observed in southern Alberta.

Jan	Feb	Mar	Apr	May	Jun	Jul	Aug	Sep	Oct	Nov	Dec

SSHA ☐   Date: _____

COOPER'S HAWK

Accipiter cooperii

L: 415 mm W: 310 g Egg: 49 x 38 mm

Etymology: *Accipiter*(L.) - "hawk;" *cooperii* (L.) - for William Cooper, 19th century American collector.

Status and Distribution: The status of this species is unknown in the province although future clearing of parkland aspen-bluffs threatens nesting habitat. This bird has been observed in various regions of the province; however, the northern limit of nesting seems to be Lesser Slave Lake.

● ●

Field Checklist

Habitat: It prefers dense pure or mixed forests as opposed to the forest edge. The nest is in dense cover, often near water, but rarely in conifers.

✓✓✓**Sight:** The male is bluish-gray above, with a grayish-black head and white throat. The rounded, long tail has four broad, dark brown bands and the wings are short, rounded and barred below. The female is larger and has broader breast bars.

✓✓**Sound:** A fast succession of "kiek, kiek, kiek, kiek." The male will "sing" to the female during incubation using a soft, modulated version of its cackling call.

Behavior: This unobtrusive bird is very rarely seen in the open. During the breeding season these inconspicuous birds are even more shy and secretive.

● ●

Similar species: Sharp-shinned Hawk and Goshawk.

Remarks: This hawk is similar to the Sharp-shinned but is larger and has a rounded as opposed to a square tail and stouter legs. Less than half the length of the Cooper's leg is feathered while that of the larger Goshawk is feathered more than half-way down its length. Individuals have been observed overwintering as far north as Edmonton and Wabamun Lake.

Jan	Feb	Mar	Apr	May	Jun	Jul	Aug	Sep	Oct	Nov	Dec

COHA ☐   Date: _____

Hawks and Eagles

NORTHERN GOSHAWK

Accipiter gentilis

L: 565 mm   W: 917 g   Egg: 59 x 45 mm

Etymology: *Accipiter*(L.) - "hawk;" *gentilis*(L.) - "noble."

Photo: K.Morck

Status and Distribution: The current status of this raptor is unknown in the province although there were several breeding records from the Alberta Bird Atlas survey. This species breeds most commonly in the densely wooded parts of northern and western Alberta.

● ●

Field Checklist

✓**Habitat:** They are found in a variety of forested habitats, usually in dense mixed forests, but sometimes in areas interspersed with clearings and cultivation.

✓✓✓**Sight:** This is a large hawk that is bluish-gray above and has white lower parts barred with gray. The head is darker with a white band above the eye. It has rounded wings that are uniformly barred below and a long tail that has four dark, broad bands.

✓**Sound:** A repetitive "kaek, kaek, kaek."

✓✓**Behavior:** Its typical flight pattern is short, rapid wing-strokes followed with a glide. When hunting it will make a quiet, concealed approach gliding in low and fast. It is often involved in dramatic aerial pursuits of avian prey. They are fierce defenders of their nesting site.

● ●

Similar species: Juveniles can be confused with Cooper's Hawk.

Remarks: They are generally migratory but individuals may overwinter in their breeding grounds or move south into the parklands and prairies. Overwintering is recorded from a number of localities throughout the province, north to Wembley and Fort McMurray. Failure of cyclic northern food species will also cause a substantial movement southward.

Jan	Feb	Mar	Apr	May	Jun	Jul	Aug	Sep	Oct	Nov	Dec

NOGO ☐   Date: _____

BROAD-WINGED HAWK

Buteo platypterus

L: 403 mm   W: 359 g   Egg: 49 x 39 mm

Etymology: *Buteo* (L.) - "hawk;" *platypterus* (Gr.) - *platys,* "broad" and *pteron,* "wing."

Status and Distribution: This hawk is classified as uncommon, with a decline noted in aspen parkland, particularly around urban areas. It breeds in an east-west strip in the southern boreal forest and parkland regions.

Field Checklist

✓**Habitat:** It requires large stands of mature forest where it prefers to nest in dense cover. It will forage at the forest edge, near clearings and wet areas.

✓✓✓**Sight:** This is a crow-sized hawk with dark brown upperparts, whitish throat and a dark brown band along the lower jaw. On the underparts, it is dull reddish brown, irregularly barred with white. The underside of the wings is bordered in black. The underside of the tail is dark brown with two conspicuous light tail-bars.

✓✓✓**Sound:** Melancholy cry (like an Eastern Wood Pewee) compared to the squeak of a rusty hinge.

Behavior: This hawk usually hunts from a perch where it pounces on its prey of small mammals, birds and insects.

Similar species: Cooper's Hawk.

Remarks: It is similar in size to the Cooper's Hawk but does not have any bluish-gray coloration on its upperparts. On the nest, the bird tends to sit silently allowing a close approach. Although this bird is shy during the breeding season, it can be observed in large numbers during migrations.

Jan	Feb	Mar	Apr	May	Jun	Jul	Aug	Sep	Oct	Nov	Dec

Hawks and Eagles

SWAINSON'S HAWK

Buteo swainsoni

Photos: K.Morck

L: 494 mm   W: 840 g   Egg: 56 x 44mm

Etymology: *Buteo* (L.) - "hawk;" *swainsoni* (ML.) - for William Swainson, 19th century English naturalist.

Status and Distribution: It is the commonest hawk of our grasslands. It is found mainly south of Lac la Biche in the parkland and prairies. It has been observed as far north as Peace River and Fort MacKay but may be in decline in the south.

●●●

Field Checklist

✓✓**Habitat:** It breeds in dry, open country where trees and shrubs are available for nesting. It uses moderately cultivated areas where it can hunt the fields and grassy borders.

✓✓✓**Sight:** It is extremely variable in appearance with pale and dark phases. The adult is usually dark brown above with a white throat patch. Distinguishing marks are a broad, dark band across the brownish white chest and a white area on the sides of the rump (in flight). The upper tail is gray while the underside is light with a dark terminal band.

✓**Sound:** It produces a harsh scream just a little less intimidating than the call of the Red-tail.

✓**Behavior:** This hawk hunts small mammals from the air but may also hop on the ground after insects. It holds its wings in a slight "V" while soaring.

●●

Similar species: Rough-legged Hawk and Red-tailed Hawk

Remarks: The distinguishing feature between this and the Rough-leg is that its leg is not feathered. It is smaller than the Red-tail, which is more of a forest species.

Jan	Feb	Mar	Apr	May	Jun	Jul	Aug	Sep	Oct	Nov	Dec

SWHA ☐   Date: _____

RED-TAILED HAWK

Buteo jamaicensis

L: 530 mm   W: 929 g   Egg: 59 x 47 mm

Etymology: *Buteo* (L.) - "hawk;" *jamaicensis* (ML.) - of Jamaica where the first specimens were collected.

Status and Distribution: This is one of the most widely distributed, numerous and commonly observed raptors in the province. The Red-tailed Hawk is found in all regions of Alberta with the highest concentrations found in the central parklands.

Field Checklist

✓**Habitat:** It is found in woodlands near open country.

✓✓✓**Sight:** The Red-tailed Hawk is highly variable in appearance. The upper parts are dark reddish brown, while below it is creamy white with a dark band across the abdomen, and dark along the sides of the breast and flanks. The tail is brick-red above and reddish-white below with a narrow, dark subterminal band. The wings are round and broad.

✓✓**Sound:** It produces a harsh, drawn out scream "kaer," which is repeated several times in flight.

✓**Behavior:** It is commonly observed soaring over open fields or perched on a high tree that allows it an unobstructed view of the field.

Similar species: Swainson's Hawk.

Remarks: It is slightly larger than Swainson's and the dark band on the underbody is across the abdomen as opposed to the breast. The darker phase of this bird (the common one in Alberta) is known as Harlan's Hawk whereas the pale phase is called Krider's Hawk. This is the common soaring hawk of Alberta's parkland and boreal regions. Overwintering has been recorded in a variety of areas of the province.

Jan	Feb	Mar	Apr	May	Jun	Jul	Aug	Sep	Oct	Nov	Dec

RTHA ☐   Date: _____

Hawks and Eagles

FERRUGINOUS HAWK

Buteo regalis

Photo: K.Morck

L: 607 mm   W: 1239 g   Egg: 62 x 49 mm

Etymology: *Buteo* (L.) - "hawk;" *regalis* (L.) - "royal."

Status and Distribution: This hawk is on Alberta's Blue List which classifies it as endangered, with a 1991 estimate of 1400 - 1700 pairs in the province. It is found in the grassland region of the province with a few records in the aspen parkland.

Field Checklist

✓✓**Habitat:** This is a bird of the dry mixedgrass prairie and is most abundant in grasslands under moderate cultivation. It nests in elevated areas such as coulee ledges, rock piles, riverbanks, hillsides and in trees.

✓✓✓**Sight:** These are the largest and heaviest of Alberta's hawks. The majority are light-phased with a white, slightly streaked underbody, reddish-brown shoulders, back and rump. The tail is white and does not have a terminal band. Dark-phase birds, which are rare in the province, are a uniform chocolate brown.

✓**Sound:** These birds make a loud, clear "cre-ah."

✓**Behavior:** They will hunt from perches and in flight. They have been known to lie down or crouch at a ground squirrel burrow waiting for prey.

Similar species: Rough-legged Hawk

Remarks: It is distinguished from the Rough-legged Hawk by the amount of pure white on the breast and the absence of the dark band on the abdomen. The spread of agriculture and the encroachment of the parkland into the grassland ecosystem have caused the Ferruginous Hawk to abandon 40% of its former range. Key nesting and feeding habitats must be secured to allow for its recovery. There are few overwintering records in Alberta.

Jan	Feb	Mar	Apr	May	Jun	Jul	Aug	Sep	Oct	Nov	Dec

FEHA ☐   Date: _____

ROUGH-LEGGED HAWK

Buteo lagopus

Photo: D. Wood

L: 556 mm   W: 883 g   Egg: 57 x 44 mm

Etymology: *Buteo* (L.) - "hawk;" *lagopus* (Gr.) - *lagos*, "a hare" and *pous*, "foot."

Status and Distribution: This hawk is relatively common in the province during its spring and fall migrations.

Field Checklist

Habitat: During migration it prefers open areas and fields where it hunts rodents.

✓✓✓**Sight:** There are two color phases. The predominant light phase has a buff-colored head and chest streaked with brown. It has a dark brown-black abdominal band, wrist patch and terminal tail band. Its legs are feathered down to the base of the toes, hence its name. The dark phase is solid dark brown to black.

Sound: This bird is virtually silent during migration and on its wintering grounds.

✓✓**Behavior:** When hunting, it will often hover with rapidly beating wings which is unusual for hawks. During migration it is observed circling in loose groups high in the air.

Similar species: Ferruginous Hawk, especially in the dark phase.

Remarks: It is smaller than the Ferruginous and has a narrower bill. In the light phase, it has irregular spots or streaks that are not evident in the Ferruginous Hawk. Although it is large, it possesses small, weak talons, which forces it to hunt small, mammalian prey. Winter records in the province are common, occurring as far north as Donnelly. The feathered tarsi provide insulation for this species which breeds in the high Arctic.

Jan	Feb	Mar	Apr	May	Jun	Jul	Aug	Sep	Oct	Nov	Dec

RLHA ☐   Date: _____

Hawks and Eagles

GOLDEN EAGLE

Aquila chrysaetos

Photo: D. Wood

L: 840 mm W: 3953 g Egg: 77 x 59 mm

Etymology: *Aquila* (L.) - "eagle;" *chrysaetos* (Gr.) - *chrysos*, "golden" and *aetos*, "eagle."

Status and Distribution: This bird is on Alberta's Yellow List as it is a rare and local breeder with less than 250 pairs in the province. It nests in the lower reaches of the major southern river systems and in the Rocky Mountains. It is uncommon in the northern areas of the province.

● ●

Field Checklist

✓✓**Habitat:** It prefers rocky outcrops, sparsely treed mountain slopes and grassland habitats with coulees, steep riverbanks, and canyons. In forested areas, territories contain large openings such as meadows, burns and marshes.

✓✓✓**Sight:** The adult bird is entirely dark brown except for the golden brown of the nape and hindneck. The legs are entirely feathered to the talons. The basal half of the juvenile's tail is mostly white.

✓**Sound:** It is not vocal but its call has been compared to the yelp of a small dog.

✓**Behavior:** The Golden Eagle is often observed soaring at high altitudes for hours. It hunts from flight using a low-level, high-speed glide or less frequently a steep vertical descent. It is known to pirate food from other Golden Eagles and Red-tailed Hawks.

● ●

Similar species: Juvenile Bald Eagle.

Remarks: The juvenile Bald Eagle has more gray on the underside of the wing. The nest is usually located in isolated areas on cliff ledges, escarpments or rocky bluffs. This eagle preys mostly on marmots, rabbits and ground squirrels but is known to take young of wild sheep and goats. The Golden Eagle can overwinter as far north as Grande Prairie and Wembley.

Jan	Feb	Mar	Apr	May	Jun	Jul	Aug	Sep	Oct	Nov	Dec

GOEA ❏ Date: _____

Order: Falconiformes - Family: Falconidae

Falcons

AMERICAN KESTREL

Falco sparverius

L: 265 mm   W: 100 g   Egg: 35 x 29 mm

Etymology: *Falco* (L.) - "falcon;" *sparverius* (L.) - pertaining to a sparrow.

Status and Distribution: This is Alberta's most common falcon and is widely distributed throughout the province.

Field Checklist

✓**Habitat:** They favor semi-open to open country where trees, structures and cliffs provide cavities for nesting. They are also common in urban environments. In the grasslands they are found along watercourses which provide trees for nest cavities.

✓✓✓**Sight:** It is a jay-sized falcon with black and white face-markings and reddish plumage on the crown, back and tail. The wings and head of the male are slate gray. The upperparts of the female are reddish brown. It has the falcon characteristics of pointed wings and a long tail.

✓✓**Sound:** This falcon is quite vocal, uttering a loud "killy, killy, killy."

Behavior: It hunts from a perch or hovers in the air with its tail spread and wings beating rapidly. It dives head-first to take mammal prey and feet-first for an insect, but always uses its feet to capture prey.

Similar species: Merlin and Sharp-shinned Hawk.

Remarks: The black and white face markings and the red plumage on its back distinguish it from the Merlin; long pointed wings prevent confusion with the Sharp-shinned Hawk. This bird was formerly known as the "Sparrow Hawk" which was a misnomer as its favorite prey are insects and small mammals. Wintering has been recorded as far north as Grande Prairie.

Jan	Feb	Mar	Apr	May	Jun	Jul	Aug	Sep	Oct	Nov	Dec

77   AMKE ☐   Date: _____

Falcons

Order: Falconiformes - Family: Falconidae

MERLIN

Falco columbarius

L: 290 mm   W: 157 g   Egg: 40 x 31 mm

Etymology: *Falco* (L.) - "falcon;" *columbarius* (L.) - "pertaining to pigeons."

Status and Distribution: Populations are healthy and increasing. It is found throughout Alberta in open woodlands. Individuals can overwinter in cities.

● ●

Field Checklist

✓**Habitat:** It requires open to semi-open habitat, an adequate avian prey base, woodlands or cliffs for isolated nest sites, and abandoned corvid nests. In the grassland-parkland areas it nests in small stands of trees and wooded valleys. In boreal areas, it uses sparse woodland edges.

✓✓✓**Sight:** The female is larger and heavier than the male. She has a brown upperbody with a buffy underbody that is streaked with brown. The male has a grayish-blue upperbody, and a black and gray barred tail. Below, it is buff, heavily streaked with brown. In both sexes, the throat is whitish and slightly streaked.

✓✓**Sound:** During the breeding season it utters a sometimes annoyingly loud series of "kik, kik, kik" calls.

Behavior: They are rapid and agile in flight, looking like fast-flying domestic pigeons.

● ●

Similar species: Sharp-shinned Hawk and American Kestrel.

Remarks: It is distinguished from the Sharp-shinned Hawk by its pointed as opposed to rounded wings and from the American Kestrel by the absence of red. There are two subspecies in the province, Richardson's Merlin *F. c. richardsonii* in the grassland - parkland, and the Taiga Merlin *F. c. columbarius* which breeds locally in the boreal areas. The movement of crows and magpies into urban areas has allowed the Merlin to follow.

Jan	Feb	Mar	Apr	May	Jun	Jul	Aug	Sep	Oct	Nov	Dec

MERL ❐   Date: _____

PRAIRIE FALCON

Falco mexicanus

Photo: K.Morck

L: 415 mm   W: 445 g   Egg: 52 x 42 mm

Etymology: *Falco* (L.) - "falcon;" *mexicanus* (ML.) - "of Mexico."

Status and Distribution: There is a concern for the long-term decline of this species in the province, especially in the northern parts of its historic range. It breeds in the prairie areas, west into the mountains and north to Calgary, Red Deer and Rumsey.

● ●

Field Checklist

✓✓**Habitat:** This falcon prefers dry, open country in the vicinity of canyons and coulees of the badlands, or cliffs of southern river valleys up to the mountains. It nests in cliffs, using shallow caves or ledges with overhangs.

✓✓✓**Sight:** The upperparts of the body are brown, the head has a light line over the eye and a brown "moustache streak." The throat is white and the light underparts are streaked with brown. In flight, a distinctive dark axillary patch (wingpit) is evident.

✓**Sound:** The Prairie Falcon utters a single, harsh "kreee" when agitated.

✓**Behavior:** In flight, it has a rapid wing beat without a glide.

● ●

Similar species: Peregrine Falcon.

Remarks: It is similar in size to the Peregrine but it is much paler. There are historical nesting records north to the North Saskatchewan River. In its core range in southern Alberta, the Prairie Falcon is dependent on the availability of secure nest sites and an adequate ground squirrel population. Overwintering has been recorded throughout most of its breeding range.

Jan	Feb	Mar	Apr	May	Jun	Jul	Aug	Sep	Oct	Nov	Dec

PRFA ☐   Date: _____

Falcons

PEREGRINE FALCON

Falco peregrinus

L: 466 mm W: 738 g Egg: 53 x 41 mm

Photo: K.Morck

Etymology: *Falco* (L.) - "falcon;" *peregrinus* (L.) - "wandering."

Status and Distribution: The Peregrine Falcon remains on Alberta's Red List, denoting a species at risk. There are less than 50 breeding pairs in Alberta, with known breeding Peregrines in the northeastern corner, the Rocky Mountains, Edmonton, Calgary and on cliffs along rivers in the southern part of the province.

● ●

Field Checklist

✓✓**Habitat:** It uses cliffs near water for nesting and open fields, swamps and marshes for hunting. Tall buildings or bridges replace cliffs in urban areas.

✓✓**Sight:** The sexes are similar, grayish-blue on top, darkening to almost black on the crown and tail. It is creamy white below, barred with black on the abdomen and thighs. The dark bar down the side of the face can be seen from a distance. It has long, triangular wings and a fairly long tail that is not spread in flight.

✓**Sound:** It is vocal only around the nest site where a harsh "kec, kec, kec, kec" is heard.

✓✓**Behavior:** It is specialized for hunting by direct aerial pursuit, or from a swift dive.

● ●

Similar species: Prairie Falcon

Remarks: Similar in size to the Prairie Falcon but distinguished by its gray-blue rather than brown plumage. It is one of the fastest birds reaching nearly 300 kph when diving at prey. Recovery will depend on lower pesticide levels in prey, releases of captive-reared chicks and protection of wetlands. Overwintering has been recorded in south and central parts of the province.

Jan	Feb	Mar	Apr	May	Jun	Jul	Aug	Sep	Oct	Nov	Dec

PEFA ☐ Date: _____

Order: Falconiformes - Family: Falconidae

Falcons

GYRFALCON
Falco rusticolus

L: 574 mm   W: 1388 g   Egg: 58 x 46 mm

Etymology: *Falco* (L.) - "falcon;" *rusticolus* (L.) - "a country dweller."

Status and Distribution: This is an uncommon winter resident in Alberta that has been observed south to Calgary and into the mountains at Lake Louise and Jasper. Records of breeding in the Lake Athabasca area are unconfirmed.

● ● ● ● ● ● ● ● ● ● ● ● ● ● ●

Field Checklist

Habitat: In winter it prefers open terrain across the parkland and prairie and into mountain valleys, but can be seen in cities.

✓✓✓**Sight:** This large falcon has a light and a dark color phase; both can be seen in Alberta. In the light phase, it is generally white with dark brown spotting on the crown, back and sides, and black bars on the wings and tail. In the dark phase it is blackish-brown above and below with fine white barring on the underparts. There are intermediate stages between these two phases. The bill has a hook, or "tooth," and the wingtips are pointed.

Sound: Usually silent in winter, it may utter a harsh "kak-kak."

✓**Behavior:** Around urban areas in winter, it is observed preying on Rock Doves and waterfowl.

● ●

Similar species: Dark phase is similar to immature Peregrine Falcon and the light phase is colored like a Snowy Owl.

Remarks: It is more uniform in color than the immature Peregrine Falcon and lacks the "moustache streak" of the latter. The small head, pointed wingtips, and rapid wing beats will help separate the Gyrfalcon from a flying Snowy Owl.

Jan	Feb	Mar	Apr	May	Jun	Jul	Aug	Sep	Oct	Nov	Dec

81

GYRF ☐   Date: _____

Partridges

GRAY PARTRIDGE

Perdix perdix

L: 290 mm   W: 374 g   Egg: 36 x 27 mm

Etymology: *Perdix* (L.) - "partridge."

Status and Distribution: Populations appear to be stable; however, they are susceptible to sharp drops during severe winters. The Gray Partridge is a resident throughout its range in the grassland and parkland regions of the province. There is a disjunct population in the Peace River area.

• •

Field Checklist

✓**Habitat:** It resides in areas of open grassland and agricultural land which have adjacent areas of woody cover. It prefers the border between scrub and cultivation.

✓✓✓**Sight:** This smallest of Alberta's game birds is generally gray with a reddish brown eyeline, cheeks and throat. The breast is finely vermiculated with black, white and brown. It is distinguished by its unmarked, chestnut outer feathers visible in flight and a chestnut "horseshoe" on the male's breast. The female's coloration is similar but duller.

Sound: A raspy "kir-ip."

✓✓**Behavior:** Flushing warily, it explodes from cover with a clatter of wings and a rapid cackle, assuming a low and fast flight path. Prior to courting, the males engage in prolonged battles to establish breeding territories.

• •

Similar species: None in Alberta.

Remarks: This is the only partridge-like bird to have the vermiculated breast. When the reddish tail is spread in flight, it is very conspicuous. The bird was imported from Hungary in 1908, when 70 pairs were released near Midnapore, hence the local name, Hungarian Partridge.

Jan	Feb	Mar	Apr	May	Jun	Jul	Aug	Sep	Oct	Nov	Dec

GRPA ☐   Date: _____

Order: Galliformes - Family: Phasianidae **Pheasants**

RING-NECKED PHEASANT

Phasianus colchicus

Photo: B. Carroll

L: 740 mm   W: 1183 g   Egg: 46 x 35 mm

Etymology: *Phasianus* (Gr.) - *phasianos*, "a pheasant;" *colchicus* (ML.) - after the location Colchis.

Status and Distribution: On the provincial Yellow List, it has decreased considerably because of habitat loss. It is a resident of the grassland and parkland regions.

• •

Field Checklist

✓✓**Habitat:** It prefers farmland or grassland which has adjacent cover. This includes hedgerows and woodland borders, similar dense cover along irrigation ditches, and in city parks and golf courses.

✓✓✓**Sight:** The male has a long tapering tail, iridescent green crown on a black head with a white collar. The bronze body is variegated in complex patterns with maroon, cream, black and metallic green. The face is bare red skin and there are short black ear tufts. The female is variegated light and darker brown with the heaviest markings on the back. She has a much shorter tail than the male.

✓✓**Sound:** A crowing "kok, kok," is often followed by a rapid beating of the wings.

Behavior: Relying on her coloration, the female will remain motionless when approached on the nest.

• •

Similar species: Female Sharp-tailed Grouse and female Sage Grouse.

Remarks: The female pheasant is distinguished from the female Sharp-tailed by her buffier appearance, lack of white patches, longer tail and naked legs. Naked legs and no black abdominal patch separate it from the female Sage Grouse. The brilliant coloration of the male makes it distinct from all other species in the same habitat. To ensure stable populations of this introduced gamebird, habitat preservation on farmland is essential.

Jan	Feb	Mar	Apr	May	Jun	Jul	Aug	Sep	Oct	Nov	Dec

RGNP ☐   Date: _____

Grouse

RUFFED GROUSE

Bonasa umbellus

L: 418 mm W: 578 g Egg: 40 x 30 mm

Etymology: *Bonasa* (Gr.) - *bonasos,* "a wild ox;" *umbellus* (L.) - "a sunshade," referring to the ruffs.

Status and Distribution: This common grouse is found throughout the province with the exception of the grassland areas. Two subspecies are found in Alberta, *B. u. yukonensis* in the north and *B. u. umbelloides* in the central and southwestern part of the province.

• •

Field Checklist

✓**Habitat:** This grouse prefers aspen-dominated mixed forests with openings and a heavy understorey.

✓✓✓**Sight:** The Ruffed is a large brown and gray grouse with broad, soft, black feathers on the sides of the necks producing ruffs, lightly barred underparts, feathered legs, naked toes and a longish tail with a broad, dark subterminal band that is noticeable in flight. The female is smaller, has a shorter ruff and tail and an incomplete tail band.

✓✓✓**Sound:** When disturbed, it will utter a cackling sound repeated several times. The drumming of the male Ruffed Grouse is a familiar sound in the spring.

✓✓**Behavior:** When flushed the rapid wing beats produce a whirring sound as the grouse flies low and straight, then it glides to land usually within a hundred metres.

• •

Similar species: None

Remarks: The black ruffs on both sides of the neck and the broad barred tail are quite distinctive. This grouse appears in both a gray and red phase, although the dominant color is brown. The gray phase is associated with northern areas or higher elevations, while the reddish-brown phase is more characteristic of southern and lower elevation populations.

Jan	Feb	Mar	Apr	May	Jun	Jul	Aug	Sep	Oct	Nov	Dec

RUGR ☐   Date: _____

Order: Galliformes - Family: Phasianidae

SAGE GROUSE

Centrocercus urophasianus

Photo: K.Morck

L: 635 mm   W: 2228 g   Egg: 55 x 38 mm

Etymology: *Centrocercus* (Gr.) - *kentron,* "a point" and *kerkos,* "tail;" *urophasianus* (Gr.) - *oura,* "tail" and *phasianos,* "pheasant."

Status and Distribution: Listed on the Alberta Blue List, the Sage Grouse is a species at risk. It is found only in the extreme southeast corner of the province east of the Milk River and south of the Cypress Hills.

● ●

Field Checklist

✓✓**Habitat:** It requires large stands of sagebrush, which exist only in the shortgrass prairie. Wet areas, river valleys or green areas are required for foraging.

✓✓✓**Sight:** The male is a large grouse with the upperparts finely marked in brown, black and dull white without an evident pattern and a black patch on the abdomen. The tail is rounded and variegated with sharply tapered feathers. The female is similar but black the abdomen patch may be smaller.

✓✓**Sound:** A sharp popping or booming sound is produced by quickly releasing air from two brightly colored, distensible sacs flanking the bird's larynx.

✓**Behavior:** Reluctant to fly when alarmed, it prefers to run, but will resort to a grouse-like flutter and cackle when pressed.

● ●

Similar species: None

Remarks: This bird is unique in its habitat. In April, males form territorial leks on traditional dancing grounds where they defend mating spots and passively attract females with displays of strutting, hooting, snorting and grunting. As sage leaves are their predominant winter food, this grouse is totally dependent on the distribution of sagebrush in the province.

Jan	Feb	Mar	Apr	May	Jun	Jul	Aug	Sep	Oct	Nov	Dec

SAGR ☐   Date: _____

Grouse

SPRUCE GROUSE

Falcipennis canadensis

L: 400 mm   W: 529 g   Egg: 44 x 32 mm

Etymology: *Falcipennis* (L.) - *falci,* "sickle shaped," and *pennis,* "wing or feather;" *canadensis* (ML.) - "of Canada."

Status and Distribution: Two subspecies of this bird are found in Alberta. *F. c. canadensis* is found in central and northern Alberta while *F. c. franklinii* is in the Rocky Mountains. Although it is designated as having a healthy stable population, the constant removal of its habitat by clearing and logging is a restricting factor.

● ●

Field Checklist

✓**Habitat:** It lives in coniferous and mixed wood forests with bogs and openings, edges and old burns.

✓✓✓**Sight:** The male is generally barred in black and brown with a black throat, breast and tail and a small red comb. The female is generally barred brown, gray and rust. The legs are feathered to the toes. The mountain subspecies is differentiated by its lack of rusty-ochre tips of the tail feathers and the presence of white-tipped feathers on the upper tail coverts.

✓**Sound:** Males give an extremely low-pitched "wwhoot." You can hear the sound of their wings as the males perform a rapid flutter flight ended by a wingclap.

✓✓**Behavior:** The Spruce Grouse is known for its tameness.

● ●

Similar species: Blue Grouse

Remarks: The conspicuous black and white markings on the underparts of the male distinguish it from the Blue Grouse. Its lack of fear of man has given it the name "Fool Hen." This has led to its elimination in the parts of its historic range that overlapped with human settlement.

Jan	Feb	Mar	Apr	May	Jun	Jul	Aug	Sep	Oct	Nov	Dec

SPGR ☐   Date: _____

Order: Galliformes - Family: Phasianidae

BLUE GROUSE

Dendragapus obscurus

L: 485 mm   W: 1057 g   Egg: 50 x 35 mm

Etymology: *Dendragapus* (L.) - *dendron*, "a tree" and *agape* (Gr.), "love;" *obscurus* (L.) - "dark."

Status and Distribution: The population of this permanent resident is deemed to be stable. It is found in the Rocky Mountains and the adjoining foothills from the Smoky River in the north, south to the United States border.

• •

Field Checklist

✓✓**Habitat:** A bird of the montane region, in spring and summer it is mainly terrestrial, living in treed habitats in or near openings at low elevations. In fall and winter it moves higher to thick coniferous forests where it becomes more arboreal.

✓✓✓**Sight:** The adult male is a large slate-colored bird, with the throat and neck mixed with white, large orange-yellow combs over the eyes and legs feathered to the toes. The female is similar to the male but the chest and sides are lightly barred with brown.

✓✓**Sound:** The male utters a hollow "whoot, whoot" produced by filling the yellow or plum-colored neck sacs with air.

✓**Behavior:** Males establish territories, but the females are not fixed to a particular territory and often wander through. The female will feign injury to distract an intruder away from her brood.

• •

Similar species: Spruce Grouse

Remarks: The Blue Grouse is larger than the Spruce Grouse and the male lacks the black breast patches of the latter. Females of the two species are similar, but the female Blue Grouse lacks the dark breast patches and is less extensively barred on the underparts.

Jan	Feb	Mar	Apr	May	Jun	Jul	Aug	Sep	Oct	Nov	Dec

BLGS ☐   Date: _____

Ptarmigan

WILLOW PTARMIGAN

Lagopus lagopus

L: 375 mm   W: 526 g   Egg: 44 x 32 mm

Etymology: *Lagopus* (Gr.) - *lagos,* "a hare" and *pous,* "foot."

Status and Distribution: It is a rare breeder in a very localized part of the province. The breeding range of this bird includes northern Jasper National Park, north into the Kakwa region and east to Grande Prairie. In winter, flocks from the NWT move into the far northern parts of the province.

• •

Field Checklist

✓**Habitat:** It prefers willow-dwarf birch meadows and willow-covered stream banks near timberline. In winter, they move into timbered areas along water courses where more food is available.

✓✓✓**Sight:** This largest of the ptarmigan is all white in winter except for the black tail, eye and heavy bill. In summer, the male is dark reddish-brown on the throat and breast, the crown and back of the neck are barred. The female is heavily barred with dark brown and ochre. In both sexes, the wings are mostly white and feet are feathered to the toes.

✓**Sound:** Call is a barking "to-bee, to-bee" that sounds like the bird is on helium.

Behavior: The male's territorial display includes showing off his plumage, hooting, booming and descending flight spirals.

• •

Similar species: White-tailed Ptarmigan.

Remarks: Although similar, the Willow Ptarmigan can be distinguished in winter by its black tail. In summer, compared to the White-tail, the male Willow is more reddish-brown on its head, back and breast and the female is grayer overall and more heavily barred on her breast and flanks.

Jan	Feb	Mar	Apr	May	Jun	Jul	Aug	Sep	Oct	Nov	Dec

WIPT ☐   Date: _____

WHITE-TAILED PTARMIGAN

Lagopus leucurus

L: 325 mm   W: 340 g   Egg: 43 x 29 mm

Etymology: *Lagopus* (Gr.) - *lagos*, "a hare" and *pous*, "foot;" *leucurus* (Gr.) - *leukos*, "white" and *oura*, "tail."

Status and Distribution: A fairly common year-round resident of the Rocky Mountain region with a breeding range from the Willmore Wilderness Area south to Waterton Lakes National Park.

● ●

Field Checklist

✓✓**Habitat:** It favors open rocky areas and alpine meadows in summer including open scree with nearby water. In winter it moves downslope into the open forest and willow meadows.

✓✓✓**Sight:** This is the smallest ptarmigan. In winter the plumage is completely white. In summer the male is heavily barred with black on the throat and breast and the back is finely barred with black and brown. The females are more heavily barred with black and white. Both sexes have a white tail and wings in summer and their legs and toes are completely feathered.

✓✓**Sound:** It utters a cackling, squealing call.

Behavior: The male on territory will use a courtship chase, a succession of quick and slow strutting and a display of swollen red eye combs to attract females.

● ●

Similar species: Willow Ptarmigan

Remarks: The all-white tail of the White-tailed Ptarmigan is the major characteristic that distinguishes it from other ptarmigan. This species is a mountain resident as opposed to an arctic bird. The female nests in open areas on the ground and relies on camouflage to hide from predators.

Jan	Feb	Mar	Apr	May	Jun	Jul	Aug	Sep	Oct	Nov	Dec

WTPT ❑   Date: _____

Grouse

Order: Galliformes - Family: Phasianidae

SHARP-TAILED GROUSE

Tympanuchus phasianellus

L: 436 mm W: 801 g Egg: 43 x 32 mm

Etymology: *Tympanuchus* (Gr.) - *tympanon*, "a drum" and *nucha* (ML.), "neck;" *phasianellus* (Gr.) - *phasianos*, "little pheasant."

Status and Distribution: Although relatively common throughout the central and southern portions of its range, it remains on the provincial Yellow List because of the long term impact of agriculture on its habitat in central Alberta.

●●●●●●●●●●●●●●●●●●●●●●●●●●●●●●●●●●●●●●

Field Checklist

✓**Habitat:** In grassland regions it uses open prairie, shrubby sandhills, coulees, margins of water courses and farmland. In the parkland and boreal regions, it prefers open woodland.

✓✓✓**Sight:** The upper parts of this medium-sized grouse are grayish and mottled with brown, black and white. The underside is lighter with black V marks on the breast and flanks. The short pointed tail has long dark middle feathers and short white outer feathers.

✓✓**Sound:** Males produce a booming sound through the release of air from inflated purple neck sacs. A shrill "chilk" is used to attract prospective mates.

✓**Behavior:** In April, males gather on traditional dancing grounds and defend territory within the lek, carrying out dancing duels for nearby females by rapidly stamping their feet, lowering their heads and fluffing their plumage.

●●●●●●●●●●●●●●●●●●●●●●●●●●●●●●●●●●●●●

Similar species: None

Remarks: The light color, sharp, short tail and dark V marks on the breast are distinctive. It is mistakenly referred to as a "prairie chicken," but the true Prairie Chicken (*Tympanuchus cupido*) has been extirpated from Alberta. Larger flocks form in the fall and move into birch and aspen stands to feed.

Jan	Feb	Mar	Apr	May	Jun	Jul	Aug	Sep	Oct	Nov	Dec

STGR ☐ Date: _____

Order: Galliformes - Family: Phasianidae

WILD TURKEY

Meleagris gallopavo

L: 1240 mm   W: 7400 g   Egg: 63 x 45 mm

Photo: W.Burgess

Etymology: *Meleagris* (Gr. and L.) - "a Guinea-fowl;" *gallopavo* (L.) - *gallus*, "a cock" and *pavo*, "a pea fowl."

Status and Distribution: There is no management concern for this introduced bird. Wild Turkeys were introduced into the Cypress Hills, the Porcupine Hills and into the Lees Lake and Todd Creek areas. Turkeys sighted in other areas are probably birds released locally and are not thought to be breeding.

• •

Field Checklist

✓**Habitat:** The turkey prefers open deciduous forest, forest edges and agricultural fields. It remains on the breeding grounds overwinter, but is quite dependent on supplemental feeding during harsh winters, when it frequents cattle feeding sites and barnyards.

✓✓✓**Sight:** It is a large bronze and brown bird with a naked neck and long tail barred with bronze and brown.

✓✓✓**Sound:** As with the domestic species, the familiar "gobble, gobble, gobble" is uttered.

✓**Behavior:** The turkey roosts in trees at night and when alarmed it is more likely to run than fly. Two to three females will often share a common nest and share incubation.

• •

Similar species: Domestic Turkey

Remarks: The Domestic Turkey originated from Mexican stock and always shows a little white at the tip of the tail, whereas the tail of the Wild Turkey, sometimes called the Merriam's Turkey, ends in a light brown. Birds generally flock together from early fall to early spring with the males separated from the females and young.

Jan	Feb	Mar	Apr	May	Jun	Jul	Aug	Sep	Oct	Nov	Dec

WITU ☐   Date: _____

Rails and Coots

YELLOW RAIL

Coturnicops noveboracensis

L: 165 mm   W: 62 g   Egg: 28 x 21 mm

Photo: M.Robert

Etymology: *Coturnicops* - *coturnix* (L.) - "a quail" and *opsis* (Gr.) - "appearance;" *noveboracum* (ML.) - "New York," *ensis* (L.) - "belonging to" and *novus* (L.) - "new."

Status and Distribution: This species is thought to be locally common. The historical range has been concentrated in east-central Alberta with occurrences north to Fort MacKay and south to Calgary. There are early records from Jasper.

●●

Field Checklist

✓**Habitat:** It prefers larger, denser grass or sedge marshes with little or no standing water. To build its nest, it uses drier habitat than other rails.

✓✓**Sight:** This is the smallest of the rails and is distinguished by its short, stout, yellow bill, overall buffy plumage, and white tips on the secondaries. Fine white lines create bars on the back. White wing patches are prominent in flight. The female is slightly smaller.

✓✓✓**Sound:** A repetitive metallic "tik, tik - tik, tik, tik" is most often heard at night.

✓**Behavior:** When confronted alone, it prefers to freeze and rely on its coloration to hide, but will quietly slip off the nest when alarmed and disappear into dense vegetation.

●●●

Similar species: Sora

Remarks: The Yellow Rail is smaller than the Sora, and the fine white barring on the back and the white-tipped secondaries are absent in the Sora. The immature birds of both species are identical except for the white wing patch of the Yellow Rail. Like all rails, it is secretive; its long toes and laterally compressed body help it to move quietly through thick marsh vegetation.

Jan	Feb	Mar	Apr	May	Jun	Jul	Aug	Sep	Oct	Nov	Dec

YERA ❑   Date: _____

Order: Gruiformes - Family: Rallidae

VIRGINIA RAIL

Rallus limicola

L: 240 mm   W: 105 g   Egg: 32 x 24 mm

Photo: T.Thormin

Etymology: *Rallus* (ML.) - "a rail;" *limicola* (L.) - *limus*, "mud" and *colo,* "to inhabit."

Status and Distribution: Its status is poorly known in Alberta with few historical records. This species has been recorded in eastern Alberta north to Fort Chipewyan and south to Brooks. The westernmost sighting was in the Valleyview area.

Field Checklist

✓**Habitat:** The breeding habitat of the Virginia Rail includes areas of freshwater lakes, ponds, marshes, sloughs and bogs, with an extensive cover of bulrushes, cattails and sedges.

✓✓✓**Sight:** The rail's reddish bill is longer than its head. Its upper parts are dark brown, flanks are barred black and white and the foreneck and breast are a light cinnamon-brown. The cheeks are gray and almost black in front of the eye.

✓✓**Sound:** A loud quacking "ki-dik, ki-dik."

✓**Behavior:** If approached on the nest, it will slip off before being seen or heard. If the intruder nears the nest, the bird will splash the water with its wings to create a distraction. When approached off the nest, it will freeze and due to its coloration will blend into the background of dry marsh vegetation.

Similar species: None in Alberta

Remarks: The long red bill and the reddish-brown coloration separate it from other members of its family in Alberta. It is best observed at dawn or dusk when it may be seen in the open probing in the mud for earthworms, insect larvae, slugs and snails. This low-flying migrant is especially secretive during migration providing little definitive data on its migration periods in the province.

Jan	Feb	Mar	Apr	May	Jun	Jul	Aug	Sep	Oct	Nov	Dec

VIRA ☐   Date: _____

Rails and Coots

SORA

Porzana carolina

L: 210 mm W: 77 g Egg: 31 x 22 mm

Etymology: *Porzana* (L.) - "the crake;" *carolina* (ML.) - "of Carolina."

Status and Distribution: The Sora is the most common rail in Alberta. The population in the province is stable. It is found in all regions of the province where suitable wetlands exist.

• •

Field Checklist

✓✓**Habitat:** The Sora has adapted to a variety of wetland habitats. It breeds in freshwater ponds, meandering streams, marshes, sloughs, or wet meadows, with at least a partial margin of extensive sedges, rushes or cattails. Flooded willow swamps are less popular.

✓✓✓**Sight:** This rail is chunky and has a short yellowish bill. The upper parts are olive brown, the breast is gray and the throat and front of the face are black.

✓✓✓**Sound:** A sharp upslurred whistle and a descending series of loud notes, often described as a whinny or maniacal laugh.

✓**Behavior:** In common with other rails, the Sora is reluctant to take flight when disturbed and prefers to take advantage of its laterally compressed body and slip quietly into the tangled vegetation.

• •

Similar species: Yellow Rail.

Remarks: It is larger than the Yellow Rail and lacks the white patch on the wing. It has more olive on its back as opposed to the brown of the Yellow Rail. This is the most common and least secretive of the rails in the province. The Sora will usually build its nest in deeper water than other rails, where it is anchored to a tuft of rushes. In the fall, they are less secretive.

Jan	Feb	Mar	Apr	May	Jun	Jul	Aug	Sep	Oct	Nov	Dec

SORA ☐   Date: _____

AMERICAN COOT

Fulica americana

L: 377 mm   W: 600 g   Egg: 49 x 39 mm

Etymology: *Fulica* (L.) - *fuligo*, "soot," referring to the bird's color; *americana* (ML.) - "of America."

Status and Distribution: This waterbird is common in marshes across the province. It breeds in all regions of Alberta but is more widespread in the northern parts of the province.

Field Checklist

✓✓**Habitat:** The coot breeds in freshwater bodies that have bulrush, cattail and sedge margins. It prefers an area of open water adjacent to its breeding ground. Its nest is in or near rushes, but is designed to move in response to changes in water level.

✓✓✓**Sight:** The coot is generally a dark slate color with a black head and neck, a whitish bill with a black spot on the tip and whitish-brown frontal shield. Although closely related to rails, with which it shares the characteristic long toes and short round wings, the coot is duck-like in appearance.

✓✓**Sound:** A cackling "kuc, kuc, kuc."

✓**Behavior:** On land or in the water the coot nods its head in time with its leg movements. It is hard to flush it when it is disturbed; it prefers to hide or dive.

Similar species: None in Alberta.

Remarks: From a distance, the local "mud hen" may be mistaken for a duck, but the distinctive silhouette of the smaller, rounder head and the bobbing motion of the head help separate it from the ducks. In the fall they gather in large flocks on lakes prior to migration. Some overwintering in open water areas has been recorded for Alberta.

Jan	Feb	Mar	Apr	May	Jun	Jul	Aug	Sep	Oct	Nov	Dec

95

AMCO ❐   Date: _____

Cranes

SANDHILL CRANE

Grus canadensis

L: 930 mm   W: 3379 g   Egg: 94 x 60 mm

Etymology: *Grus* (L.) - "crane;" *canadensis* (ML.) - "of Canada."

Status and Distribution: It is on the provincial Yellow List because little is known of its population size and distribution in the foothills and boreal regions. The normal breeding range extends as far south as the Bottrell area, but there have been extralimital records in the extreme southwest portion of the province. On migration, it can be seen anywhere.

Field Checklist

✓**Habitat:** Breeding habitat includes marshes, bogs adjacent to ponds, and large marshes with some open water, tall grasses and rushes. The area must be secluded and undisturbed.

✓✓**Sight:** These metre-tall birds are slate-blue overall, with water staining adding a rust color. They have black wing tips and a bald red upper face and forehead. Juveniles are similar with many tawny-tipped wing and body feathers.

✓✓**Sound:** In flight its repetitive rolling "karooo" can be heard for long distances.

✓✓**Behavior:** In courtship it carries out a ritual hopping dance with a lowered head and raised wing. In migration it will often be seen in huge flocks soaring on thermal updrafts or moving linearly in a noisy V formation.

Similar species: Great Blue Heron, and geese in flight.

Remarks: The fully extended neck of this crane in flight and the quicker upstroke of the wings distinguish it from the Great Blue Heron. Trailing legs, its call and its habit of soaring differentiate the Sandhill from migrating geese. It is sensitive to human disturbance and the pressure of resource extraction within its breeding range is of concern.

Jan	Feb	Mar	Apr	May	Jun	Jul	Aug	Sep	Oct	Nov	Dec

SACR ☐   Date: _____

WHOOPING CRANE

Grus americana

L: 1345 mm   W: 7000 g   Egg: 100 x 63 mm

Etymology: *Grus* (L.) - "crane;" *americana* (ML.) - "of America."

Status and Distribution: With 21 individuals left in 1941, extensive management has raised the population of this endangered species to only about 150 in almost 60 years. Its breeding range within the province is restricted to Wood Buffalo National Park where all nest sites are protected.

● ●

Field Checklist

✓✓**Habitat:** The large, relatively open marshy areas of the national park provide the isolation required for successful nesting.

✓✓✓**Sight:** Standing over one metre tall, it has long black legs, a long neck and a relatively long and heavy bill. Adults are all white with black-tipped primaries and coverts that show in flight. A red facial patch splits from the bill up over the crown and down under the eye. Immatures are a mix of white and rusty brown and have no facial patches.

✓✓**Sound:** The deep trumpeting "ker-laa, ker-laa" is given in flight.

Behavior: This crane is wary and highly territorial.

● ●

Similar species: None

Remarks: It can be distinguished in flight from the Great Blue Heron as it flies with its neck outstretched. The trailing long legs in flight distinguish it from the other two large white birds with black wing tips, the White Pelican and the Snow Goose. In fall, migrants fly singly, by family unit, or in small groups, sometimes mixed with Sandhill Cranes. Sightings of this bird should be recorded. Look for any identifying tags and report them to the provincial wildlife agency or the Canadian Wildlife Service.

Jan	Feb	Mar	Apr	May	Jun	Jul	Aug	Sep	Oct	Nov	Dec

WOCR ❐   Date: _____

Plovers

BLACK-BELLIED PLOVER

Pluvialis squatarola

Photo: G.Beyersbergen

L: 295 mm   W: 209 g   Egg: 51 x 36 mm

Etymology: *Pluvialis* (L.) - "rainy;" *squatarola* - a Venetian name for the bird.

Status and Distribution: This is a regular spring and fall migrant in Alberta. It is observed in all regions with the exception of the mountains where it occurs rarely.

• •

Field Checklist

✓**Habitat:** It prefers mud flats, beaches and sand bars.

✓✓✓**Sight:** The male has a white crown above the eye, with the face, throat and breast a solid black. The back is checked with white, black and brown. The rear abdomen and undertail coverts are white, while the axillars (arm-pits) are black. The female has less white in the underparts and she is more brown than black. A small rear toe is present. In fall, the white on the head and neck may not be as prominent and the underparts are whitish-gray.

✓✓**Sound:** Its call, a mournful "tee-oo-ee," drops in pitch in the middle syllable.

Behavior: This plover is wary and takes flight quickly when approached.

• •

Similar species: American Golden Plover.

Remarks: The Black-bellied Plover is larger than the Golden with a distinctive white rather than golden crown, back and rear abdomen. The black axillars are prominent in flight. The hind toe is absent in the American Golden Plover. The adults return on their fall migration in late July with the birds of the year appearing at the end of August. Fall birds are harder to distinguish but the Black-bellied is larger and does not have gold flecking.

Jan	Feb	Mar	Apr	May	Jun	Jul	Aug	Sep	Oct	Nov	Dec

BBPL ❑   Date: _____

AMERICAN GOLDEN-PLOVER

Pluvialis dominica

Photo: G.Beyersbergen

L: 268 mm   W: 142 g   Egg: 48.6 x 33 mm

Etymology: *Pluvialis* (L.) - "rainy;" *dominica* (ML.) - "of Santo Domingo."

Status and Distribution: These plovers are regular spring and fall migrants that can be observed in the province east of the mountains and foothills. It is most often seen in open fields in the grassland and parkland regions.

• •

Field Checklist

✓**Habitat:** When migrating through the province, it prefers drier habitats including grassland, cultivated fields, pastures and tilled fields where they can feed on worms and insects.

✓✓✓**Sight:** In breeding plumage, it has a black face, throat, chest, abdomen and undertail coverts. It has a white forehead that extends in a line over the eye and down the cheek and neck. The upperparts including the crown are a mixture of black, gold and white.

✓**Sound:** It has two regular calls: "cue-wit" heard mainly in flight and a loud "tue-e-e."

Behavior: They are very difficult birds to approach.

• •

Similar species: Black-bellied Plover

Remarks: The main distinctive features are the solid black underparts, unlike the Black-bellied which has a distinctive white rear abdomen and the gray instead of black axillars. The American Golden Plover also lacks the rear toe of the Black-bellied Plover and is smaller. The adult birds migrate north through Alberta but return to their wintering grounds by a route that takes them farther east. The young birds of the year migrate south through Alberta, retracing the route taken north by their parents.

Jan	Feb	Mar	Apr	May	Jun	Jul	Aug	Sep	Oct	Nov	Dec

AGPL ☐   Date: _____

Plovers

SEMIPALMATED PLOVER

Charadrius semipalmatus

Photo: G.Beyersbergen

L: 169 mm   W: 47 g   Egg: 33 x 23 mm

Etymology: *Charadrius* (L.) - "a plover;" *semipalmatus* (L) - *semi*, "half," and *palma*, "palm of the hand," literally half-webbed, referring to the feet.

Status and Distribution: It is a rare breeder in Alberta, where it is at the southern periphery of its breeding range and is most commonly observed as a migrant. There has been confirmed breeding in Wood Buffalo National Park and possibly in the Birch River delta.

● ●

Field Checklist

✓**Habitat:** It prefers mud flats, sandy beaches and open margins of water bodies during migration. For breeding it uses sandy or gravelly shores where it nests on dry ground.

✓✓✓**Sight:** A small shorebird with a short orange bill with a black tip, brown upperparts, narrow black patch from base of the bill to cheeks, a white forehead and a single black breast band. The orange feet of this plover have some webbing between the three toes giving it the name "semipalmated."

✓✓**Sound:** "Chu-weee, chu-weee"

✓**Behavior:** Parents give a broken-wing display near the nest, running ahead of an intruder for long distances before taking flight. When feeding, the bird runs, stops and trembles its foot to make prey move.

● ●

Similar species: Killdeer and Piping Plover.

Remarks: It is smaller than the Killdeer, has a single rather than a double breast band, lacks the Killdeer's rufous rump and has an orange bill with a black tip. It is darker than the Piping Plover and its face is dark rather than light.

Jan	Feb	Mar	Apr	May	Jun	Jul	Aug	Sep	Oct	Nov	Dec

SEPL ☐   Date: _____

PIPING PLOVER

Charadrius melodus

L: 179 mm W: 55 g Egg: 32 x 34 mm

Etymology: *Charadrius* (L.) - "a plover;" *melodus* (L.) - "a melody."

Status and Distribution: This bird is on Alberta's Red List as an endangered species as there are only 100 - 150 breeding pairs in the province. It is regarded as a rare and local summer resident in the grassland and parkland regions north to the North Saskatchewan River and south to the Oldman and South Saskatchewan rivers east of Red Deer to the Saskatchewan border.

• •

Field Checklist

✓✓**Habitat:** It prefers extensive sandy, gravelly beaches on a saline lake or pond with dry, open beach areas for nesting and wet mudflats close to water, for feeding.

✓✓✓**Sight:** The Piping Plover has pale, gray-brown upperparts, light-colored cheeks, white forehead, small black bar above the forehead, white lowerparts and a pale, sometimes broken black, breast band.

✓✓**Sound:** A melodic piping call "queep, queep" from which it gets its name.

Behavior: The female abandons the family before the young fledge, leaving parental duties to the male.

• •

Similar species: Semipalmated Plover

Remarks: It is much paler than the Semipalmated Plover and lacks any black or dark brown on the cheeks. It is the only single-ringed plover to breed south of the arctic tundra. The present decline of this plover is linked to increased recreational use of beaches used as nesting habitat, fluctuating water levels, and disturbance by cattle. The present world population is about 6,000 with distinct populations centered on the prairies and the northeast coast of the U.S. and Canada.

Jan	Feb	Mar	Apr	May	Jun	Jul	Aug	Sep	Oct	Nov	Dec

PIPL ❏   Date: _____

Sandpipers

SOLITARY SANDPIPER

Tringa solitaria

L: *203 mm* W: *49 g* Egg: *36 x 26 mm*

Etymology: *Tringa* (Gr.) - *tryngas*, "a sandpiper;" *solitaria* (L.) - "solitary."

Status and Distribution: The Solitary is relatively common in the southern boreal forest and foothills regions of the province, wide spread in the northern parts of these regions and in the mountain areas north of Banff. On migration, it is also observed in the southern part of Alberta.

● ●

Field Checklist

✓✓**Habitat:** This sandpiper prefers open, wet woodlands, nesting near wetlands, ponds and lakes. It nests in an old nest of a Robin, Rusty Blackbird or similarly sized bird, at any height in a tree. It feeds at the edge of shallow pools and muskeg ponds, or along the muddy margins of sloughs and rivers.

✓✓✓**Sight:** A slender, straight-billed sandpiper, it has a blackish-brown back and rump, with a greenish sheen and fine light speckling. It has heavy black and white barring of the axillars under the wing, dark green legs and a white eye-ring.

✓✓**Sound:** The call that is usually heard is a whistled "peet-weet".

✓✓**Behavior:** These birds are usually observed alone, but may be observed in groups of two or three during migration.

● ●

Similar species: Spotted Sandpiper

Remarks: It differs from the Spotted Sandpiper as the upper body is darker and in flight it lacks the white wing bar and shows more white on the tail. This species forages at water's edge or in shallow water, often vibrating the leading foot as it walks. This stirs up the bottom enough to disturb insects. In migration, it can be confusing as it shows up in more traditional sandpiper habitat.

Jan	Feb	Mar	Apr	May	Jun	Jul	Aug	Sep	Oct	Nov	Dec

SOSA ☐   Date: _____

WILLET

Catoptrophorus semipalmatus

L: 365 mm　W: 265 g　Egg: 55 x 39 mm

Etymology: *Catoptrophorus* (Gr.) - *katoptron,* "mirror" and *phero,* "to bear;" *semipalmatus* (L.) - *semi,* "half" and *palma,* "palm of the hand," literally half-webbed, referring to the feet.

Status and Distribution: Although surveys in the mid-eighties indicated an increase in the population of this species, it is on the provincial Yellow List because of indications of a recent decline over the grassland portion of its range. It breeds in central and southern Alberta west to the foothills and north to St. Paul.

● ●

Field Checklist

✓**Habitat:** It favors moist and wet meadows and the grassy edges of sloughs and lakes, rarely wandering far from water. It nests on the upper edges of beaches or on drier grassy areas near marshes.

✓✓✓**Sight:** It is a large shorebird with brownish-gray coloration that is lightly streaked with black. It has a straight bill, white rump, light tail and gray-blue legs. The dark wings have a conspicuous white wing bar visible in flight that contrasts with the black tips, producing a showy pattern.

✓✓✓**Sound:** A rolling, loud "pill-will-willet" or "pill-willet".

✓**Behavior:** It can be seen standing with its distinctive black and white wings raised above its back.

● ●

Similar species: None.

Remarks: As long as its wings are spread or it gives a call, there is no other species in the province that the Willet should be confused with. It is semi-colonial with pairs maintaining separate nesting and feeding territories. It feeds by walking along, pecking or probing in the mud and turning over rocks and debris with its bill to find insects.

Jan	Feb	Mar	Apr	May	Jun	Jul	Aug	Sep	Oct	Nov	Dec

　　WILL ☐　　**Date:** _____

Sandpipers

WHIMBREL

Numenius phaeopus

L: 410 mm   W: 450 g   Egg: 59 x 41 mm

Etymology: *Numenius* (Gr.) - *neos*, "new" and *mene*, "moon;" *phaeopus* (Gr.) - *phaios* "dusky" and *pous* "foot," for the grayish feet and legs.

Status and Distribution: The main migration routes for this bird are up the Pacific coast or the shores of the Great Lakes. The Whimbrel is a scarce but regular spring migrant through east-central Alberta, with observations at Buffalo, Beaverhill, and Miquelon lakes and Lac la Nonne.

• •

Field Checklist

Habitat: On migration through the province, it frequents cultivated and short grassy fields, lakeshores, rocky shores, sandy beaches and the sparsely vegetated areas around marshes.

✓✓✓**Sight:** This large shorebird has a down-curved bill, heavy dark brown striping on the front neck, a dark stripe on the crown and another through the eye. The upper parts are grayish-brown, with a pale fringe on the feathers providing a mottled effect. The underparts are buffish white and the rump is white.

✓✓**Sound:** Its call is a clear whistled "ti-ti-ti-ti-ti."

Behavior: It feeds in small groups and tends to pick at visible prey more than probing through the sand and mud to find food.

• •

Similar species: Long-billed Curlew and Marbled Godwit.

Remarks: It is separated from the Long-billed Curlew by a shorter down-curved bill, a dark stripe through the eye, a light medial crown stripe, grayish (less pinkish-cinnamon) plumage and smaller overall size. The Marbled Godwit has a straighter bill, which is slightly upturned, and is darker buff on the undersides.

Jan	Feb	Mar	Apr	May	Jun	Jul	Aug	Sep	Oct	Nov	Dec

WHIM ❒   Date: _____

LONG-BILLED CURLEW

Numenius americanus

L: 539 mm   W: 531 g   Egg: 65 x 46 mm

Etymology: *Numenius* (Gr.) - *neos*, "new" and *mene*, "moon;" *americanus* (ML.) - "of America."

Status and Distribution: Numbers are low and probably declining as native grasslands are converted to agriculture. This bird is on the province's Blue List which denotes a species at risk. It is found in isolated populations in the grasslands of southern Alberta.

• •

Field Checklist

✓✓**Habitat:** It requires large tracts of open, dry grassland with low vegetative cover and no visual barriers for its nesting habitat. In fall migration it frequents wetter habitats.

✓✓✓**Sight:** The largest shorebird in the province, it is mottled dark brown and pinky-buff above, pale, pinky-buff below, with a creamy breast and throat. There are fine dark streakings on the neck and the head is grayish-brown. In flight the cinnamon-colored trailing edge of the wing and the barred tail are visible.

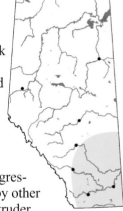

✓✓**Sound:** One of its calls is a drawn out "curl-e-e-e-e-e-e-u-u-u."

Behavior: Breeding adults are vocal and aggressive in defending the nest and will be joined by other Long-billed Curlews in defence against an intruder.

• •

Similar species: Whimbrel and Marbled Godwit.

Remarks: Its size, long legs, long down-curved bill and buffy color make this shorebird distinctive during the breeding season. The Whimbrel, which is only present during spring migration, has a dark eye stripe and shorter bill. The Marbled Godwit has a straighter, slightly upturned bill. Extralimital breeding has been recorded at Glenbow and Beaverhill lakes.

Jan	Feb	Mar	Apr	May	Jun	Jul	Aug	Sep	Oct	Nov	Dec

LBCU ❑   Date: _____

Sandpipers

SANDERLING

Calidris alba

L: 194 mm   W: 60 g   Egg: 37 x 24 mm

Etymology: *Calidris* (Gr.) - "a gray speckled sandpiper;" *alba* (L.) - "white."

Status and Distribution: A common migrant that is very local in its distribution during migration. It is not seen in the Rocky Mountains.

• •

Field Checklist

Habitat: In migration it frequents the sandy windswept shores of large lakes, less often it forages on rocky shorelines and mudflats.

✓✓✓**Sight:** In the spring, the breeding plumage shows variegated rusty-brown upperparts including the head. The Sanderling has a short, heavy, black bill. The breast and front of the neck are rust-colored, the belly is white and the legs are black. In the fall, the rusty tints are absent with the upper parts an ashy-gray and white below and in front. In this plumage, the dark eye is conspicuous. In all seasons a white line along the base of the flight feathers is evident.

✓✓**Sound:** The bird uses a short, distinctive "twick" call when in flight.

✓**Behavior:** It follows the receding waves on a shoreline, feeding with a probing action on stranded food particles. As the wave returns the bird runs quickly ahead of it and begins the cycle again.

• •

Similar species: Other sandpipers.

Remarks: The breeding plumage and profile of this small shorebird are distinctive and unlike other sandpipers. This species lacks a hind toe. In its winter plumage, it is the palest of any of the sandpipers.

Jan	Feb	Mar	Apr	May	Jun	Jul	Aug	Sep	Oct	Nov	Dec

SAND ❑   Date: _____

SEMIPALMATED SANDPIPER

Calidris pusilla

L: 146 mm   W: 24 g   Eggs: 31 x 20.5 mm

Etymology: *Calidris* (Gr.) - "a gray speckled sandpiper;" *pusilla* (L.) "very small."

Status and Distribution: This sandpiper is a common migrant in the province in spring and fall. It is rare in the mountain areas.

• •

Field Checklist

Habitat: In migration this sandpiper is found on mudflats near lakes and marshes

✓✓✓**Sight:** It is named for the partial webbing between its toes. Its upperparts are a mixture of dull gray, black and buff, with these feathers having a pale outer fringe. The throat is white, the breast band is extensively streaked (this is lighter in the fall) and there is a dark streak through the eye. The underparts are white. It has a short, straight, black bill with a deep base, and black legs. In flight a narrow white wing bar and white sides are visible.

Sound: The call of this shorebird is a harsh, low-pitched "cheh."

Behavior: This is one of the earliest migrants to return in the fall.

• •

Similar species: Western Sandpiper, Least Sandpiper.

Remarks: In the fall it is distinguished from other sandpipers by its white throat band, black legs and short stout bill. The plumage of the Western Sandpiper is rustier and more heavily streaked, but in the fall it is very difficult to separate these two birds. The Least Sandpiper has a darker breast band and yellowish legs, but no web between toes.

Jan	Feb	Mar	Apr	May	Jun	Jul	Aug	Sep	Oct	Nov	Dec

    SESA ❑   Date: _____

WHITE-RUMPED SANDPIPER

Calidris fuscicollis

L: 184 mm   W: 41 g   Egg: 33 x 23 mm

Photo: G.Beversbergen

Etymology: *Calidris* (Gr.) - "a gray speckled sandpiper;" *fuscicollis* (L.) - *fuscus,* "dusky" and *collum,* "neck."

Status and Distribution: This shorebird is a rare but regular migrant through eastern Alberta, most commonly observed in the spring. It is regularly found staging in the Provost-Chauvin area and at Beaverhill Lake.

Field Checklist

Habitat: On migration it favors muddy lake shores and edges of marshes, mudflats, beaches and wet fields.

✓✓✓**Sight:** The upperparts are mottled gray, buff and black, with the crown and ear patches a cinnamon color. The throat and breast are streaked and spotted with dark brown-black. It is white below with a conspicuous white rump patch, usually hidden by the long wings, extending beyond the tail. It has a short straight bill and short legs. In the fall, the breast band is somewhat lighter and appears a light gray or buff.

✓✓**Sound:** The call is a high-pitched "jeet."

Behavior: They are usually seen in the company of other small sandpipers.

Similar species: Baird's Sandpiper and Stilt Sandpiper.

Remarks: It is the only small, short-legged sandpiper with a white rump. It is generally grayer than the Baird's, which has a black rump. The Stilt Sandpiper has a white rump but is narrower overall, has much longer legs and a longer bill. The fall migration is in a more southeasterly direction from their Arctic breeding grounds making them a very rare fall migrant in Alberta.

Jan	Feb	Mar	Apr	May	Jun	Jul	Aug	Sep	Oct	Nov	Dec

WRSA ☐   Date: _____

BAIRD'S
SANDPIPER

Calidris bairdii

L: 175 mm   W: 38 g   Egg: 33 x 23 mm

Etymology: *Calidris* (Gr.) - "a gray speckled sandpiper;" *bairdii* (ML.)- for Spencer F. Baird.

Status and Distribution: On migration it appears across the province but only rarely in the mountain areas. An important staging area is in the Chauvin-Provost area, where there are shallow saline lakes in sandy soil.

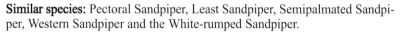

Field Checklist

✓**Habitat:** It prefers the drier parts of wet areas, frequenting beaches, mudflats of larger lakes, as well as the margins of sloughs.

✓✓✓**Sight:** Upperparts are brown with feather edges variegated with rust and white. It has a white chin, buff breast band slightly streaked, grayish brown rump, white underparts, a straight and short bill, and black legs with unwebbed toes.

✓✓**Sound:** The call is a low "kriet, kriet."

✓**Behavior:** Baird's rarely feeds in water and frequently accompanies flocks of other small sandpipers.

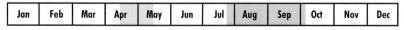

Similar species: Pectoral Sandpiper, Least Sandpiper, Semipalmated Sandpiper, Western Sandpiper and the White-rumped Sandpiper.

Remarks: It is separated from the Pectoral and the Least Sandpipers by the black legs and fainter streaking on its breast. It is larger than the Semipalmated and Western, has a more obvious buff breast band and lacks the webbing between the toes. The black rump separates it from the White-rumped Sandpiper.

Jan	Feb	Mar	Apr	May	Jun	Jul	Aug	Sep	Oct	Nov	Dec

BASA ☐   Date: _____

Sandpipers

Order: Charadriiformes - Family: Scolopacidae

STILT SANDPIPER

Micropalama himantopus

L: 203 mm W: 54 g Egg: 35.5 x 25.4 mm

Etymology: *Micropalama* (Gr.) - *mikros,* "small" and *palame,* "a web;" *himantopus* (Gr.) - *himatos,* "strap" and *pous,* "feet."

Status and Distribution: They are a regular spring and fall migrant across the province, using areas in central Alberta such as Beaverhill Lake as staging areas. It is only rarely recorded in the mountains and foothills.

●●

Field Checklist

Habitat: It prefers fresh water ponds, marshes and lakes with extensive shallow areas.

✓✓✓**Sight:** The long bill is spatulated at the blunt tip and slightly downcurved and the longish legs are a pale olive-yellow. In breeding plumage, it has a dark regularly barred lower breast and abdomen, a heavily streaked neck and a rust-colored cheek patch with a white stripe above the eye. The upper parts are dark brown with the feathers bordered with white and rust. In winter plumage, the barring is absent and the underparts are a grayish-white. In flight a white rump patch is evident. The female is larger than the male.

✓**Sound:** A single, low noted "wru."

✓✓**Behavior:** Stilt Sandpipers are waders and feed in water up to their bellies, usually with their head and neck submerged, as they probe the bottom.

●●

Similar species: Lesser Yellowlegs and dowitchers

Remarks: It is distinguished from the Lesser Yellowlegs by the pale greenish rather than bright yellow legs, its smaller size and the white stripe over the eye. It has a white rump patch, unlike dowitchers in which the white extends up the back. It lacks the white wing stripe of the dowitcher.

Jan	Feb	Mar	Apr	May	Jun	Jul	Aug	Sep	Oct	Nov	Dec

SLSA ☐   Date: _____

BUFF-BREASTED SANDPIPER

Tryngites subruficollis

Photo: G.Beyersbergen

L: 207 mm   W: 69 g   Egg: 36.8 x 26.7 mm

Etymology: *Tryngites* (Gr.) - *tryngas,* "a sandpiper;" *subruficollis* (ML.) - "reddish below the neck."

Status and Distribution: It is a regular but uncommon spring and fall migrant in the province. The largest numbers occur at Beaverhill Lake, but they are also found irregularly at lakes around Hanna, Calgary and Strathmore, and in Wood Buffalo National Park. Very rarely are they observed in the mountain areas.

● ●

Field Checklist

✓**Habitat:** This bird prefers uplands near water when migrating. These include grassy areas, stubble and cultivated fields and meadows.

✓✓**Sight:** A small sandpiper with a long thin body shape. The buff color below extends up the neck to the head. It is dark brown above with the feathers fringed with reddish brown. The head, with a dark-flecked crown, is small and there is a short black bill. In flight, the white underwings, with a dark grayish trailing edge, are quite evident. The legs are a dull yellow. The male is a little larger than the female.

Sound: In flight or alarm, this sandpiper utters a "prreeet."

Behavior: They are reluctant to fly when disturbed but when they do, they do not fly very far.

● ●

Similar species: Baird's Sandpiper

Remarks: The buff of this species is more evident than on the Baird's, and it lacks the white throat and black legs of the latter. The bird is shaped like an Upland Sandpiper, a species it can be seen with on migration.

Jan	Feb	Mar	Apr	May	Jun	Jul	Aug	Sep	Oct	Nov	Dec

BBSA ☐   Date: _____

Sandpipers

SHORT-BILLED DOWITCHER

Limnodromus griseus

L: 290 mm   W: 130 g   Egg: 41 x 29 mm

Etymology: *Limnodromus* (Gr.) - *limne,* "Marsh" and *dromos,* "running;" *griseus* (ML.) - "gray."

Status and Distribution: This shorebird is an uncommon breeder in the boreal forest. It is found breeding very locally from Edmonton northward and is a transient in the southern part of Alberta.

● ●

Field Checklist

✓**Habitat:** Breeding habitat is muskegs, edges of lakes and open bogs with low vegetation. Sloughs and ponds with muddy edges are favored in migration.

✓✓✓**Sight:** A medium-sized sandpiper with a straight bill about twice as long as the head and a pale line above the eye. It has reddish underparts, white lower back barred with black on the rump and tail. The back is mottled brown-buff with no distinctive pattern. In the fall the bird is more grayish.

✓✓**Sound:** The call of this dowitcher is a raspy "tu-tu-tu."

✓**Behavior:** It forages by probing the water with rapid up-and-down bill movements while standing in shallow water.

● ●

Similar species: Common Snipe and Long-billed Dowitcher.

Remarks: The subspecies in Alberta is *L. g. hendersoni.* It is distinguished from the Common Snipe by its reddish breast, the white patch on the rump and back and the lack of buffy stripes on the back. It is so similar to the Long-billed Dowitcher that it is very difficult to separate them in the field although the subspecies in the province is somewhat lighter than the Long-billed. The Short-billed Dowitcher nests in Alberta while the Long-billed is a migrant. The calls of the two species are distinctive.

Jan	Feb	Mar	Apr	May	Jun	Jul	Aug	Sep	Oct	Nov	Dec

126   SBDO ☐   Date: _____

LONG-BILLED DOWITCHER

Limnodromus scolopaceus

L: 282 mm   W: 107 g   Egg: 44.5 x 29 mm

Etymology: *Limnodromus* (Gr.) - *limne,* "Marsh" and *dromos,* "running;" *scolopaceus* (Gr.) - *scolopax,* "Woodcock."

Status and Distribution: This common and widespread migrant can be observed in all parts of the province on its migration north and south, but is rare in the mountain areas.

• •

Field Checklist

Habitat: In migration it favors edges of freshwater ponds and impoundments where it feeds in shallow pools and mudflats.

✓✓**Sight:** Like the Short-billed Dowitcher it is medium-sized with a straight bill about twice as long as the head and a pale line above the eye. It has reddish underparts that extend down over the belly, sides are barred, and the white lower back is barred with narrow buff bands on the rump and tail. The back is mottled brown-buff with no distinctive pattern. In the fall the bird is grayer.

✓✓**Sound:** A high-pitched "keek" is usually uttered only in a single note.

✓**Behavior:** They are not wary and tend to stay together in conspecific flocks even when feeding on the ground, rarely mixing with other species.

• •

Similar species: Short-billed Dowitcher

Remarks: Distinctions are detailed under the Short-billed Dowitcher. The Long-billed is somewhat darker than the subspecies of Short-billed found in Alberta and does not have as much white on the belly. The call of the Long-billed is higher-pitched than that of the Short-billed. In the fall the adult birds return to Alberta in early August, with the birds of the year moving south from their breeding grounds in late August or early September.

Jan	Feb	Mar	Apr	May	Jun	Jul	Aug	Sep	Oct	Nov	Dec

LBDO ☐   Date: _____

COMMON SNIPE

Gallinago gallinago

L: 259 mm   W: 92 g   Egg: 39 x 28 mm

Etymology: *Gallinago* (L.) - *gallina*, "a hen."

Status and Distribution: This is a common breeder in the parkland, foothills and southern boreal forest regions of the province. In all other areas it breeds locally where suitable wetlands are available.

Field Checklist

Habitat: This species is found in woodland bogs, fens, grassy margins of sloughs, moist meadows, and similar areas that provide soft mud and low cover. The nest is usually in drier areas.

✓✓✓**Sight:** The Common Snipe has an extremely long bill and dark and light stripes on the head. The upperparts are various shades of browns and buffs with buff stripes down the back, the tail is short and orange-red with a black subterminal stripe. The breast is light with darker streaks and bars. The undersides are white.

✓✓✓**Sound:** The male's tail feathers produce a hollow drumming sound from its "winnowing" aerial display in the spring. The call, a raspy "scape, scape" is used when the bird is disturbed.

✓✓**Behavior:** It can be recognized by its erratic zig-zag flight when flushed. The Snipe feeds by probing with its bill in the mud as it pivots around in a small semi-circle.

Similar species: Dowitchers

Remarks: It has the same long bill as the dowitchers, but the brick-red tail barred with black differs from the largely white tail of the dowitchers. The Common Snipe was formerly known as Wilson's Snipe and is the only game species of shorebird in the province. It is sensitive to nest disturbance and often abandons the nest after a single visitation by humans.

Jan	Feb	Mar	Apr	May	Jun	Jul	Aug	Sep	Oct	Nov	Dec

Order: Charadriiformes - Family: Scolopacidae

WILSON'S PHALAROPE

Phalaropus tricolor

Photo: G. Beyersbergen

Phalaropes

L: 227 mm   W: 60 g   Egg: 37 x 24 mm

Etymology: *Phalaropus* (Gr.) - *phalaris*, "a coot," *pous*, "feet;" *tricolor* - "three colors."

Status and Distribution: This is a common breeder in the grassland, parkland and southern boreal forest regions north of Cold Lake and Lesser Slave Lake and west into the mountains. In the northern parts of Alberta it is local and widespread.

Field Checklist

Habitat: This phalarope favors sloughs and shallow lakes with wet meadows and grassy marshes.

✓✓✓**Sight:** The female is larger than the male and is more brightly colored. She has a black stripe through the eye and down the side of the neck extending into a rust neck stripe. The crown and back of the neck are light gray, chin is white, wings dark with no white stripe, and the rump is white. The male is duller and has a more prominent white line above the eye.

✓✓**Sound:** A low, nasal "cawurk" is distinctive from sounds made by the other phalaropes.

✓**Behavior:** The female initiates courtship and, after laying the eggs, leaves all the brooding and tending of the young to the male as she goes off to find another mate.

Similar species: Other phalarope species.

Remarks: The Wilson's Phalarope is separated from the other phalaropes by the lack of a white stripe on the spread wing. The sharp needle-like bill separates it from the Red Phalarope which has a broader bill. Although the phalaropes are known for their swimming habits, this species forages more on land than in the water.

Jan	Feb	Mar	Apr	May	Jun	Jul	Aug	Sep	Oct	Nov	Dec

WIPH ❑   Date: _____

Order: Charadriiformes - Family: Scolopacidae

RED-NECKED PHALAROPE

Phalaropus lobatus

L: *191 mm W: 37 g Egg: 30 x 21 mm*

Etymology: *Phalaropus* (Gr.) - *phalaris,* "a coot" and *pous,* "feet;" *lobatus* - "lobed."

Status and Distribution: The northern edge of the province is at the southern extremity of this phalarope's breeding range. It is an extremely rare breeder with the only confirmed breeding taking place in the Caribou Mountains. During migration it frequents lakes in east-central Alberta.

● ●

Field Checklist

✓**Habitat:** It breeds in tundra and tundra-forest transition zones, preferring small lakes, bogs and marshes where adjacent sedges and mossy hummocks provide suitable nesting sites.

✓✓**Sight:** The female of this small phalarope has a dark crown and face, black breast, a brick-red line that extends down the neck and then across the breast below the white throat patch. The upperparts are dark gray and the underparts are white. There is a white wing stripe that is visible in flight. The male is smaller and duller.

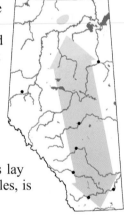

Sound: A sharp "kip, kip, kip."

✓**Behavior:** Serial polyandry, where females lay two successive clutches for two different males, is common with this species.

● ●

Similar species: Red Phalarope and Wilson's Phalarope

Remarks: The lack of extensive red on the underparts and a very slender, needle-like bill distinguishes this species from the Red Phalarope. A darker crown and the brick red on the sides of the neck rather than black, and the white wing stripe visible in flight separates it from Wilson's Phalarope. This species was formerly known as the Northern Phalarope.

Jan	Feb	Mar	Apr	May	Jun	Jul	Aug	Sep	Oct	Nov	Dec

RDNP ☐   Date: _____

FRANKLIN'S GULL

Larus pipixcan

L: *359 mm* W: *265 g* Egg: *52 x 36 mm*

Etymology: *Larus* (L.) - "a gull;" *pipixcan* - *pipican,* an Aztec word whose meaning is unknown.

Status and Distribution: Franklin's gull breeds commonly in Alberta east of the mountains. It is found primarily in south and central Alberta, but is also found locally in the northern part of the province.

●●●

Field Checklist

✓**Habitat:** This gull frequents larger, reedy lakes and marshes, and forages over water, grassy fields, meadows, ploughed land and other open areas. It nests on a floating mass of old reeds anchored to emergent vegetation.

✓✓✓**Sight:** It is a white-bodied, black-headed gull with a gray wing that has a white band bordering the black wing tips. The dark red bill is conspicuous and the legs are dark orange-to-maroon. In juvenile Franklin's Gulls, the primary wing feathers are solid black and the face and crown are gray.

✓✓**Sound:** The typical, continuously screamed call is "kuk-kuk-kuk."

✓**Behavior:** This is the common black-headed white-bodied gull often seen following farm equipment during cultivation or flycatching over open fields.

●●●

Similar species: Bonaparte's Gull.

Remarks: Although quite similar to the Bonaparte's, the Franklin's is larger, has a red not black bill, darker wings and lighter-colored legs. The juvenile Franklin's has darker primaries, darker head and face and lacks the dark ear patch of the juvenile Bonaparte's. From late July to late September these gulls are seen in large numbers on lakes in southern Alberta.

Jan	Feb	Mar	Apr	May	Jun	Jul	Aug	Sep	Oct	Nov	Dec

FRGU ☐   Date: _____

BONAPARTE'S GULL

Larus philadelphia

Photo: R. Gehlert

L: 345 mm   W: 192 g   Egg: 49 x 34 mm

Etymology: *Larus* (L.) - "a gull;" *philadelphia* (ML.) - Philadelphia, where it was first described.

Status and Distribution: This gull is common locally and is widespread in the boreal and foothills regions of the province. It has been recorded from Caroline north to the 60th parallel. It is a rare migrant and summer visitor in the mountain areas, and is observed on migration in the parkland and prairie.

● ●

Field Checklist

✓✓✓**Habitat:** It breeds in the vicinity of lakes, ponds and muskegs in the coniferous woodlands. It nests in conifers near water.

✓✓**Sight:** This smallest of Alberta's gulls is white-bodied, black-headed and black-billed. The primary feathers of the wing are predominantly white, with a thin black line on the trailing edge of the outer wing. In winter plumage and in juveniles, the head is lighter with a conspicuous darker patch.

✓**Sound:** This gull's call is a nasal tern-like "cheerr".

✓✓**Behavior:** The flight pattern is light, buoyant and tern-like. These gulls hawk insects from the air or drop onto insects and fish from a hover.

● ●

Similar species: Franklin's Gull.

Remarks: It is smaller than the Franklin's Gull, has a black not red bill, more white in a triangular patch on the leading edge of the outer wing and lacks the conspicuous black patch on the wing tip. The juvenile of the Bonaparte's has a lighter color on the head and a distinctive dark ear patch. The small muskeg lakes near which the Bonaparte's Gull breeds are the type of wetland habitat that is easily impacted by the cutting of northern forests.

Jan	Feb	Mar	Apr	May	Jun	Jul	Aug	Sep	Oct	Nov	Dec

MEW GULL

Larus canus

L: 440 mm W: 368 g Egg: 57 x 41 mm

Etymology: *Larus* (L.) - "a gull;" *canus* (L.) - "grayish-white."

Status and Distribution: Mew Gulls are rare and local breeders in the northeast corner of the province which is at the southern periphery of their breeding range. Breeding evidence has been recorded in the Caribou Mountains, Fort McMurray, Bocquene and Rock Island lakes. It has been recorded in migration at landfill sites in Edmonton and Calgary.

• •

Field Checklist

✓**Habitat:** In breeding season, it uses marshy areas, shallow lakes, ponds and rivers in northern forested areas of the province. The nest is usually on the ground, on marshy or rocky shores but will sometimes be in trees.

✓✓✓**Sight:** A small gull with a round, white head and breast, and a gray mantle. It is distinguished by the lack of markings on its short, yellow bill, a dark eye and a larger white patch on black wing tips. The legs are greenish-yellow

✓✓✓**Sound:** It has a distinctive "mewing " call.

✓**Behavior:** It dives for fish more than other gulls, but rarely plunges below the surface.

• •

Similar species: Ring-billed Gull

Remarks: It is difficult to distinguish from the similar white-headed Ring-billed Gull, but it is slightly smaller, has a short, yellow unmarked bill, shows more white on its wing tips and has a darker eye. It is a more graceful bird than the Ring-billed. The birds are common summer residents on some northern lakes, but most individuals seen are subadults. In southern Alberta it is recorded more often during fall migration. It was previously called the Short-billed Gull.

Jan	Feb	Mar	Apr	May	Jun	Jul	Aug	Sep	Oct	Nov	Dec

MEGU ☐   Date: _____

Gulls

RING-BILLED GULL

Larus delawarensis

L: 456 mm   W: 500 g   Egg: 59 x 42 mm

Etymology: *Larus* (L.) - "a gull;"
delawarensis (ML.) - "of Delaware."

Status and Distribution: This is the most abundant gull in North America and breeds locally in eastern Alberta, from Pakowki Lake in the south to Lake Athabasca in the north and west to the foothills. It is observed in the foothills and mountains but there are no confirmed breeding records.

● ●

Field Checklist

✓**Habitat:** It breeds on the shores and islands of larger fresh-water and alkaline lakes, and forages over fields, mudflats, water and landfill sites.

✓✓✓**Sight:** This gull has the typical white head, gray mantle and black wing tips, but has the conspicuous black ring on its bill. It has a light-colored eye, a red eye-ring and yellow-green legs. The juvenile of this species is the whitest of the larger gulls and has a tail bar.

✓**Sound:** A high-pitched "ki-eow."

✓**Behavior:** In late summer and autumn, it is a common sight at urban locations such as garbage dumps, parking lots, parks and golf courses where it scavenges for food.

● ●

Similar species: Mew Gull, Herring Gull and California Gull

Remarks: It is larger than the Mew Gull, lighter-colored and has the distinctive marking on the bill. It is smaller than the Herring Gull and has a black ring and not a red spot on the bill, and yellow not pinkish legs. It is smaller than the California Gull, has a lighter eye and lacks the red spot on the bill. Large colonies with more than 1000 pairs are found at Miquelon Lake, Lake Newell, Keho Lake, Frank Lake, Irricana Reservoir, Dowling Lake and Buffalo Lake.

Jan	Feb	Mar	Apr	May	Jun	Jul	Aug	Sep	Oct	Nov	Dec

RBGU ❑   Date: _____

CALIFORNIA GULL

Larus californicus

Photo: T. Thormin

L: 540 mm   W: 758 g   Egg: 68 x 46 mm

Etymology: *Larus* (L.) - "a gull;" *californicus* (ML.) - "of California."

Status and Distribution: Populations are stable and widespread. It breeds east of the foothills from Ross Lake and the St. Mary's Reservoir north to Margaret Lake in the Caribou Mountains. It is observed in mountain areas during migration.

• •

Field Checklist

✓**Habitat:** It breeds near freshwater and alkaline lakes, marshes and rivers, preferring a treeless island where spring vegetation is sparse, but may be seen around ploughed fields and landfills.

✓✓✓**Sight:** It has the same general coloration as the Herring Gull but has a darker gray mantle. It is distinguished by the red spot with a black fleck on its bill, and a dark eye with a reddish eye-ring. The legs are yellow.

✓**Sound:** The call is a repetitive "'ke-yah."

✓**Behavior:** It nests in large colonies. Some with over 10,000 pairs are found at Irricana Reservoir, Lake Newell, Miquelon Lake, Keho Lake and Chip Lake.

• •

Similar species: Herring Gull and Ring-billed Gull

Remarks: It is intermediate in size between the smaller Ring-billed and larger Herring Gull and has a dark eye unlike the light eyes of the other two species. Unlike the Herring Gull, it has a black fleck in the red spot on the bill and its legs are yellow, not flesh-colored. However, first-year California and Herring gulls are very similar. The main distinctions between the California and the Ring-billed are the larger size of the former and the black ring on the bill of the latter. Overwintering of this species has been recorded in Alberta.

Jan	Feb	Mar	Apr	May	Jun	Jul	Aug	Sep	Oct	Nov	Dec

CAGU ❐   Date: _____

Terns

COMMON TERN

Sterna hirundo

Photo: K.Morck

L: 358 mm W: 130 g Egg: 42 x 30 mm

Etymology: *Sterna* (ML.) - "a tern;" *hirundo* (L.) - "a swallow," for the resemblance in shape and flight to the swallow.

Status and Distribution: These colonial breeders are commonly observed in southern and central Alberta and breed locally in the rest of the province east of the foothills. Colonies have been recorded on Lake Newell, Buffalo, Nakama, Eagle, Pakowki, Beaverhill, Miquelon, Burstall, St. Agnes, Bistcho and Andrew lakes.

• •

Field Checklist

✓**Habitat:** It is found in the vicinity of large bodies of open water, rivers, canals and creeks, which it patrols for food. It breeds on islands, peninsulas and shorelines of lakes.

✓✓✓**Sight:** This small tern has a black crown and nape, gray mantle, white underparts with a grayish tinge, white forked tail, red bill with a black tip and orange legs and feet. In winter plumage, the forehead is lighter and the black coloration extends from in front of the eye to the back of the head forming a band across the nape.

✓**Sound:** A trilly, raspy "kee-arr."

✓**Behavior:** During the early phase of courtship, the male displays his fishing skills by holding a fish in its beak and flying back and forth over the colony, uttering a "fish" call.

• •

Similar species: Forster's Tern and Arctic Tern

Remarks: The three medium-sized terns in Alberta are very similar with only slight differences in appearance. The Common differs from the Forster's by having a grayer tinge to the underparts, a white rather than gray tail and a softer call. The black bar extending around its head is a distinguishing feature of the Common Tern in winter plumage. The difference between the Common and Arctic terns is the bill. The Common has a black tip while that of the Arctic Tern is solid red.

Jan	Feb	Mar	Apr	May	Jun	Jul	Aug	Sep	Oct	Nov	Dec

COTE ☐   Date: _____

ARCTIC TERN
Sterna paradisaea

L: 360 mm   W: 115 g   Egg: 42 x 30 mm

Etymology: *Sterna* (ML.) - "a tern;" *paradisaea* (L.) - *paradisus,* "an enclosure, a park."

Status and Distribution: This marathoner of migrants annually logs about 30,000 km on its round trip and is a rare migrant through the province, although it is regularly observed near the west end of Lake Athabasca. A specimen was also collected at Lac la Nonne.

• •

Field Checklist

Habitat: Look for the Arctic Tern foraging over larger bodies of water as it moves through Alberta.

✓✓✓**Sight:** It has the same basic coloration of the Common Tern. The Arctic Tern has a black crown, white face and neck, a gray mantle, a deeply forked white tail, short red legs and a deep red bill with no black on the tip. The underparts are more distinctively gray which extends up on the lower face.

✓**Sound:** A high pitched "keek-keek."

Behavior: Banding records may document the longevity a species. One Arctic Tern died in its natal colony 27 years after being banded as a fledgling.

• •

Similar species: Common Tern and Forster's Tern

Remarks: It differs from the Common Tern having a darker gray mantle across the wings and back, shorter legs and a deeper reddish bill, lacking any black on the tip. It is grayer on the underparts. It is darker than the Forster's and their ranges are different. Although it has not been recorded as breeding in Alberta, breeding has been documented on the Saskatchewan side of Lake Athabasca.

Jan	Feb	Mar	Apr	May	Jun	Jul	Aug	Sep	Oct	Nov	Dec

ARTE ☐   Date: _____

FORSTER'S TERN
Sterna forsteri

L: 396 mm   W: 138 g   Egg: 43 x 31 mm

Etymology: *Sterna* (ML.) - "a tern;"
forsteri (ML.) - for Johann R. Forster, a
German naturalist.

Status and Distribution: This is an
uncommon breeder in Alberta which is
at the northern edge of its breeding
range. It breeds locally north to Cold
Lake, west to the foothills. Recent
records indicate that its range is expanding northward.

• •

Field Checklist

✓✓**Habitat:** It inhabits marshes and the marshy bays of lakes,
nesting in the deeper portions of large cattail marshes.

✓✓✓**Sight:** Forster's is a medium-sized tern with black crown
and nape. The bill is orange with a black tip,
breast and abdomen are white, the mantle over
the back and wings is gray and the tail is
white. On the wing, the primaries are lighter
than the rest of the wing. In late autumn and
winter, the crown is white and there is a black
eye-bar extending to the ear, but not around
the back of the head.

✓✓**Sound:** A raspy "zaaaah" and a
"kyeeer." Both calls are more nasal than those
of other terns.

✓**Behavior:** When diving for fish, it folds its wings
and submerges completely. Upon emerging, it will
shake off the water in mid-flight.

• •

Similar species: Common Tern and Arctic Tern

Remarks: Very similar to the Common Tern, its underparts are whiter (no
grayish tinge) and the tail is gray rather than white. The nasal call once
heard will also help in identifying this species. It is a lighter gray across the
mantle than the Arctic Tern, which is an uncommon migrant in the province.
The bill of the Arctic is red rather than orange.

Jan	Feb	Mar	Apr	May	Jun	Jul	Aug	Sep	Oct	Nov	Dec

Order: Charadriiformes - Family: Laridae

Terns

BLACK TERN
Chilidonias niger

L: 238 mm   W: 62 g   Egg: 43 x 25 mm

Etymology: *Chilidonias* (Gr.) -
chelidon, "a swallow;" *niger* (L.) -
"black."

Status and Distribution: The
populations of this tern across North
America are in decline because of loss
of habitat and as such it is on the
provincial Yellow List. Although it is
found in all regions of the province, it is most abundant in the parkland and
southern boreal forest regions. It is widespread in the northern parts of the
province and rare in the mountains and foothills.

Field Checklist

✓**Habitat:** The Black Tern inhabits shallow lakes, marshes,
sloughs, ponds and wet meadows where there are extensive
open shallows and moderate amounts of
emergent vegetation.

✓✓✓**Sight:** This small tern is slate gray with
a black head, neck and underparts. The tail is
only slightly forked. In the late summer, the
black areas are mostly white with a gray
crown and a connecting dark patch extending
down behind the eye.

✓**Sound:** A sharp "kip" is repeated frequently.

✓✓**Behavior:** The Black Tern is a noisy and fierce
defender of the nest and will dive-bomb intruders,
sometimes spraying them with red excrement.

Similar species: None

Remarks: The size and coloration of this species make it distinctive. It is
more of an insect feeder than other terns and is seen hovering over open
water or open fields waiting to pick its prey off the surface or hawking them
in mid-air. The habitat of this species is under pressure mainly due to marsh
drainage for agricultural purposes.

Jan	Feb	Mar	Apr	May	Jun	Jul	Aug	Sep	Oct	Nov	Dec

141   BLTE ☐   Date: _____

GREAT HORNED OWL

Order: Strigiformes - Family: Strigidae

Photo: J.Kristensen

Bubo virginianus

L: 541 mm W: 1339 g Egg: 56 x 47 mm

Etymology: *Bubo* (L.) - "horned owl;" *virginianus* (ML.) - "of Virginia," where it was first described.

Status and Distribution: The provincial bird of Alberta is common in the grassland and parkland regions and the southern part of the boreal region. It is widely distributed throughout the rest of the province.

• •

Field Checklist

Habitat: It uses many different habitats including both deciduous and coniferous woodlands, isolated stands of trees in rural and urban settings and wooded coulees and river valleys.

✓✓✓**Sight:** This large, fierce-looking owl has prominent ear tufts. Its coloration can vary from dark brown, variegated with small amounts of white, to almost white with touches of dark brown. Most commonly, the upperparts are pale brown to gray, finely barred with black and white. There is a pale facial disc outlined in black, light throat, and underparts that are light buff barred with black and brown.

✓✓**Sound:** It has many different vocalizations but the most common is the familiar, low "whoo-whoo-whoo-whoo."

✓**Behavior:** The indigestible parts of prey are regurgitated as pellets found under nesting and roosting sites.

• •

Similar species: Snowy Owl and Long-eared Owl.

Remarks: In winter, the lighter individuals of this species may be confused with the Snowy Owl at a distance, but closer observation will reveal the prominent tufts of the Great Horned Owl and the finely vermiculated pattern of the underparts. It is separated from the Long-eared by its larger size and ear tufts that are more to the outside of the head and pointed more laterally.

Jan	Feb	Mar	Apr	May	Jun	Jul	Aug	Sep	Oct	Nov	Dec

GHOW ❑   Date: _____

SNOWY OWL

Nyctea scandiaca

Photo: D. Wood

L: 572 mm   W: 1740 g   Egg: 57 x 45 mm

Etymology: *Nyctea* (Gr.) - "nocturnal;" *scandiaca* (L.) - *scandia*, an ancient name for the southern part of Sweden.

Status and Distribution: This winter resident generally resides in its arctic breeding ground, but lack of prey forces it south. It is a regular visitor in the province in all areas except the mountains and the far south.

Field Checklist

Habitat: During the winter it prefers open fields and marshes for hunting.

✓✓✓**Sight:** A large owl with a round head and no ear tufts, yellow eyes and heavily feathered legs and feet. The males are mostly pure white, but usually with some dark bars except on the face and throat. Females, and especially young, have more barring overall.

Sound: It usually vocalizes only during the breeding season and as such is not often heard when it is in Alberta.

✓✓**Behavior:** It is an active hunter during the day and can often be seen perched along a roadway on a fence post or power pole scanning the open terrain. As it glides off these perches it is vulnerable to collisions with vehicles.

Similar species: None.

Remarks: From a distance, a light-colored Great Horned Owl may be confused with this species. There are observational records for this bird in the province during its breeding season but no confirmed breeding. In some winters, large numbers of these owls will move into the southernmost parts of the province and into the northern United States.

Jan	Feb	Mar	Apr	May	Jun	Jul	Aug	Sep	Oct	Nov	Dec

SNOW ☐   Date: _____

Owls

NORTHERN HAWK OWL

Surnia ulula

L: 370 mm   W: 315 g   Egg: 40 x 32 mm

Etymology: *Surnia* (Gr.) - "owl;" *ulula* (L.) - "I howl," for the bird's cry.

Status and Distribution: This owl is uncommon and widely distributed in its breeding range. It has been recorded breeding frequently in the boreal forest and foothills natural regions, less often in the northern Rocky Mountains, south to Banff.

●●●●●●●●●●●●●●●●●●●●●●●●●●●●●●●●●●●●●●●

Field Checklist

✓**Habitat:** A bird of the northern coniferous forests, it frequents open coniferous or mixed woodlands, muskeg, brushy edges of clearings and old burns. It usually nests in cavities in trees, taking advantage of abandoned Pileated Woodpecker holes.

✓✓✓**Sight:** This is a medium-sized owl that has dark brown upper parts spotted with white, a small inconspicuous facial disc that is buffy-white with a black border, sharply barred underparts and a long, wedge-shaped, pointed tail. It has the yellow iris of most owls and a yellow-tipped beak.

✓✓**Sound:** A chattering "kip, kip, kip" and a harsh rising "skreee-e-e-e-yep" are the two common calls of this species.

✓✓**Behavior:** Its "hawk-like" posture and flight give the Hawk Owl its name. This species is more active during the day than most woodland owls.

●●●●●●●●●●●●●●●●●●●●●●●●●●●●●●●●●●●●●●●

Similar species: None.

Remarks: Unlike other owls, this bird will sometimes construct its own crude nest of interwoven branches. Not regularly migratory, it may move south to a wintering territory. It has been recorded wintering in several locations from Edmonton south to the Montana border. The increase of logging activity in northern Alberta poses a threat to the older stands of trees required by this species for nesting.

Jan	Feb	Mar	Apr	May	Jun	Jul	Aug	Sep	Oct	Nov	Dec

NHOW ☐   Date: _____

NORTHERN PYGMY-OWL

Glaucidium gnoma

L: 170 mm   W: 48 g   Egg: 29 x 34 mm

Etymology: *Glaucidium* (Gr.) - *glaukidion*, "glaring;" *gnoma* (L.) - "a spirit or sprite," or *gnome* (Gr.), "intelligence."

Status and Distribution: An uncommon species in Alberta with the first confirmed nesting recorded in 1971. Its status is not well known, but it is found breeding in the southwest part of the boreal region and the adjacent foothills. It is rare breeder in the mountain parks and is observed in central and southern Alberta in the winter.

● ●

Field Checklist

✓✓**Habitat:** Heavy stands of coniferous forest or mixed wood with a good percentage of spruce, pine or fir that have meadows or other openings are the preferred habitat. The nest is in the abandoned hole of a Hairy Woodpecker or Northern Flicker.

✓✓✓**Sight:** A very small owl (bluebird size) heavy in stature with a small head and no ear tufts. The upperparts are dark brown with small light spots on the head, back and wing. The underparts are white and heavily streaked with brown. As shown above, it has black patches bordered with white on the hind neck that are like eyes in the back of its head.

✓✓**Sound:** The primary call of this species is a whistled series of "hoook" notes repeated every few seconds.

✓**Behavior:** The calling is usually at night but this owl hunts during the day.

● ●

Similar species: None.

Remarks: The small size, sharply streaked underparts and its unique display from the back of the head make this owl species quite unmistakable.

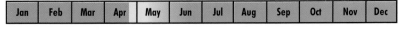

Jan	Feb	Mar	Apr	May	Jun	Jul	Aug	Sep	Oct	Nov	Dec

Order: Strigiformes - Family: Strigidae

BURROWING OWL

Athene cunicularia

Photo: K.Morck

L: 230 mm   W: 141 g   Egg: 31 x 26 mm

Etymology: *Athene* (Gr.) - from Athene, Greek goddess of wisdom; *cunicularia* (L.) - "a miner or burrower ."

Status and Distribution: It is on the provincial Red List and considered endangered as there are only 700 - 900 breeding pairs. Its current range is mainly limited to the grassland region of Alberta with some extension north and west into the parklands.

Field Checklist

✓✓**Habitat:** The typical habitat is level, open, short grass areas that are grazed. The nest is usually in the unoccupied burrow of a ground squirrel or badger.

✓✓✓**Sight:** It is generally a light brown color with white spots and has a rounded head with poorly defined facial disc and no ear tufts. The underparts are a buffy white barred with brown. The long, unfeathered legs and a stubby tail are distinctive. It has a prominent white chin stripe.

✓✓**Sound:** The most common call is a deep melodious "coo-coo-o-o." It also issues a defensive call when disturbed in the burrow that is an accurate mimicry of the rattle of a rattlesnake.

✓**Behavior:** It can be seen standing on a mound near its nest or at dusk on a fence post as it prepares to hunt.

Similar species: Short-eared Owl.

Remarks: It shares the same habitat as the Short-eared but is smaller and has barred not streaked underparts. The population of this owl is declining across the grasslands as agricultural practices are eliminating nest sites and ground squirrels. Pesticide use is taking its toll on insect prey and body chemistry of the Burrowing Owl.

Jan	Feb	Mar	Apr	May	Jun	Jul	Aug	Sep	Oct	Nov	Dec

BUOW ☐   Date: _____

BARRED OWL

Strix varia

L: 488 mm   W: 680 g   Egg: 50 x 42 mm

Photo: R.Gehlert

Etymology: *Strix* (L.) - "a screech owl;" *varia* (L.) - "variegated," for the plumage.

Status and Distribution: This species is on the provincial Yellow List as it is uncommon with fewer than 1000 breeding pairs in Alberta. It is found mainly in the southern boreal areas of Alberta and the coniferous foothills and montane forests west of Calgary north through Jasper National Park. Extralimital breeding has been recorded in the La Crete - Fort Vermilion area.

● ●

Field Checklist

Habitat: Breeding habitat is mature, mixed woods with nearby open country for foraging. It requires large deciduous trees for nesting cavities and favors areas along lakeshores and stream valleys.

✓✓✓**Sight:** It is a large grayish-brown owl with a large, rounded head, large dark eyes, a gray facial disc and no ear tufts. The upper throat and breast are barred laterally with vertical striping on the lower body.

✓✓✓**Sound:** This is the most vocal of all owls in our area and the owl with the widest range of calls. The most common and often heard call is a resonant hoot for which it gets its common name of Hoot Owl. The call is a two-part phrase that sounds like "who-cooks-for-you, who-cooks-for-you-all."

Behavior: It drinks water frequently and bathes often even in winter when open water is available.

● ●

Similar species: None.

Remarks: This is one of the rarest owls in the province and forest fragmentation by industrial development poses a threat to this species which requires large blocks of dense mature mixed forest.

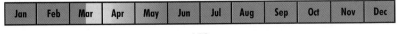

Jan	Feb	Mar	Apr	May	Jun	Jul	Aug	Sep	Oct	Nov	Dec

BAOW ☐ Date: _____

GREAT GRAY OWL

Strix nebulosa

L: 620 mm   W: 1056 g   Egg: 54 x 35 mm

Etymology: *Strix* (L.) - "a screech owl;" *nebulosa* (L.) - "clouded," as it has the color of a dark cloud.

Status and Distribution: The status of the Great Gray Owl in Alberta is unknown. It is an uncommon inhabitant of northern and western parts of the province with breeding in the foothills south to the Calgary area and in the parkland south to Buffalo Lake.

Field Checklist

✓**Habitat:** It is found in coniferous, deciduous, and mixed woodlands, usually near water sources, nesting in the abandoned nests of a crow, raven or hawk. It hunts the forest margin in brushy clearings and natural forest openings.

✓✓✓**Sight:** Measured by wingspan, it is the largest owl in the province. It is dark gray, lightly mottled with light gray and white, with a large round head, no ear tufts, circular facial discs, yellow eyes and a long tail that is barred with light and dark gray.

✓✓**Sound:** A deep "whoo-whoo-whooo" repeated at irregular intervals.

✓**Behavior:** This is the only species in the genus *Strix* that is not primarily nocturnal, its particularly small eyes being an adaptation for daylight hunting.

Similar species: None.

Remarks: The size, lack of ear tufts and general coloration of this species make it easily identifiable. Migrations of this bird are sporadic and are dependent on the cyclic levels of prey species. Some winters find them quite a bit south of their breeding area in a variety of woodland habitats in more settled parts of the province.

Jan	Feb	Mar	Apr	May	Jun	Jul	Aug	Sep	Oct	Nov	Dec

GGOW ☐   Date: _____

LONG-EARED OWL

Asio otus

L: 348 mm   W: 231 g   Egg: 42 x 33 mm

Etymology: *Asio* (L.) - "a kind of horned owl;" *otus* (Gr.) - "an eared owl."

Status and Distribution: It appears to be widespread and locally common in the central and southern parts of the province and rare in the southern mountains. Extralimital breeding has been recorded near Grande Prairie.

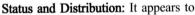

Field Checklist

✓**Habitat:** During breeding it uses woodlands, forest edges or patches where it has dense tree cover for nesting and roosting and adjacent open areas for hunting. It prefers these well timbered areas to be in close association with water sources.

✓✓✓**Sight:** Distinctive long ear tufts, reddish brown facial disc with narrow black markings around the eyes and stripes on the abdomen identify this species.

✓✓**Sound:** Its usual call, an extended series of "kwoo-kwoo-kwoo," is heard infrequently. It may also give a drawn-out cat-like scream when disturbed.

Behavior: Hunting takes place in open areas on the edge of woodlands. Difficult to locate as it remains hidden during daylight. It will pretend to be wounded to move intruders away from the nest.

Similar species: Great Horned and Short-eared owls.

Remarks: Tufts on the head are positioned much closer together than in other eared owls. It is the same general coloration as the Great Horned but is smaller and lacks the fine vermiculation on the upper body. The ear tufts of this owl are longer than the Short-eared and it does not have the bold brown striping on the breast.

Jan	Feb	Mar	Apr	May	Jun	Jul	Aug	Sep	Oct	Nov	Dec

LEOW ☐   Date: _____

Owls

SHORT-EARED OWL

Asio flammeus

Photo: R. Gehlert

L: 365 mm W: 302 g Egg: 40 x 31 mm

Etymology: *Asio* (L.) - "a kind of horned owl;" *flammeus* (L.) - "flame-colored," for its tawny plumage.

Inset: PMA

Status and Distribution: This owl is on the provincial Blue List as a species that may be at risk. The status of the provincial population is unknown but is suspected to be in decline. It is found locally in the grassland and parkland natural regions and is uncommon in the forested areas northwest to Peace River.

● ●

Field Checklist

✓**Habitat:** It breeds in relatively open country such as grasslands, marshland, brushy meadows and previously forested areas that have been cleared. The nest is on the ground in a little rise of land, well hidden by surrounding vegetation.

✓✓✓**Sight:** It is a medium-sized owl that is buffy white with broadly streaked upperparts. The underparts have narrower more sharply defined striping. The ear tufts are quite short or may be absent. It has small facial discs with dark areas around the yellow eyes and a distinctive black patch on the underwing near the wrist.

✓**Sound:** The call is a barking "keow," but this owl is relatively silent in comparison to the other owl species in the province.

✓✓**Behavior:** This owl flies low over its territory and pauses often to hover before swooping down on its prey. It is most active in the evening.

● ●

Similar species: Long-eared Owl.

Remarks: The habitat preferences, light coloration, much shorter and less prominent ear tufts and the sharper striping on the body are the distinguishing features of the Short-eared Owl.

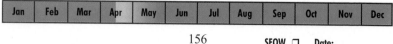

Jan	Feb	Mar	Apr	May	Jun	Jul	Aug	Sep	Oct	Nov	Dec

156   SEOW ☐   Date: _____

BOREAL OWL

Aegolius funereus

L: 240 mm   W: 102 g   Egg: 32 x 37 mm

Etymology: *Aegolius* (Gr.) - *aigolios,* "a kind of owl," or *aigos,* "a goat," as its call is similar to the bleating of a goat; *funereus* (L.) - "mournful."

Status and Distribution: There is no detailed information available on the status of this species in the province. It is uncommon and widely distributed in the forested parts of Alberta south to Bragg Creek and Priddis. In winter it may wander into the more settled areas of the province.

● ●

Field Checklist

✓**Habitat:** It prefers coniferous and mixed forests for breeding areas but tends to avoid large unbroken stands of pine. It commonly nests in abandoned Northern Flicker or Pileated Woodpecker holes.

✓✓✓**Sight:** It is a small, flat-headed owl with deep brown upperparts. There are small white spots on the crown and large, less distinct spots on the back. Its underparts are light with grayish-brown streaking. It has grayish-white facial discs with a black outer border, a pale horn-colored beak and yellow eyes.

✓**Sound:** The call is heard only during courtship and the nesting season. It is a soft bell-like sound that is repeated in series.

Behavior: It uses low perches from which it dives to take small animals.

● ●

Similar species: Northern Saw-whet Owl.

Remarks: The Boreal Owl is a larger, deeper brown bird than the reddish brown Northern Saw-whet. The white on the forehead is spotted not streaked. The Boreal has a pale-colored bill, not black like that of the Saw-whet.

Jan	Feb	Mar	Apr	May	Jun	Jul	Aug	Sep	Oct	Nov	Dec

BOOW ☐   Date: _____

Order: Strigiformes - Family: Strigidae

NORTHERN SAW-WHET OWL

Aegolius acadicus

L: 185 mm W: 70 g Egg: 30 x 25 mm

Etymology: *Aegolius* (Gr.) - *aigolios*, "a kind of owl," or *aigos*, "a goat," as its call is similar to the bleating of a goat; *acadicus* (L.) - "of Acadia," for Nova Scotia where the first specimen was found.

Status and Distribution: It is fairly common locally in the central part of the province. Its breeding range goes north to Manning and south in the mountains and foothills to Pincher Creek. It is rare in the grassland region of the province.

• •

Field Checklist

✓**Habitat:** It uses mature forests with a mixture of large trees. The Saw-whet prefers moist areas, alder thickets and tamarack bogs to drier deciduous areas.

✓✓✓**Sight:** This small owl has a relatively large, flattened head with no ear tufts but with fine white streaks on the crown. The upperparts are brown with some white and the underparts are white with broad reddish-brown streaking. The facial disc is white above the eye and buffy towards the outside. The bill is black.

✓✓✓**Sound:** The metallic squeal, which sounds like the filing of a saw, is not its most common call. During breeding, a more melodious, whistled "too-too-too" is repeated monotonously.

Behavior: The male brings food to the female throughout the incubation period.

• •

Similar species: Boreal Owl.

Remarks: The distinguishing features are detailed in the account on the Boreal Owl. The winter status of this species is not well known, but the scarcity of winter records may suggest that it is somewhat migratory.

Jan	Feb	Mar	Apr	May	Jun	Jul	Aug	Sep	Oct	Nov	Dec

NSWO ☐   Date: _____

COMMON NIGHTHAWK

Chordeiles minor

Photo J.Kristensen

L: 235 mm   W: 77 g   Egg: 30 x 22 mm

Etymology: *Chordeiles* (Gr.) - *choros*, "a circular dance" or "moving about" and *deile*, "evening;" *minor* (L.) - "smaller."

Status and Distribution: The population of the Common Nighthawk in the province is rated as stable. It is found in virtually all parts of the province.

● ●

Field Checklist

✓✓Habitat: It breeds in or near open habitat in a variety of areas including forest clearings, cultivated fields, barren rock and beaches. It nests on sand, gravel, leaf litter and in urban areas, on tar and gravel roofs.

✓✓Sight: The nighthawk has a barred belly, a white wing bar and blackish upper parts marbled in gray, white and buff. The male has a white tail bar, a white throat and chin which appears buffy on the female. It has a large head, large eyes and a small weak beak.

✓✓✓Sound: Their flight call is a nasal sounding "peent." During nesting the male will create a localized sonic "boom" near the nest, by forcing air through the flight primaries as he rounds out of a steep dive.

✓✓✓Behavior: This bird has a large mouth adapted for scooping insects in flight. These birds are normally seen in flight at dawn and dusk.

● ●

Similar species: Common Poorwill

Remarks: It is larger than the Common Poorwill, has a white rather than dark throat and chin and more pronounced barring below. It also has a longer tail, which is slightly forked instead of round. The Nighthawk is readily identified in flight by its dark appearance, slightly forked tail, long pointed wings and distinctive call.

Jan	Feb	Mar	Apr	May	Jun	Jul	Aug	Sep	Oct	Nov	Dec

Nightjars

Order: Caprimulgiformes - Family: Caprimulgidae

COMMON POORWILL

Phalaenoptilus nuttallii

L: 190 mm   W: 50 g   Egg: 26 x 20 mm

Etymology: *Phalaenoptilus* (Gr.) - *phalaina*, "a moth" and *ptilon*, "a feather;" *nuttallii* (ML.) - in honor of Thomas Nuttall, an English immigrant and American ornithologist.

Status and Distribution: The status is still unknown as Alberta is on the periphery of its range. With many recorded observations of this bird over the last fifty years, confirmation of breeding has not occurred. There have been several sightings in the Cypress Hills, Calgary, and near Dinosaur Provincial Park.

• •

Field Checklist

✓**Habitat:** A bird of the open, it breeds in semi-arid sagebrush benchlands and the grassy openings in warm arid valleys.

✓✓**Sight:** It is dark brown above frosted over with a fine pattern of light gray. The flanks and abdomen are light and finely barred and the breast and throat are dark with a white triangular throat patch. The tail is short, rounded and white-tipped.

✓✓✓**Sound:** It is more often heard at night than seen in the day. The repertoire includes a whistled "poor-will," which at close range sounds like "poor-willuck."

✓✓**Behavior:** Unlike the Common Nighthawk, this species will more frequently be seen in bat-like flight below the tree tops.

• •

Similar species: Common Nighthawk.

Remarks: The poorwill is distinguished by its smaller size, lack of white on the wings, rounded wings and tail, absence of any white tail band and the presence of white-tipped outer tail feathers. It spends the majority of the day dozing inconspicuously on the ground, often under grass or a shrub, and when it cools down in the evening, it becomes active hawking insects on the wing.

Jan	Feb	Mar	Apr	May	Jun	Jul	Aug	Sep	Oct	Nov	Dec

COPW ☐   Date: _____

BLACK SWIFT

Cypseloides niger

Photo: G. Holroyd

L: 184 mm   W: 45 g   Egg: 29 x 19 mm

Etymology: *Cypseloides* (Gr.) - *kypselos*, "European Swift" and *eidos*, "like;" *niger* (L.) - "black."

Status and Distribution: Extremely rare in the province with only two confirmed nesting locations: a long term site in Johnston's Canyon in Banff National Park and a more recently confirmed site in Maligne Canyon, Jasper National Park. There are historical sightings at Sunwapta and Athabasca Falls, Canmore, Kananaskis and Bragg Creek.

● ●

Field Checklist

✓✓**Habitat:** It breeds in areas with cliff faces in canyons, in a moist situation near some seepage such as a waterfall.

✓✓✓**Sight:** This is Canada's largest swift. The male is dark sooty above and below, faintly lighter on the forehead and crown with a small black area in front of the eyes. The wing line in flight is regularly bowed, and the tail is slightly forked. The female has a less forked tail and the feathers of the abdomen and undertail coverts are tipped in white.

Sound: Its call is a "plik, plik, plik."

✓**Behavior:** It flies quickly with a rapid, even and continuous wing beat followed by long glides. It forages at great heights during good weather but lower during overcast weather.

● ●

Similar species: Purple Martin and Vaux's Swift.

Remarks: In comparison to the Purple Martin, the Black Swift's wings are relatively longer. It also tends to forage at far greater heights. The Vaux's Swift is smaller, has faintly pale underparts and has spines on the tips of its tail feathers.

Jan	Feb	Mar	Apr	May	Jun	Jul	Aug	Sep	Oct	Nov	Dec

161   BLSW ❑   Date: _____

Hummingbirds

RUBY-THROATED HUMMINGBIRD

Archilochus colubris

L: 87 mm   W: 2.8 g   Egg: 13 x 8 mm

Etymology: *Arch* (Gr.)- "chief" and *lochos*, "a body of people," here meaning "first among birds;" *colubris* (L.)- "serpent." It is likely that Linnaeus intended "*colibri*," (Fr.)- "hummingbird."

Status and Distribution: This species' distribution is broad. It is most commonly found in central Alberta in the parkland and southern boreal regions. It has been observed as far north as High Level and Fort Chipewyan.

• •

Field Checklist

✓**Habitat:** Optimal habitats are woodland clearings, edges and gardens. They require treed or shrubby areas for nesting, perching, shelter and availability of nectar-producing flowers.

✓✓✓**Sight:** The male has an iridescent orange to red throat with a metallic green upper body and dull white underparts. The female has a plain white throat, green upper-parts and rounded tail with white feather tips.

✓✓**Sound:** Vocalization is a high "chick" call. The humming noise is created by its wings which beat at over 70 beats per second, accelerating to 200 beats per second during courtship.

Behavior: This species is highly territorial.

• •

Similar species: Calliope Hummingbird (female).

Remarks: The male is easily distinguished. The distinction between the females is detailed in the Calliope account. It is the most common "hummer" seen in the gardens and flower beds of east-central and southern Alberta. Only the female tends the young as the male leaves after the eggs are laid. The Ruby-throat is attracted to sugar water feeders.

Jan	Feb	Mar	Apr	May	Jun	Jul	Aug	Sep	Oct	Nov	Dec

RTHU ☐   Date: _____

CALLIOPE HUMMINGBIRD

Stellula calliope

L: 80 mm   W: 2.4 g   Egg: 12 x 8 mm

Etymology: *Stellula* (L.) - "little star;" *calliope* (Gr.) - "the muse responsible for epic poetry."

Status and Distribution: In Alberta, this species is at the eastern limit of its breeding range. It is found in the mountains and foothills of the province with breeding records north to the Wapiti River and south to Waterton Lakes National Park.

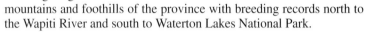

Field Checklist

✓✓**Habitat:** In the mountains it frequents open areas, shrubby meadows and open forest where flowers are abundant. It nests in open woodland.

✓✓✓**Sight:** The male of our smallest hummingbird is iridescent green above, dull white below and has long reddish-purple feathers on the sides of the throat that are fanned out for display. The female is iridescent green above and dull white below.

✓**Sound:** The male emits a loud whistle or squeak when defending territory.

✓**Behavior:** In courtship, the male flies back and forth in a deep "U" like a pendulum, vocalizing at the bottom of the pattern. The female vigorously defends her nesting territory alone.

Similar species: Female Ruby-throated and Rufous hummingbirds.

Remarks: The male Calliope is easily recognized with its brilliant reddish-purple markings on the throat but, although the female Calliope is smaller, it is almost indistinguishable from the female Rufous. She can be distinguished from the female Ruby-throated by her more rounded tail and the reddish-brown coloration on her flanks. It is a marvel that all this energy is packaged in a bird that weighs less than 1/10 of an ounce.

Jan	Feb	Mar	Apr	May	Jun	Jul	Aug	Sep	Oct	Nov	Dec

CAHU ☐   Date: _____

Kingfishers

BELTED KINGFISHER

Ceryle alcyon

L: 305 mm   W:149 g   Egg: 34 x 27 mm

Etymology: *Ceryle* (Gr.) - "The King-fisher;" *alcyon* (L.) - "kingfisher."

Status and Distribution: The Belted Kingfisher is a common breeder in Alberta. It breeds in suitable habitat throughout the province, but is rarer and more irregular in the grassland areas.

● ●

Field Checklist

✓✓**Habitat:** Kingfishers are found in the vicinity of lakes, ponds, rivers and streams where there are good populations of small fish, the water is clear and shallow and there are suitable perching and nesting sites.

✓✓✓**Sight:** It has a distinctive ragged head crest, a large heavy bill, a slatey-blue body with a white collar, white spots in front of the eyes, light underparts. The male has a blue breast band while the female (above) has an additional rufous band below the blue one.

✓✓**Sound:** A harsh rattling call.

✓**Behavior:** A solitary bird often seen near water where it will sit motionless on a perch watching for prey below. It also hunts from the air, where it will hover for a moment before hitting the water with a splash.

● ●

Similar species: None in North America

Remarks: Very distinctive and easy to identify. To nest, it digs a burrow in a steep vertical bank, preferably close to water. It will use cliffs along rivers or lakes, or sometimes road and railway cut banks. Sawdust piles, tree cavities and the earth-filled roots of upturned trees have also been used. This species frequently overwinters in Alberta where open water is present.

Jan	Feb	Mar	Apr	May	Jun	Jul	Aug	Sep	Oct	Nov	Dec

BEKI ❐   Date: _____

YELLOW-BELLIED SAPSUCKER

Sphyrapicus varius

L: 206 mm   W: 47 g   Egg: 22 x 17 mm

Etymology: *Sphyrapicus - sphyra* (Gr.), "a hammer" and *picus* (L.) - "a wood-pecker;" *varius* (L.) - "variegated."

Status and Distribution: This is a common summer resident in Alberta. It is found predominantly in the parkland, boreal and foothills regions of the province.

Photo: T.Thormin

• •

Field Checklist

✓**Habitat:** They prefer deciduous or mixed woodlands, especially where birches and poplars are prevalent. Most nest sites are at the forest edge adjacent to water bodies or near other forest openings.

✓✓**Sight:** The adult male has a red crown and throat patch, the female a red crown (occasionally black) and white throat. Both sexes have a black breast patch and yellowish-white abdomen. The upper body is a variegated black and white with a broad white stripe on the closed wing.

✓**Sound:** It utters a "wee-urr, wee-urr" and is especially noisy at the nest.

✓✓**Behavior:** The rolling staccato of the sapsucker drilling, with three or four solitary taps at the end, is distinctive from other woodpeckers.

• •

Similar species: Red-naped Sapsucker.

Remarks: The male Red-naped has a red bar across the nape separated from the crown by a black patch and the female Red-naped has a red throat. They nest in cavities preferring deciduous trees to conifers and will usually excavate a new nest every year although they may use the same tree. A sign of sapsucker activity is the drilling of holes in horizontal lines or checkerboard pattern through the outer bark of a tree.

Jan	Feb	Mar	Apr	May	Jun	Jul	Aug	Sep	Oct	Nov	Dec

     YBSA ☐   Date: _____

Woodpeckers

HAIRY WOODPECKER

Picoides villosus

L: 247 mm W: 86 g Egg: 25 x 19 mm

Etymology: *Picoides - picus* (L.) - "a wood-pecker" and *oides* (Gr.) - "like;" *villosus* - "hairy."

Status and Distribution: This is a permanent resident with a stable population, found in all forested parts of the province. The two subspecies in Alberta are *P.v. septentrionalis* which nests east of the Rocky Mountains and *P. v. monticola* which nests in southwestern Alberta.

● ●

Field Checklist

✓**Habitat:** It inhabits deciduous, mixed and, occasionally, coniferous forests, often near openings.

✓✓✓**Sight:** A four-toed black and white woodpecker with a broad white stripe down the middle of the back, white outer tail feathers and a bill almost as long as the head. The adult male has a small red bar on the nape. Young birds may have red or yellow spots on the head. *P. v. monticola* has reduced white spotting on the wing.

✓✓**Sound:** Its call is a sharp "peek, peek, peek," with the notes barely separated.

✓**Behavior:** This species is more wary than the Downy Woodpecker and will generally not allow a close approach.

● ●

Similar species: Downy Woodpecker and Three-toed Woodpecker.

Remarks: It can be distinguished from the Downy Woodpecker by its larger size, longer bill relative to the head and by the white outer tail feathers. The Three-toed Woodpecker has one less toe and is more heavily barred on its sides and flank. It derives its common name from the white feathers on its back that fall over the black areas looking unkempt. It is found throughout Alberta in winter.

Jan	Feb	Mar	Apr	May	Jun	Jul	Aug	Sep	Oct	Nov	Dec

HAWO ❐ Date: _____

THREE-TOED WOODPECKER

Picoides tridactylus

L: 211 mm   W: 54 g   Egg: 21 x 19 mm

Photo: R.Gehlert

Etymology: *Picoides - picus* (L.) - "a woodpecker" and *oides* (Gr.) - "like;" *tridactylus* (Gr.) - *trios*, "three" and *daktylos*, "toe."

Status and Distribution: Although not abundant anywhere in its Alberta range, its population is not considered at risk. The subspecies in Alberta, *P. t. fasciatus,* is found in suitable habitat in the mountain, foothills and boreal regions of western and northern Alberta.

• •

Field Checklist

✓**Habitat:** It prefers mature coniferous forest with open areas near burns and clearcuts. Although it is found in areas of spruce, fir and pine, it prefers mature spruce forest with stands of dead trees.

✓✓✓**Sight:** As its name implies, it has three toes, similar only to the Black-backed Woodpecker in Alberta. This black and white woodpecker has a black back barred with white and heavily barred sides and flanks. The male has a yellow cap that is conspicuous.

✓**Sound:** Its single-noted "kik" is rarely heard, except in the vicinity of the nest. The drumming of this species, a roll increasing in tempo, is similar to that of the Black-backed Woodpecker.

✓**Behavior:** The Three-toed Woodpecker is solitary and quiet and relatively wary of humans.

• •

Similar species: Hairy Woodpecker and Black-backed Woodpecker.

Remarks: The yellow crown of the male separates the Three-toed from the male Hairy, but females are often confused. The three toes and barring on the back of the Three-toed female are useful identifiers. The lack of barring in the Black-backed helps distinguish these two species. Overwintering of this woodpecker has been recorded in several locations around the province.

Jan	Feb	Mar	Apr	May	Jun	Jul	Aug	Sep	Oct	Nov	Dec

Woodpeckers

BLACK-BACKED WOODPECKER

Picoides arcticus

L: 240 mm Wt: 74 g Egg: 24 x 19

Etymology: *Picoides - picus* (L.) - "a woodpecker" and *oides* (Gr.) - "like;" *arcticus* (L.) - "northern."

Status and Distribution: The status of this uncommon resident is unknown in the province. Its reliance on mature and burnt-over conifer stands makes it a species sensitive to northern logging. It is found in the foothills and boreal forests.

• •

Field Checklist

✓✓**Habitat:** It breeds in dense, mixed or coniferous forests, often choosing nest sites in stumps or decaying trees.

✓✓✓**Sight:** It is one of only two three-toed woodpecker species in the province. It is entirely black above, whitish below and has a broad white stripe below the eye. The male Black-backed has a yellow crown patch.

✓**Sound:** A sharp "keik."

✓**Behavior:** Its flight pattern is rapid, gliding and undulating with a sharp call sometimes given during the glide. It is shy and usually can be spotted only when feeding or flying.

• •

Similar species: Three-toed Woodpecker.

Remarks: It is distinguished from the Three-toed by its lack of barring on the back. It is the only woodpecker with a white breast and throat and black back. It is a difficult bird to observe because its coloration blends with its dark surroundings. Evidence of this woodpecker's activity is a dead conifer with large areas where the bark has been scaled. This bird was formerly known as the Arctic Woodpecker and the Black-backed Three-toed Woodpecker. It overwinters in much of its breeding range and has been recorded east and south into the aspen parkland region.

Jan	Feb	Mar	Apr	May	Jun	Jul	Aug	Sep	Oct	Nov	Dec

172   BBWO ☐   Date: _____

NORTHERN FLICKER

Colaptes auratus

L: 308 mm   W: 147 g   Egg: 28 x 22 mm

Photo: D. Godkin

Etymology: *Colaptes* (Gr.) - "to chisel;" *auratus* (L.) - "golden."

Status and Distribution: Both sub-species, the Yellow-shafted and Red-shafted flickers, breed in Alberta. The Yellow-shafted Flicker, *C. a. borealis,* breeds in most parts of the province, except the mountain regions of the southwest where the Red-shafted, *C. a. collaris,* occurs. Interbreeding is common with very few pure Red-shafted Flickers now found in Alberta.

● ●

Field Checklist

✓**Habitat:** It breeds in a variety of habitats including mixed, deciduous and coniferous forests that are moderately open.

✓✓✓**Sight:** It is a large woodpecker with brown underparts, a spotted breast and a black crescent on the throat. In flight, the white rump is conspicuous. The two subspecies are separated by the yellow or red under the tail and wing linings. The male Yellow-shafted has a black mous-tache mark as opposed to a red one in the Red-shafted.

✓✓✓**Sound:** The name was derived from the "flicka, flicka, flicka" call of the male during courtship. It is also known to utter a loud "pieew-w-w."

✓**Behavior:** It drums out a long reverberating roll that can be heard a long distance away.

● ●

Similar species: None.

Remarks: In Alberta the two subspecies interbreed so that various combi-nations of the color characteristics occur. The abandoned nest cavities of this bird are used by the American Kestrel, Tree Swallows and small owls. It regularly overwinters in various parts of the province. Look for the Flicker feeding, almost Robin-like, on the ground.

Jan	Feb	Mar	Apr	May	Jun	Jul	Aug	Sep	Oct	Nov	Dec

NOFL ☐   Date: _____

Woodpeckers

PILEATED WOODPECKER

Dryocopus pileatus

L: 440 mm   W: 336 g   Egg: 33 x 25 mm

Etomology: *Dryocopus* (Gr.) - *drys*, "a tree" and *kopis*, "a cleaver;" *pileatus* (L.) - "capped."

Status and Distribution: The population is thought to be stable, however, it is on the provincial Yellow List as it is associated with habitats (old growth forest) that are deteriorating. It breeds in the forested areas of the province. In the grassland regions it is observed in wooded river valleys.

• •

Field Checklist

✓✓**Habitat:** It prefers older, mature dense canopied forests, particularly mixed and deciduous woods where there are large, dead or dying trees for nesting. It is very rarely found in burns or areas of downed timber.

✓✓✓**Sight:** It is Alberta's largest woodpecker (crow-sized) with mainly black plumage, a white stripe on the side of the head and neck, and a prominent flame-red crest.

✓✓**Sound:** Its call is a loud "kek kek kek kek" that rises and falls. It is similar to but harsher than the call of the Northern Flicker.

✓**Behavior:** Its loud call and slow heavy drumming are distinctive. It is difficult to approach.

• •

Similar species: Northern Flicker (vocally).

Remarks: Once seen, it cannot be confused with any other woodpecker in the province. The abandoned nest cavities of this woodpecker provide essential habitat for several other boreal species including the American Kestrel, Tree Swallows and small owls. Management agencies have indicated that the maintainence of breeding habitat needs to be incorporated into forest management on both public and private lands to allow for the long term benefit of this species.

Jan	Feb	Mar	Apr	May	Jun	Jul	Aug	Sep	Oct	Nov	Dec

PIWO ❑   Date: _____

RED-HEADED WOODPECKER

Melanerpes erythrocephalus

Photo: T.Thormin

This uncommon woodpecker is regularly observed locally in the Medicine Hat, Foremost and Brooks area and is suspected of breeding in the area. It has been documented breeding on the Saskatchewan side of the Cypress Hills.

The head, neck and upper breast are a crimson-red, upperparts are black and the rump and underparts are white. There are large white patches on the black wings. The young woodpeckers have a dusky-brown head but are identified by the large white patches on the wing. It differs from other woodpeckers in its feeding habits as it will often hawk insects from a perch and is known to prey on the eggs and young of other birds.

The call is a harsh, raspy "churr, churr".

Flycatchers

YELLOW-BELLIED FLYCATCHER

Empidonax flaviventris

L: 132 mm   W: 12 g   Egg: 17 x 13 mm

Etymology: *Empidonax* (Gr.) - "King of the gnats;" *flaviventris*, (L.) - "yellow-bellied."

Status and Distribution: It is uncommon and scattered in central and northern Alberta. The Yellow-bellied

may occur throughout the boreal forest and in the mountain parks, at least south to Jasper, but it is relatively poorly documented throughout its range.

• •

Field Checklist

✓**Habitat:** This flycatcher prefers bogs and the edges of any coniferous and mixed wood forests and thickets bordering lakes and streams.

✓✓✓**Sight:** It is distinctively yellow-bellied and yellow-throated and bright green above.

✓**Sound:** Soft two-note monotone "che-bek" and rising "pe-wheep" slower and less emphatic than Least Flycatcher's "che-bek."

Behavior: There are few behavioral differences that help separate *Empidonax* flycatchers. As a group, they share the practice of picking insects off foliage, or hawking them from the air, then returning to the same perch.

• •

Similar species: All *Empidonax* flycatchers, especially the Cordilleran Flycatcher.

Remarks: Good detectability but relatively few records document the biology of this species in Alberta. It is a late spring migrant and may be missed in field trips taken before the end of March. It is quiet during migration and not a vigorous singer on the breeding grounds. Five years of the Bird Atlas surveys confirmed only two nests. This is not surprising given its behavior and nesting habitat but the paucity of possible and probable records (about 25) make it a species whose status should be assessed carefully.

Jan	Feb	Mar	Apr	May	Jun	Jul	Aug	Sep	Oct	Nov	Dec

YBFL ❏   Date: _____

ALDER
FLYCATCHER

Empidonax alnorum

L: 143 mm   W: 13 g   Egg: 18 x 13 mm

Etymology: *Empidonax* (Gr.) - King of
the gnats;" *alnorum* (L.) - "of the
alders," for the bird's habitat.

Status and Distribution: The Alder is
found throughout Alberta except in the
extreme southeast and high elevations.
It is common in central Alberta and the southern boreal forest. The range of
the Alder overlaps with the range of the similar Willow Flycatcher in the
southwestern part of province.

• •

Field Checklist

✓**Habitat:** Look for the Alder in wet alder and willow thickets
near muskegs, bogs, marshes, streams and lakes. It loves
mosquito-rich environments but can also be found in drier areas.

Sight: More green above and yellow below
than the Least Flycatcher but not as green
above or as yellow below as the Yellow-
bellied Flycatcher.

✓✓✓**Sound:** Slightly burry, three-part "fee-
bee-o" or wheezy, two-part "zwee-oo." The
second call is heard more frequently and
often mistaken for the harsher staccato, two-
note "fitz-bew" of the Willow.

Behavior: It perches high or low on the periphery
of willow or alder bushes and forages by flying out to
capture an insect, often returning to the same perch.

• •

Similar Species: All *Empidonax* Flycatchers (visually).

Remarks: This species can only be distinguished from the Willow Flycatcher by song. Where the species overlap in southwestern Alberta, the
distribution and habitat preferences of the two remain to be determined.
Older field guides may list Traill's Flycatcher which was split into two
species - the Alder and Willow Flycatchers in the 1970s.

Jan	Feb	Mar	Apr	May	Jun	Jul	Aug	Sep	Oct	Nov	Dec

ALFL ❐   Date: _____

Flycatchers

Order: Passeriformes - Family: Tyrannidae

HAMMOND'S FLYCATCHER

Empidonax hammondii

L: 135 mm   W: 11 g   Egg: 17 x 13 mm

Etymology: *Empidonax* (Gr.) - "King of the gnats;" *hammondii* - for William Hammond, a colleague of John Xantus who collected the first specimen of this species.

Status and Distribution: This species breeds throughout the Rocky Mountains from Jasper to Waterton. Its status is not well known, most records being concentrated near town-sites in the National Parks. Unlike many montane species, Hammond's is not found in the Cypress Hills.

• •

Field Checklist

✓✓**Habitat:** Hammond's Flycatchers prefer coniferous woods usually at high elevations but, lower in the dry valleys of the western slopes of the Rocky Mountains, they are found nesting in Lodgepole Pine, Douglas Fir and White and Engelmann Spruce. Dusky Flycatchers, which are similar to Hammond's, tend to be in deciduous woods usually at lower elevations.

Sight: Hammond's exhibits typical *Empidonax* coloration, but the breast is grayer than that of the Dusky Flycatcher. The Hammond's bill is a little shorter and the lower mandible is darker than the Dusky's.

✓✓✓**Sound:** A raspy three-part "sweep, tsurp, seep," with the pitch of the last note rising. It is a hoarse version of the song of the Dusky.

✓**Behavior:** It flicks its wings and tail vigorously.

• •

Similar Species: All *Empidonax* flycatchers.

Remarks: Fair vocal detectability, hard to spot. In the hand, the grayish plumage and lack of whitish outer tail feathers can distinguish this species from the Dusky Flycatcher. Field identification is far more difficult.

Jan	Feb	Mar	Apr	May	Jun	Jul	Aug	Sep	Oct	Nov	Dec

HAFL ☐   Date: _____

DUSKY FLYCATCHER

Empidonax oberholseri

L: 141 mm   W: 12 g   Egg: 17 x 13 mm

Etymology: *Empidonax* (Gr.) - "King of the gnats;" *oberholseri* - for Dr. Harry Oberholser who worked for the United States Fish and Wildlife Service and was the Curator of Ornithology at the Cleveland Museum of Natural History.

Status and Distribution: Dusky Flycatchers are relatively common in the mountain parks, foothills and Cypress Hills . Records for the five years of the Alberta Breeding Bird Atlas were evenly distributed throughout the National Parks.

• •

Field Checklist

✓✓**Habitat:** Deciduous woods at lower elevations in the mountains and foothills are preferred habitat.

✓**Sight:** Compared to the Hammond's, the underparts of the Dusky are paler and less uniform. The throat is whitish instead of gray and contrasts more with the gray of the breast. The outer web of the outer tail feathers is more whitish. The bill of the Dusky is a little longer and the lower mandible lighter and more variable in color than that of Hammond's.

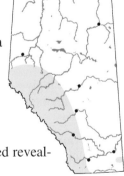

✓✓✓**Sound:** Three-part clear, soft or raspy "tsyrup tsurp, seep."

Behavior: It often flicks its tail while perched revealing grayish outer feathers.

• •

Similar species: All *Empidonax* species, especially the Hammond's Flycatcher.

Remarks: Good vocal detectability but difficult to spot. Fall migration dates are uncertain because confirming identification outside the breeding season is so difficult. Call is variable but normally less wheezy than that of Hammond's.

Jan	Feb	Mar	Apr	May	Jun	Jul	Aug	Sep	Oct	Nov	Dec

CORDILLERAN FLYCATCHER

Empidonax occidentalis

L: 140 mm W: 12 g Egg: 18 x 13 mm

Etymology: *Empidonax* (Gr.) - "King of the gnats;" *occidentalis* (L.) - "western."

Status and Distribution: Cordilleran Flycatchers are found in the south-western part of Alberta primarily in the mountains and foothills north to Jasper. Records for the five years of Atlas surveys were concentrated in the mountains immediately west of Calgary. The status of the species in Alberta is uncertain as the species limits for this and the closely related Pacific-slope Flycatcher (*Empidonax difficilis*) are not well known.

● ●

Field Checklist

✓✓**Habitat:** It is found in shady, coniferous and deciduous woodlands along streams or ravines in the mountains and foothills.

✓**Sight:** The tear-shaped, buff-colored eye-ring is distinctive among *Empidonax* species. The yellow belly is prominent and confusable only with that of the Yellow-bellied Fly-catcher.

✓**Sound:** It gives a high thin "pseet, ptsick seet" with the last note pitched higher than the first two.

Behavior: Catches insects on the wing like all other flycatchers. May nest on a ledge.

● ●

Similar species: All *Empidonax* flycatchers, especially the Yellow-bellied.

Remarks: Only fair detectability - habitat seems to be critical. The former Western Flycatcher was divided into two new species, the Cordilleran Flycatcher and the Pacific-slope Flycatcher. It is possible that the Pacific-slope Flycatcher wanders into Alberta. The song is the only means of separating these two forms. The best clue for this species is habitat, a steeply banked mountain stream is its likely home.

Jan	Feb	Mar	Apr	May	Jun	Jul	Aug	Sep	Oct	Nov	Dec

COFL ❑   Date: _____

Order: Passeriformes - Family: Tyrannidae

EASTERN PHOEBE

Sayornis phoebe

L: 174 mm   W: 20 g   Egg: 19 x 15 mm

Etymology: *Say* - after Thomas Say, naturalist and entomologist who worked in the Rocky Mountains in 1819-20; *ornis* (Gr.) - "bird;" *phoebe* (Gr.) - "one of the twelve Titans."

Status and Distribution: Found throughout Alberta, the Eastern Phoebe is uncommon in the mountain parks and southern grasslands. It is common in the aspen parkland and southern boreal forest.

● ●

Field Checklist

✓**Habitat:** The Phoebe breeds in open wooded areas including mixed deciduous and coniferous forests often near streams and lakes. It prefers forest edges and nests frequently under the eaves of barns, cottages and outhouses.

✓**Sight:** It has a dark head, and neither an eye ring nor distinctive wing bars.

✓✓**Sound:** The call is a whistled, slurred two- or three-syllable, "zwee bee," or "zwee bubee."

✓**Behavior:** Phoebes characteristically pump and spread their tail when perched. A female builds a bulky mud, grass and moss nest usually attached to a vertical surface. She is very tame at the nest.

● ●

Similar species: Western Wood-Pewee, all *Empidonax* flycatchers.

Remarks: Good vocal and visual detectability especially in early spring. The Eastern Phoebe (pronounced fee bee) is the earliest flycatcher to return in the spring. It can be caught in late spring snowstorms making its flexible diet an asset. Cup nests under eaves belong to either this species, its relative, Say's Phoebe or the Barn Swallow, but the Swallows tend to nest in groups. By late May or June when other species are at their peak of singing, Eastern Phoebes are quiet. The best time to hear them is late April or early May.

Jan	Feb	Mar	Apr	May	Jun	Jul	Aug	Sep	Oct	Nov	Dec

Flycatchers

SAY'S PHOEBE

Sayornis saya

Photo: K.Morck

L: 192 mm   W: 26 g   Egg: 20 x 15 mm

Etymology: *Say* - after Thomas Say, naturalist and entomologist who worked in the Rocky Mountains in 1819-20; *ornis* (Gr.) - "bird;" *saya* (L.) - another honorific for Say.

Status and Distribution: The Say's Phoebe breeds in the southeastern prairies but can be found in the aspen parkland and southern boreal forest. A separate subspecies *Sayornis saya yukonensis* may breed in extreme northern Alberta and undoubtedly migrates through the province.

●●

Field Checklist

✓**Habitat:** This species is a bird of the dry prairies particularly badlands and open rangeland of southeastern Alberta. The subspecies *yukonensis* is a northern variety that can be found above treeline, near cliff faces or dry slopes.

✓✓**Sight:** Look for the rust-colored belly, black tail, dusky head and back.

✓**Sound:** A plaintive, soft two-note "pee-urr," or three-note "pu, pee-urr."

Behavior: To capture its prey, it will hover like an American Kestrel or sit on a low perch, catching most insects on the wing. It will nest under the eaves of farm buildings.

●●●

Similar Species: None.

Remarks: Say's Phoebe, despite its reputation as a prairie species, shows fairly wide habitat tolerances. The split between *saya* forms and *yukonensis* forms is blurred. There are foothills and boreal forest nesting records for Alberta which imply either *yukonensis* breeds farther south than assumed or that *saya* can occupy forest habitats. The distribution and status of this species in Alberta merits further study.

Jan	Feb	Mar	Apr	May	Jun	Jul	Aug	Sep	Oct	Nov	Dec

186   SAPH ❑   Date: _____

Order: Passeriformes - Family: Tyrannidae

GREAT CRESTED FLYCATCHER

Flycatchers

Myiarchus crinitus

L: 214 mm   W: 40 g   Egg: 23 x 17 mm

Etymology: *Myiarchus* (Gr.) - literally "flying chief or ruler;" *crinitus* (L.) - hair, here referring to the crest.

Status and Distribution: There are a variety of sightings in central and east-central Alberta. Areas of concentration appear to be St. Paul and Pine Lake. This species was first recorded in Alberta about 1940. It is now a regular breeder though its status is unknown.

Field Checklist

✓**Habitat:** It is common in eastern deciduous forests but only recently has expanded from Saskatchewan into Alberta. It selects forests that most resemble eastern deciduous woods. These include stands of tall aspen, balsam poplar and birch, where a thick understorey has developed.

✓✓**Sight:** Prominent features are the bright yellow underside of the belly, gray throat and upper breast, and rufous on the tail. It is distinguished from the Western Kingbird by its crest, dark upper parts, white wing bars and rusty-colored tail and wings.

✓✓✓**Sound:** Their call is a distinctive, ascending whistled note, "wreep," sometimes proceeded by a short series of "whits."

✓**Behavior:** It captures flying insects by dashing out on quivering wings, much like a kingbird, with its tail spread to show the rufous coloration.

Similar species: Western Kingbird (visually).

Remarks: Being noisy, it has high vocal detectability and is easy to spot once heard. In addition to being a large, colorful flycatcher, the Great Crested has the interesting behavior of decorating its nest. Onion skins, plastic, cellophane and cast snake and lizard skins are common nest ornaments. It nests in tree cavities.

Jan	Feb	Mar	Apr	May	Jun	Jul	Aug	Sep	Oct	Nov	Dec

187

GCFL ☐   Date: _____

Flycatchers

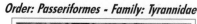

WESTERN KINGBIRD

Tyrannus verticalis

L: 210 mm   W: 44 g   Egg: 23 x 17 mm

Etymology: *Tyrannus* (L.) - a tyrant; *verticalis* (L.) "the top of the head," referring to the red patch

Status and Distribution: The Western Kingbird is found in the grasslands and southern aspen parkland. Thirty-one percent of Atlas squares surveyed in the grasslands recorded this species. Northward movement of this species reflects clearing of aspens for agriculture.

● ●

Field Checklist

✓**Habitat:** Open country but near trees, poles or buildings. This species is relatively common in native grasslands, pastures, parks and golf courses in southern Alberta.

✓✓**Sight:** It is identified by the yellow belly, pale gray head and breast, black tail with white on the outer edges and a pale gray head.

✓✓**Sound:** The call is a series of harsh twitters and squeaks, ending with an emphatic "ker-whip" or a single aggressive "kip."

✓**Behavior:** Hawks from its perch or pounces on prey on the ground. It invariably returns to its perch after a hunting foray. The Kingbird attacks larger birds near its territory.

● ●

Similar species: The Great Crested Flycatcher has a yellow belly, but its reddish tail and preference for deciduous forests makes confusion unlikely.

Remarks: High vocal and visual detectability. Western Kingbirds are not shy, they make their presence clearly known to all visitors to their territory. This species and the Eastern Kingbird use a distinctive fluttering almost hovering flight combined with a variety of harsh calls when alarmed. This species closely resembles a number of tropical Kingbirds giving our prairies a southern look in the summer.

Jan	Feb	Mar	Apr	May	Jun	Jul	Aug	Sep	Oct	Nov	Dec

WEKI ❑   Date: _____

Order: Passeriformes - Family: Tyrannidae

Flycatchers

EASTERN KINGBIRD

Tyrannus tyrannus

L: 210 mm W: 41 g Egg: 24 x 18 mm

Etymology: *Tyrannus tyrannus* (L.) - a tyrant twice.

Status and Distribution: Common throughout the grasslands, aspen parkland and southern boreal forest. They are absent from high elevations in the mountains and scattered throughout northern Alberta.

• •

Field Checklist

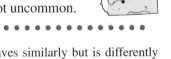

✓**Habitat:** Eastern Kingbirds prefer open country with scattered trees, as well as forest edges, shrubby fields and pastures. In forested areas, they are found in clearings, cutlines, near beaver ponds, bogs or burns.

✓✓**Sight:** Eastern Kingbirds have a black head, gray back, white band on the end of the tail and white underparts.

✓✓**Sound:** They produce a harsh "dzeet," often repeated in a series.

✓✓**Behavior:** Aggressive attacks by this species on larger birds, often high in the air, are not uncommon.

• •

Similar species: The Western Kingbird behaves similarly but is differently colored.

Remarks: High detectability both vocally and visually. They are aggressive and fearless in defending their nest. Hawks, crows, magpies, squirrels and humans will all be attacked if they get too close. "Too close" for hawks can be anywhere in sight. The quivering, hovering flight is characteristic of this species as is its habit of perching conspicuously. A trip down gravel roads in the aspen parkland or grasslands is almost guaranteed to produce Eastern Kingbirds perched on barbed-wire fences. This and its western counterpart are part of the tyrant flycatcher group. Watch them for a while; you will see how they earned the name "tyrant."

Jan	Feb	Mar	Apr	May	Jun	Jul	Aug	Sep	Oct	Nov	Dec

189   EAKI ☐   Date: _____

Shrikes

NORTHERN SHRIKE

Lanius excubitor

L: 248 mm W: 68 g Egg: 26 x 18 mm

Etymology: *Lanius* (L.) - "butcher;" *excubitor* (L.) - "a sentinel."

Status and Distribution: This shrike is a migrant and winter visitor in the south. It is a potential breeder in the far north. Birds appear to be on territories in April near Fort Vermilion with only one confirmed nest being found beyond the Shield region in extreme northeastern Alberta.

• •

Field Checklist

✓**Habitat:** In winter it sits in open areas in the boreal forest and parkland. In spring look along edges of mixed boreal forest.

✓✓**Sight:** The Northern Shrike shows a mix of light gray and black plumage, lighter gray on the underparts. Its black hooked bill, horizontal posture while perched and rapid wing beats separate it from everything except the Loggerhead.

Sound: The Northern is not often heard. It has a harsh call note and gives a wheezy repeated "snee."

✓✓**Behavior:** It perches in the open, on power lines and treetops in late spring in the boreal forest. When it flies it is direct, fast and usually in a straight line.

• •

Similar species: Loggerhead Shrike, Gray Jay, Northern Mockingbird (visually).

Remarks: This species is an aggressive predator, catching small birds on the wing, pouncing on small mammals and killing both with a blow to the back of the neck with its beak. It will also hawk insects and, characteristically, hunt from and return to a perch. It is lighter colored and has a smaller mask than the Loggerhead, but habitat is the best clue for initial identification. In most settled areas of Alberta, this is only a winter visitor.

Jan	Feb	Mar	Apr	May	Jun	Jul	Aug	Sep	Oct	Nov	Dec

NOSH ☐   Date: _____

LOGGERHEAD SHRIKE

Lanius ludovicianus

Photo: D. Wood

L: 214 mm   W: 48 g   Egg: 24 x 19 mm

Etymology: *Lanius* (L.) - "butcher;" *ludovicianus* (ML.) - "of Louisiana."

Status and Distribution: Considered in decline in southeastern Alberta but historically it was common throughout the grasslands and southern parkland. The Bird Atlas project (1986-91) produced numerous breeding records in the grasslands.

• •

Field Checklist

✓✓**Habitat:** The Loggerhead breeds in open country in the grasslands and parkland. It requires a medium sized bush for nesting.

✓✓**Sight:** It is darker than the Northern Shrike but the overall appearance is very similar. Look for the black, gray and white plumage, horizontal perching habit and rapid wing beats. The mask of the Loggerhead is bigger than the counterpart on the Northern.

Sound: Shrikes are not vocal. They give a variety of squeaky noises but are not often heard.

✓✓**Behavior:** They are often seen perching on power lines, shrub tops and barbed-wire fences. They have fast direct flight and are aggressive predators.

• •

Similar species: Northern Shrike, Gray Jay, Northern Mockingbird (visually).

Remarks: In its spring and summer habitat, the Loggerhead Shrike can be confused only with the rare Northern Mockingbird. The black mask, perching posture and rapid wingbeats of the Loggerhead Shrike easily distinguish it from the vocal mockingbird. It is unlikely that the two shrike species would be found together except during April. The cause for its recent decline is still unknown. Both shrike species are famous for their habit of impaling their prey on thorns or barbed wire for future consumption.

Jan	Feb	Mar	Apr	May	Jun	Jul	Aug	Sep	Oct	Nov	Dec

LOSK ☐   Date: _____

Vireos

BLUE-HEADED VIREO

Vireo solitarius

L: 135 mm   W: 15 g   Egg:20 x 14 mm

Etymology: *Vireo* (L.) - "green bird;"
solitarius (L.) - "solitary."

Status and Distribution: Widespread
in the boreal forest and northern
Rockies south to the latitude of
Calgary. Despite availability of good
habitat, there is no evidence of breeding in the Cypress Hills. Highest
numbers occur where sandy soils and pine trees predominate.

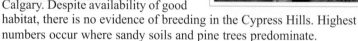

Field Checklist

✓✓**Habitat:** The Blue-headed Vireo is most common in pine-
dominated mixed woods; occasionally it is
found in spruce-aspen communities. It will
breed in a monoculture of Lodgepole or Jack
Pine.

✓**Sight:** The blue on the head contrasts with
the greenish back. White spectacles and
bright wing bars separate this from other
vireos. The similar Cassin's Vireo has a
grayer back.

✓✓✓**Sound**: The Blue-headed utters slow,
slurred, whistled phrases. They are similar to those
of a Red-eyed Vireo but distinctly slower.

✓**Behavior:** Vireos sing regularly throughout the day,
but are rarely seen without having been heard first.

Similar species: Cassin's Vireo, Red-eyed Vireo, Philadelphia Vireo
(vocally); Cassin's Vireo (visually).

Remarks: This species was formerly combined with Cassin's Vireo and
Plumbeous Vireo as the Solitary Vireo. It is very similar to Cassin's Vireo, so
the song differences have to be learned. Listen to Blue-headed Vireos in
northern Alberta and Cassin's Vireo in the Waterton area to allow you to
separate them where ranges overlap in the Rockies. The differences in
plumage are impossible to detect in the field. Blue-headed songs are clear
whistles, those of Cassin's are distinctly fuzzy (frequently modulated).

Jan	Feb	Mar	Apr	May	Jun	Jul	Aug	Sep	Oct	Nov	Dec

192   BHVI ☐   Date: _____

CASSIN'S VIREO
Vireo cassinii

L: 135 mm   W: 15 g   Egg: 20 x 14 mm

Etomology: *Vireo* (L.) - "green bird;" *cassinii* (ML.) - in honor of John Cassin, 19th century ornithologist.

Status and Distribution: Breeding range is restricted to the extreme southwest mountain region. Cassin's have been detected as far north as the Clearwater River crossing of Highway 40. The best areas to find them are in Waterton Park and the Westcastle area.

Field Checklist

✓**Habitat:** Cassin's prefers Lodgepole Pine and mixed pine, Douglas Fir and spruce stands. Pines seem to be necessary in every male's territory. It can be found in both open woodland and dense forest.

✓**Sight:** Gray head, greenish gray back and light underparts. The photo shows the subtle differences in head/back contrasts that separate the Cassin's (left) and Blue-headed (right) vireos.

✓✓**Sound:** Cassin's song is a series of slow, slurred whistled phrases. They are distinctly fuzzy. If written, the song would begin with a "z" whereas that of the Blue-headed would start with an "s."

Behavior: Vireos sing regularly throughout the day. Cassin's and Blue-headed, however, are not nearly as vocal as Red-eyed and Warbling vireos.

Similar Species: Blue-headed Vireo, Red-eyed Vireo, Philadelphia Vireo (vocally); Blue-eyed Vireo (visually).

Remarks: Cassin's was formerly combined with Blue-headed Vireo and Plumbeous Vireo as the Solitary Vireo. Historically, this (sub)species was thought to migrate only through southwestern Alberta on its way to breeding grounds in the Columbia Valley of British Columbia. Despite their external similarity, the genetic differences between these two species are pronounced.

Jan	Feb	Mar	Apr	May	Jun	Jul	Aug	Sep	Oct	Nov	Dec

CAVI ☐   Date: _____

WARBLING VIREO

Vireo gilvus gilvus
Vireo gilvus swainsonii

L: 132 mm W: 12 g Egg: 19 x 14 mm

Etymology: *Vireo* (L.) - "green bird;" *gilvus* (L.) - "pale yellow;" *swainsonii* (ML.) - for William Swainson, an early 19th century English ornithologist.

Status and Distribution: These forms are widespread and common in parkland, mountain and boreal forest regions. There are scattered breeding records in the grassland region and in extreme northeastern Alberta. In the parkland and mountains regions this is an extremely common bird.

• •

Field Checklist

✓✓**Habitat:** It is found in aspen groves in central and southeastern Alberta (*gilvus*) and in mixed wood in the boreal forest and foothills (*swainsonii*).

Sight: Warblings have green-brown upperparts, white eyebrow line and whitish to yellow underparts. In general, they have no good visual characteristics except the heavy *Vireo* bill.

✓✓✓**Sound:** Distinctive melodic, whistled warbling phrases (*gilvus*), or ones that are more rapid and choppy (*swainsonii*). It scolds with a harsh "zar" note, a sound that most vireos can produce.

✓✓**Behavior:** The male sings constantly, even while incubating eggs. It moves methodically as it forages, not rapidly like Kinglets.

• •

Similar species: Purple Finch, Western Tanager (vocally); Philadelphia Vireo, Tennessee Warbler and Ruby-crowned Kinglet (visually).

Remarks: Genetic and size differences between the two forms are substantial. Likely these birds will be separated into distinct species. The song differences are subtle but discernible. Surprisingly there is no hybridization between the two types. In the hand, the 20% larger size of *gilvus* is obvious but in the field, the only good distinguishing features are habitat and song.

Jan	Feb	Mar	Apr	May	Jun	Jul	Aug	Sep	Oct	Nov	Dec

Vireos

PHILADELPHIA VIREO

Vireo philadelphicus

L: 126 mm   W: 11 g   Egg: 19 x 14 mm

Etymology: *Vireo* (L.) - "green bird;" *philadelphicus* (ML.) - for site of first collected specimen in 1851.

Status and Distribution: A regular breeder in the northern parkland; there are scattered records throughout the boreal forest. It is surprisingly common in northwestern Alberta but its distribution will always be uncertain due to its similarity to the Red-eyed Vireo.

Field Checklist

✓✓**Habitat:** It is found in aspen forests and aspen stands in the southern boreal forest.

✓✓**Sight:** Both sexes are generally yellowish underneath and have a greenish back and gray cap. The eye is dark, not red.

✓✓**Sound:** Clear whistled phrases less variable but very similar to those of the Red-eyed Vireo. Sound separates the Philadelphia from all birds except the Red-eyed Vireo. To confirm identification, the bird must be seen.

✓**Behavior:** Phillies will respond to Red-eyed Vireo song and are often found within earshot of a Red-eyed Vireo territory.

Similar species: Red-eyed Vireo (vocally); Warbling Vireo, Tennessee Warbler (visually).

Remarks: Sound differences can be learned but do not guarantee identification. Every "unusual" -sounding Red-eyed Vireo should be checked. Unusual means slower and with fewer distinct syllables. The Philadelphia is moderately detectable but often hard to see despite constant singing. The best field marks are the yellow underparts, thick bill and lack of red eyes. Near the Chinchaga River in northwestern Alberta, this is the predominant vireo.

Jan	Feb	Mar	Apr	May	Jun	Jul	Aug	Sep	Oct	Nov	Dec

PHVI ❒   Date: _____

Vireos

Order: Passerifomes - Family: Vireonidae

RED-EYED VIREO

Vireo olivaceus

L: 150 mm   W: 17 g   Egg: 20 x 14 mm

Etymology: *Vireo* (L.) - "green bird;" *olivaceus* (L.) - "olive colored."

Status and Distribution: The Red-eyed Vireo is one of the most common woodland birds in Alberta. It is abundant in the parkland and boreal forest. It is less common but still regular in the foothills and Cypress Hills.

- -

Field Checklist

✓✓**Habitat:** It is found in aspen groves and forests in the parkland and mixed woods within the boreal forest. Normally, Red-eyed Vireos nest in mature aspens but in the far north and south they can be found inhabiting scrubby aspens and other deciduous shrubs.

✓✓✓**Sight:** The white eyebrow line bordered in black and the red eye are distinctive. Overall, the bird is brownish above and white below.

✓✓**Sound:** The Red-eye sings with clear to slurred whistles using a variety of phrasings. It scolds with a harsh "dzur."

✓✓**Behavior:** This most vocal singer of all the Alberta songbirds calls thousands of times throughout the day, well into the breeding season. After one season of listening to birds, this song should be imprinted into memory.

- -

Similar species: Philadelphia Vireo (vocally); Warbling Vireo (visually).

Remarks: The most detectable (vocally) species in the parkland and southern boreal forest. It responds aggressively to playback of its song. Song is variable and so close to the Philadelphia Vireo that visual confirmation of identification is recommended. Red-eyes are common in city and town parks. Phillies seem less tolerant of human presence. The best time to see vireos is in early spring. Once the leaves are out on the aspens these birds become perfectly camouflaged.

Jan	Feb	Mar	Apr	May	Jun	Jul	Aug	Sep	Oct	Nov	Dec

REVI ☐   Date: _____

GRAY JAY

Perisoreus canadensis

L: 280 mm   W: 70 g   Egg: 29 x 21 mm

Photo: G.Beyersbergen

Etymology: *Perisoreus* (Gr.) - "to pile or store," as in food; *canadensis* (ML.) - " of Canada."

Status and Distribution: It is most common in dense coniferous stands in the mountains and foothills, and in coniferous or mixed wood stands in the boreal forest region. In winter, it may wander into the parkland region, and occasionally, into the coulees of the grasslands region.

• •

Field Checklist

✓**Habitat:** It is found in mixed wood, black spruce and tamarack lowland bogs and dense white spruce forests, especially picnic sites and parking lots in these areas.

✓✓✓**Sight:** They are identified by their pale gray and white coloration, "soft" plumage and gliding flight. Juveniles are solid gray and are seen in early to late spring.

✓✓**Sound**: Gray Jays have a remarkably diverse vocal repertoire. It contains noisy, harsh babbles, chatters, hoots and whistles.

✓✓✓**Behavior:** Gregarious, often in family groups, they are aggressive and bold in approaching humans. Gray Jays will rob food from picnic tables but they are equally at home feeding on insects and berries.

• •

Similar Species: Northern and Loggerhead Shrikes (visually).

Remarks: They are curious and aggressive and will often approach observers. These jays can be seen dining on road kills. Their flight is a combination of rapid wingbeats and glides. By contrast, Shrikes are rarely seen gliding and are more distinctly black and white versus gray and white. If you hear strange hoots, cackles or whistles in the north, the Gray Jays have found you. They are also known by some, more colorful names; Canada Jay, Whiskey Jack, and Camp Robber.

Jan	Feb	Mar	Apr	May	Jun	Jul	Aug	Sep	Oct	Nov	Dec

GRJA ❑   Date: _____

Jays

STELLER'S JAY

Cyanocitta stelleri

L: 311 mm   W: 109 g   Egg: 31 x 22 mm

Etymology: *Cyanos* (Gr.) - "blue," *kitta* (Gr.) - "a chattering bird;" *stelleri* (ML.) - after George Wilhelm Steller, a German zoologist who collected the first specimen in the mid-1700s.

Status and Distribution: Steller's Jays are scarce breeders in the mountains and foothills. They are more common in the Waterton and Westcastle area than farther north. This species is far more common on the western side of the Rockies. In winter it has been recorded as far east as Edmonton and Red Deer.

• •

Field Checklist

✓**Habitat:** The Steller's Jay prefers coniferous woods above 1200 m. It may sometimes be found within the dense shrubbery of avalanche slopes.

✓✓✓**Sight:** This is our only predominantly dark-plumaged Jay. The front half of the bird is darker than the rear. Look for the crest and white spot or line above the eye.

✓✓**Sound:** This species is hard on the ears. It produces a harsh "shack-shack-shack-shack," delivered rapidly or a slower grating "yaak."

✓**Behavior:** Like a Blue Jay, Steller's is bold, gregarious and aggressive.

• •

Similar Species: Blue Jay (visually) and all jays vocally.

Remarks: Steller's Jays are noisy and gregarious in winter but secretive during the breeding season. They may hybridize with Blue Jays. Like the Blue Jay, they will eat almost anything from human garbage to seeds, carrion, small birds and mammals. The Blue Jay has a similar profile but is brighter blue on the back and white underneath. Blue Jay calls are slightly more musical and always higher pitched.

Jan	Feb	Mar	Apr	May	Jun	Jul	Aug	Sep	Oct	Nov	Dec

STJA ☐   Date: _____

BLUE JAY

Cyanocitta cristata

L: 295 mm   W: 101 g   Egg: 28 x 22 mm

Etymology: *Cyanos* (Gr.) - "blue," *kitta* (Gr.) - "a chattering bird;" *cristata* (L.) - "crested."

Status and Distribution: The Blue Jay is a common resident in central Alberta north to Fort McMurray. It's rare south of Calgary and in the mountains. The range of this and the Steller's Jay may meet near Jasper.

• •

Field Checklist

✓**Habitat:** The Blue Jay is an eastern species which prefers mixed woods but it has become highly urbanized. This is the most common city jay.

✓✓✓**Sight:** Look for the crest, bright blue plumage with white patches on the wings and tail, and white underparts.

✓✓**Sound:** Blue Jays utter a loud "jay-jay-jay" call but they can mimic a variety of species like the Red-tailed Hawk. They also produce a horn-like "weedle-eedle."

✓**Behavior:** This species is noisy and aggressive at feeders. They are bold in stealing food and in eating the eggs and chicks of other species. Like other jays, they fly on a level and will glide but not as regularly as do Gray Jays.

• •

Similar Species: Steller's Jay (visually and vocally).

Remarks: In profile, this species may be mistaken for only the Steller's Jay, which is a darker blue overall, but the distributions of these two jays rarely overlap. It is a permanent resident or partially migratory. It becomes more noticeable in late summer. Its call is almost a sentinel of cooler fall days. It is secretive during breeding season. In winter, Blue Jays are happy to visit feeders and seem to like scattering the other birds who are enjoying your seed.

Jan	Feb	Mar	Apr	May	Jun	Jul	Aug	Sep	Oct	Nov	Dec

CLARK'S NUTCRACKER

Nucifraga columbiana

Photo: K.Morck

L: 310 mm   W: 139 g   Egg: 33 x 23 mm

Etymology: *Nucis* (L.) - "nut," *frango* (L.) - "break;" *columbiana* (ML.) - for the Columbia River area, as the bird was first discovered along the Clearwater River which flows into the Columbia.

Status and Distribution: The Nutcracker is a common resident of the Mountain Parks.

Field Checklist

✓✓**Habitat:** This species lives in coniferous forests in mountain parks but can be found in campgrounds, picnic sites and other developed areas. Parking lots at National Park attractions are popular with Nutcrackers because tourists like to feed them.

✓✓✓**Sight:** Clark's Nutcrackers have a distinctive profile; they have a big bill and look chunky. The predominantly black wings with white edges contrast with a mostly white tail with a black centre.

✓✓**Sound:** The call is a harsh, nasal, grating "kaar-kaar, kaar, kaar."

✓✓**Behavior:** Nutcrackers are noisy, gregarious, aggressive and bold. Look for a gliding flight with slow wing beats.

Similar Species: Gray Jay (visually).

Remarks: The heavy, pointed bill and flashing white wing and tail feathers separate this species from the predominantly gray, Gray Jay. It is secretive in spring when it breeds, otherwise the Nutcracker is highly detectable. Pairs hold territories year round but often form large groups in winter. They have been closely studied for their ability to store food and subsequently find these caches.

Jan	Feb	Mar	Apr	May	Jun	Jul	Aug	Sep	Oct	Nov	Dec

Order: Passeriformes - Family: Corvidae

Crows and Allies

BLACK-BILLED MAGPIE

Pica pica

Photo: T.Thormin

L: 501 mm   W: 195 g   Egg: 33 x 23 mm

Etymology: *pica* (L.) - refers to the black and white coloration of the bird.

Status and Distribution: Magpies are common in all natural regions except the Canadian Shield in extreme north-eastern Alberta. Highest numbers are in the parkland and grassland. More and more they are being seen in the north as land is cleared and livestock raised.

● ●

Field Checklist

✓**Habitat:** They can be found almost everywhere except in solid coniferous forests. They are not a forest bird, preferring open country. Only tall bushes or small trees are needed for nesting.

✓✓✓**Sight:** They have a long tail and general black and white plumage. Look for iridescence in the tail and wings. Magpies build huge stick nests which are as distinctive as the birds themselves.

✓✓✓**Sound:** Their call is a loud "yak, yak, yak, yak" and sharp "maagh."

✓✓**Behavior:** This species is noisy, gregarious (family groups), aggressive and active in winter.

● ●

Similar Species: None.

Remarks: A much maligned bird for its predatory habits but it is no better or worse than any other corvid. Jays, nutcrackers, crows and ravens are also opportunistic omnivores and not shy about killing. Magpies are highly detectable year round. Young Magpies are probably the noisiest birds in Alberta. The biggest complaint homeowners level against magpies is the incessant, screaming demands of the young to be fed. Magpies probably flourished when bison were common but like the bison, they virtually disappeared from Alberta. Thanks to cattle and their innate adaptability, Magpies are back.

Jan	Feb	Mar	Apr	May	Jun	Jul	Aug	Sep	Oct	Nov	Dec

201

Order: Passeriformes - Family: Corvidae

AMERICAN CROW

Corvus brachyrhynchos

Photo: K.Morck

L: 450 mm W: 437 g Egg: 41 x 29 mm

Etymology: *Corvus* (L.) - "a raven;" *brachys* (Gr.) - "short," *rhynchos*, "beak."

Status and Distribution: Crows are common summer residents through central Alberta and permanent residents in much of the south. They are sporadic in northern boreal forests where their niche seems to be filled by Ravens.

••••••••••••••••••••••••••••••••••••

Field Checklist

✓**Habitat:** Crows are common near forest edges but can be seen in a variety of grassland and parkland habitats. Males have taken to perching and displaying on streetlights.

✓✓**Sight:** Their plumage is solid black. They have a fan-shaped tail and a relatively small bill (compared to a Raven).

✓✓✓**Sound:** Their "caw-caw," is diagnostic.

✓✓**Behavior:** Crows are noisy and aggressive. They rarely soar in flight. Males perch on lamp posts and utility poles and display to females by spreading their wing and tail feathers, puffing-up their body, bowing and uttering a rattling call.

••••••••••••••••••••••••••••••••••••

Similar Species: Common Raven (visually).

Remarks: Normally noisy and visible but, like jays, crows become quiet and unobtrusive during breeding season. They can often be seen harassing and chasing owls and hawks. This is one of the best ways to find birds of prey in the daytime: follow the crows. When they get really excited, they have found something interesting. Watch male crows or pairs on urban light standards; their interactions are both comical and fascinating.

Jan	Feb	Mar	Apr	May	Jun	Jul	Aug	Sep	Oct	Nov	Dec

AMCR ☐   Date: _____

COMMON RAVEN

Corvus corax

L: 630 mm   W: 1126 g   Egg: 50 x 33 mm

Etymology: *Corvus* (L.) - "a raven;" *corax* (Gr.) - "croaker."

Status and Distribution: Ravens are resident in the mountain, foothill and boreal regions. They continue to expand their winter and summer range to the east and south. Ten years ago, Ravens were uncommon in the parkland; now they are regular winter residents and will stay to breed in forested areas.

Photo: J. Kristensen

• •

Field Checklist

✓✓**Habitat:** They are found in forested areas, normally boreal and montane forest but they can winter anywhere. Forest edges in the mountains are the best places to see Ravens in the spring and summer.

✓✓**Sight:** Ravens, unlike crows, have a distinctive wedge-shaped (rounded) tail. Their heavy bill, beard and large size separate them from the Crow.

✓✓✓**Sound:** A harsh "croak" replaces the Crow's "caw." A variety of gurgles and bell-like notes can be heard especially around the nest.

✓✓**Behavior:** Ravens often soar like buteos and eagles, sometimes at great heights. They perform acrobatic rolls in flight. They frequent dumps and landfills, and eat carrion along roads.

• •

Similar Species: Common Crow (visually).

Remarks: Similar in appearance to the Crow, but the Raven is considerably larger, has a heavier bill and has pointed and elongated throat feathers. Ravens spend a lot of time on the ground and both walk and hop. They occasionally need a running start to get airborne, especially after a good feed at a dump. Ravens, like other corvids, are credited with a high level of intelligence. They are certainly adaptable and difficult to approach.

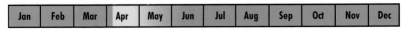

Jan	Feb	Mar	Apr	May	Jun	Jul	Aug	Sep	Oct	Nov	Dec

CORA ☐   Date: _____

Larks

HORNED LARK

Eremophila alpestris

L: 176 mm W: 33 g Egg: 23 x 17 mm

Etymology: *Eremophila* (Gr.) - *Eremos*, "lonely" and *philoe*, "love;" *alpestris* (L.) - alpine.

Status and Distribution: The Horned Lark is a migrant throughout all of Alberta but absent from the boreal forest during the breeding season. Four subspecies are found in Alberta.

● ●

Field Checklist

✓**Habitat:** This species breeds wherever there is open ground. It prefers grasslands or alpine tundra. It is extremely common in southern Alberta.

✓✓✓**Sight:** Male: white or yellow face, black stripe under the eye, black bib and tail, with white outer feathers that are exposed in flight, and black horns. Female: duller overall. Juvenile: dark above with white spotting. Mountain forms are distinctly "pinker" on their underparts.

✓**Sound:** A high, weak trilling or twittering.

✓**Behavior:** Commonly walks or runs along gravel roads or perches on rocks in open fields. Will fly down roads in front of slowly advancing automobiles.

● ●

Similar species: The Water Pipit (mountains) and Sprague's Pipit (grasslands) behave much like larks.

Remarks: The facial pattern of the adult lark is diagnostic. Juvenile larks, which are seen regularly, resemble sparrows especially the Vesper. Look for a thin rather than a seed-crunching sparrow bill and for the presence of adult larks. Their high-pitched song is easily missed. As one of our earliest migrants, the Horned Lark precedes the Robin as a harbinger of spring. The male "larks", which is a dramatic diving flight display, and "struts" for the female with his horns raised. In early spring, they are often in the company of Snow Buntings and Lapland Longspurs. Later they may mix with Chestnut-collared Longspurs and Pipts. They may raise three broods a year.

Jan	Feb	Mar	Apr	May	Jun	Jul	Aug	Sep	Oct	Nov	Dec

HOLA ☐   Date: _____

PURPLE MARTIN

Photo: K.Morck

Progne subis

L: 191 mm   W: 51 g   Egg: 24 x 17 mm

Etymology: *Progne* (Gr.) - After Procne, daughter of Pandion, the King of Athens who was transformed into a swallow; *subis* (L.) - from *Pliny*, "name for a bird that breaks eagle eggs."

Status and Distribution: The Purple Martin is restricted to the aspen parkland and southern parts of the boreal forest. Its range is expanding northwards along with urban subdivisions and artificial nest boxes.

● ●

Field Checklist

✓✓**Habitat:** This species is found in urban environments with artificial nest "apartments." Under natural conditions, the Purple Martin breeds in mature woodlands dotted with lakes, meadows and marshes. Generally Martins are seen in backyards and parks near water in cities and towns.

✓✓**Sight:** Distinguished by its forked tail, long wings compared to other swallows, wide bill, and swallow-type flight. Two-year old and older male is entirely dark, glossy purplish blue, while the female and yearling male are gray-brown below. The yearling may have some spots extending below.

✓✓**Sound:** Distinctive liquid gurgling warble and loud "chew-chew" call.

✓**Behavior:** Aerial foraging for insects, perches on its apartment; gregarious.

● ●

Similar species: Other swallows, but the Purple Martin is darker and larger. Starlings are similarly colored but they have stubby rather than forked tails and a bright yellow, pointed bill in the spring.

Remarks: Natural nest sites of the Purple Martin are hard to find throughout much of its range. It is a mosquito eater which enhances its reputation as a backyard guest but despite their best efforts, there will be lots of pests to annoy you in your yard.

Jan	Feb	Mar	Apr	May	Jun	Jul	Aug	Sep	Oct	Nov	Dec

PUMA ❑   Date: _____

Swallows

TREE SWALLOW

Tachycineta bicolor

L: 146 mm W: 22 g Egg: 19 x 13 mm

Photo: J.Kristensen

Etymology: *Tachycineta* (Gr.) - *Tachy,* " swift," *cineta* from *kinetos*, "to move;" *bicolor* (L.) - two color, referring to blue and white.

Status and Distribution: The Tree Swallow can be found anywhere in Alberta. Nest boxes have allowed this species to frequent the grasslands of southeastern Alberta although it still prefers riparian forests. It is most common in the aspen parkland.

● ●

Field Checklist

✓**Habitat:** The natural breeding habitat of Tree Swallows is a mature woodland where dead and dying trees have had nesting cavities excavated by woodpeckers. Water, which provides a source of insects, is invariably nearby. Nest boxes along fencelines near sloughs make a good substitute.

✓✓**Sight:** Dark greenish-blue above, white below; the female is duller.

✓✓**Sound:** Constant chattering twitter, if many swallows are around or "cheet-veet" and "silip" calls from individuals.

✓**Behavior:** Tree Swallows often nest in, and perch on, artificial boxes; an early spring migrant, it congregates in flocks in late summer.

● ●

Similar species: The Violet-green Swallow of southern and southwestern Alberta is similarly colored but shows more white on the face and on the rump.

Remarks: The male Tree Swallow is an early migrant to Alberta and must cope with cold weather and spring snowstorms. In inclement weather, berries supplement the insects such as stone-flies, which still seem to fly above open water. Unlike other swallows, the Tree Swallow defends a large territory and does not nest colonially.

Jan	Feb	Mar	Apr	May	Jun	Jul	Aug	Sep	Oct	Nov	Dec

TESW ☐   Date: _____

VIOLET-GREEN SWALLOW

Tachycineta thalassina

L: 132 mm W: 16 g Egg: 18 x 13 mm

Etymology: *Tachycineta* (Gr.) - *Tachy,* "swift," *cineta* from *kinetos,* "to move;" *thalassina* (L.) - "Like the sea," for its sea-green color.

Status and Distribution: The Violet-green Swallow breeds in the Rocky Mountains and east along the Red Deer, South Saskatchewan and Milk rivers to the Saskatchewan border.

• •

Field Checklist

✓**Habitat:** It can be found in mountain valleys with lakes and ponds or deeply carved river valleys.

✓✓**Sight:** The male has a bright green back, bronze tint on the head, white face and rump patches and a purplish tint to the upper tail. The female is duller and the juvenile mostly gray.

✓**Sound:** High-pitched series of "chip chip" notes.

✓**Behavior:** Often seen carrying out various aerobatic manoeuvres with wide sweeps and short turns. It does this while foraging for flying insects, seemingly using little caution around animals or buildings. It will hawk these insects high above water or flutter along the surface. This may be one of few birds seen while hiking high mountain trails.

• •

Similar species: Tree Swallows can also show greenish iridescence but are generally bluer and show less white on the face and rump.

Remarks: Moderate detectability; care is needed to distinguish it from the Tree Swallow. The Violet-green Swallow is likely more common east of the mountains than assumed. It is easy to overlook in areas where Tree Swallows are common. It is often in groups foraging high above the ground.

Jan	Feb	Mar	Apr	May	Jun	Jul	Aug	Sep	Oct	Nov	Dec

VGSW ☐   Date: _____

Swallows

NORTHERN ROUGH-WINGED SWALLOW

Stelgidopteryx serripennis

L: 131 mm W: 17 g Egg: 18 x 13 mm

Etymology: *Stelgidopteryx* (Gr.) - *Stelgi,* "a scraper," *pteryx,* "wing;" *serripennis* (L.) - *serra,* "saw," and *pennis,* "wing." Both refer to the serrated edge of the primary feathers.

Status and Distribution: The breeding range extends from southern Alberta north to Edmonton and west into the mountains, where it is uncommon.

● ●

Field Checklist

✓✓**Habitat:** Soft earth banks of creeks and irrigation canals in the grassland region are prime nesting locations, as are low stream banks in the parkland. Open areas both wet and dry are needed around the nest site to provide foraging spaces for the pair.

✓✓**Sight:** Male and female plumage are the same - brown above with a grayish wash on the chin, throat, and upper breast. This is less distinctive than the white throat and dark breast band of the Bank Swallow. Juveniles are similar, but have cinnamon wing bars.

✓**Sound:** The call is a series of single, grating "drzeet" notes.

✓**Behavior:** Rough-winged Swallows are solitary breeders. Their nests are harder to find than those of Bank Swallows, although an intruder can expect a loud and aggressive challenge.

● ●

Similar species: Bank Swallows.

Remarks: Moderate detectability but because they share similar habits, this species is commonly mistaken for the Bank Swallow. The Bank Swallow's wingbeats are quicker and shallower.

Jan	Feb	Mar	Apr	May	Jun	Jul	Aug	Sep	Oct	Nov	Dec

NRWS ☐   Date: _____

Swallows

BANK SWALLOW

Riparia riparia

L: 126 mm W: 14 g Egg: 18 x 13 mm

Etymology: *Riparia* (L.) - *ripa* "stream bank," for the nesting site, i.e., riparian.

Status and Distribution: Widespread in Alberta, most common in the parkland and least common in the extreme north. Breeding sites are determined by suitable soil cliff faces for excavation of their 60-90 cm-long burrows.

• •

Field Checklist

✓✓**Habitat:** Bank Swallows need the sides of rivers and lakes as sites for their colonial nest burrows. Similar features such as dirt or sand piles exposed by human landscaping may also be colonized. The presence of nearby water for foraging is an additional requirement.

✓✓**Sight:** Bank Swallows are dark brown above, white below, and they have a distinctive brown breast band.

Sound: Dry grating twitters. In groups the birds make a lot of noise.

✓**Behavior:** Being gregarious, Bank Swallows are found in large colonies in high river banks. They may be seen above cliffs, hawking insects over shallow waters, flying continuously, emitting soft twitters. Normally, in such social birds, aggression occurs only when neighbors appear at the same nest entrance.

• •

Similar species: White underparts and breast band distinguish it from the less widespread Northern Rough-winged Swallow.

Remarks: Highly detectable, but easily confused with the Northern Rough-winged Swallow. Colonial birds are likely Bank Swallows but Rough-wings may be mixed in with them. These birds excavate their own nest burrows. The same species is known in Europe and Asia as the Sand Martin.

Jan	Feb	Mar	Apr	May	Jun	Jul	Aug	Sep	Oct	Nov	Dec

BKSW ☐   Date: _____

BARN SWALLOW

Hirundo rustica

L: 170 mm   W: 18 g   Egg: 20 x 14 mm

Etymology: *Hirundo* (L.) - "a swallow;" *rustica* (L.) - "rustic."

Status and Distribution: Abundant throughout Alberta especially where human-built structures provide nest sites. In the mountain parks, the Barn Swallow primarily nests in the montane and lower subalpine ecoregions, though it may range into alpine regions during migration.

Field Checklist

✓**Habitat:** The Barn Swallow uses water bodies, gardens, and livestock yards for foraging, drinking, and mud gathering. Nests are on, or in, man-made structures.

✓✓✓**Sight:** The male of this commonly seen swallow is dark blue above and can be distinguished from other swallows by its long, forked tail. It also has a reddish-brown forehead and throat and cinnamon or buffy underparts. Females and juveniles are similar but with shorter tails and paler under-parts.

✓✓**Sound:** These birds are extremely vocal. Their song is a series of "surp" notes, some-times punctuated by a slightly rising, grating trill. Its flight call can be described as "kvick, kvick." In groups, their calls blend into a constant chatter.

✓**Behavior:** Highly gregarious. It usually forages near to the ground. The Barn Swallow can be seen around farm yards, over water and open land, and near marshes. On warm evenings it will fly higher, following the rise of flies, gnats, and flying ants.

Similar species: Cliff Swallow (visually).

Remarks: The Barn is our only swallow with a forked tail. It builds a distinctive mud-based cup nest under eaves.

Jan	Feb	Mar	Apr	May	Jun	Jul	Aug	Sep	Oct	Nov	Dec

BRSW ☐   Date: _____

CLIFF SWALLOW

Petrochelidon pyrrhonota

L: 143 mm W: 25 g Egg: 19 x 13 mm

Etymology: *Petrochelidon* (Gr.) - *petra*, "a rock;" *chelidon*, "a swallow;" *pyrrhonota* (Gr.) - *pyrrhos*, "flame-colored;" *notos* (Gr.) - "back."

Status and Distribution: The Cliff Swallow is abundant throughout Alberta. In the mountains, it normally breeds from the montane to the upper subalpine areas, usually near rivers or lakes. However, two colonies have been reported breeding in the alpine ecoregion.

• •

Field Checklist

✓**Habitat:** A variety of sites provides the vertical and over-hanging surfaces required for nesting: Concrete bridges, cliffs, high ledges, culverts and steep clay riverbanks. Nearby water sources provide mud, foraging and drinking water. The Cliff Swallow will also forage over open land and marshes.

✓✓✓**Sight:** Adults show a short squarish tail, white forehead, and buffy rump. Juveniles are gray-brown whereas the adults are dark with a paler throat and darker forehead.

✓✓**Sound:** The voice of the Cliff Swallow is squeakier and more grating than that of other swallows, especially in a group chorus.

✓**Behavior:** Cliff Swallows are highly colonial. They often flush in large numbers from under a bridge in response to vehicles or hikers. Look for these birds skimming over rivers, lakes, and sloughs, as they scoop up insects.

• •

Similar species: Barn Swallow.

Remarks: The white forehead and square (not forked) tail separate this swallow from the Barn Swallow with which it mixes. This is a good species to study to learn about avian social behavior. The distinctive facial patterns may help birds recognize individuals in the colony.

Jan	Feb	Mar	Apr	May	Jun	Jul	Aug	Sep	Oct	Nov	Dec

Order: Passeriformes - Family: Paridae

BLACK-CAPPED CHICKADEE

Poecile atricapillus

Photo: L. Valcourt

L: 131 mm W: 11 gm Egg: 15 x 12 mm

Etymology: *Poecile* (L.) - "variegated;" *atri* (L.) - "black" and *capillus*, (L.) - "crown."

Status and Distribution: This chickadee is common in wooded areas in every natural region in Alberta. It is less common in the mountains and extreme north. Blackcaps are joined and replaced primarily by Boreal Chickadees in the north and Mountain Chickadees in western Alberta.

• •

Field Checklist

✓**Habitat:** They are found in mixed woods but may be seen in conifers, fields and thickets, and are common in urban areas at feeders.

✓✓**Sight:** Look for the black cap and bib, and grey and white plumage. The white on the face does not extend above the eye. Chickadees are relatively small birds.

✓✓✓**Sound:** A clear "chick-a-dee-dee-dee" and clear, whistled "pee-ter" (spring) calls are unmistakable.

✓✓**Behavior:** Chickadees are gregarious, often in family groups and noisy. They are curious and will approach people especially in response to "pishing" or imitation of the "pee-ter" call. They join with other species like nuthatches and redpolls in foraging groups in the winter. They are quiet and difficult to find in the breeding season.

• •

Similar Species: Boreal Chickadee and Mountain Chickadee.

Remarks: Distinguished from the Mountain Chickadee by the lack of a white eyebrow line. Black rather than brown plumage separates it from a Boreal. Calls of Black-capped are clearer than the hoarse voices of both the Boreal and Mountain.

Jan	Feb	Mar	Apr	May	Jun	Jul	Aug	Sep	Oct	Nov	Dec

212

BCCH ☐   Date: _____

MOUNTAIN CHICKADEE

Poecile gambeli

Photo: K.Morck

L: 130 mm   W: 12 gm   Egg: 16 x 12 mm

Etymology: *Poecile* (L.) - "variegated;" *gambeli* (ML.) - for William Gambel, the first ornithologist to spend several years in California collecting and describing birds.

Status and Distribution: Mountain Chickadees are permanent residents of the Rocky Mountain and foothills natural regions. In winter they can be seen well to the east of the foothills.

Field Checklist

✓✓**Habitat:** They prefer open coniferous forests in the mountains and foothills.

✓**Sight:** The Mountain is similar to the Black-capped Chickadee with the black cap and bib. The distinctive feature of the Mountain is the white line above the eye.

✓✓**Sound:** The call of the Mountain Chickadee has the cadence of the Blackcap, but its version is a guttural "chick-a-dee-dee-dee" call. It gives a clearer three to-four-note "fee-bee-bay" whistle that changes pitch.

✓✓**Behavior:** Like all chickadees, Mountains are gregarious and active, but are less approachable than the Blackcap. It mixes with other species in the winter.

Similar Species: Black-capped Chickadee (visually). Boreal Chickadee (vocally).

Remarks: Location and habitat are the best clues for spotting this moderately detectable species. It tends to forage higher in trees than the Black-capped. Cavity nesters like all chickadees, the Mountain's nest is often less than three metres from the ground. The Mountain Chickadee performs altitudinal migrations moving annually between their high elevation nesting grounds to more moderate valleys for the winter. In some locations in the mountains all three species of chickadee can be found together in winter.

Jan	Feb	Mar	Apr	May	Jun	Jul	Aug	Sep	Oct	Nov	Dec

MOCH ☐   Date: _____

Chickadees

BOREAL CHICKADEE

Poecile hudsonicus

Photo: K.Morck

L: 130 mm   W: 11 gm   Egg: 16 x 12 mm

Etymology: *Poecile* (L.) - "variegated;" *hudsonicus* (ML.) - of Hudson Bay, alluding to its northern range.

Status and Distribution: Widespread in mountains, foothills, northern parkland and boreal forest regions. Not as common as the Black-capped but the predominant chickadee of extreme northeastern and northwestern Alberta.

• •

Field Checklist

✓**Habitat:** Boreals are found in coniferous and mixed wood forests in the mountains and throughout the north. Their preference is for conifers although they will forage in deciduous trees.

✓✓**Sight:** Brown cap, grey-brown back, brown sides and flanks.

✓✓**Sound:** Very hoarse, nasal, "chick-a-dee-dee," the last notes delivered in almost a wheeze.

✓**Behavior:** A typical chickadee, gregarious, active, noisy, it often flocks with other species in winter. During the breeding season it is quiet and hard to find.

• •

Similar Species: Black-capped or Mountain Chickadee (visually and vocally).

Remarks: There is considerable overlap in the range of the three common Alberta chickadees. In poor light, the Boreal can resemble a Black-capped. Vocal differences are the best identifiers. Boreal Chickadees forage often in the central foliage of spruce trees. As one travels north in Alberta, the numbers of Blackcaps decline and the numbers of Boreals increase. Boreal Chickadees favor solid conifer forest. In winter Boreals will visit feeders especially in backyards with mature trees.

Jan	Feb	Mar	Apr	May	Jun	Jul	Aug	Sep	Oct	Nov	Dec

BOCH ☐   Date: _____

CHESTNUT-BACKED CHICKADEE

Poecile rufescens

The Chestnut-backed Chickadee is an accidental vagrant that wanders across the British Columbia or Montana border into Alberta's southern mountain parks, particularly Waterton Lakes. It prefers coniferous forests but can be found in mixed and deciduous woods even scrubby vegetation.

It shows a similar plumage pattern to the Black-capped but it has a distinctive chestnut back, rump and flanks. The cap is brown, face white and throat black. Its song is a fast, hoarse version of the typical "chick-a-dee' call but it seems to have an extra syllable "chick-a-du-dee-dee." Typically, the Chestnut-backed Chickadee forages on the upper parts of trees. This is particularly obvious in areas where its range overlaps with that of the Black-capped which tends to forage well below the canopy.

The Chestnut-backed is primarily a coastal forest bird. It is doubtful that it will ever be permanently established in Alberta. With some luck though, you might find four chickadee species together in Waterton Park.

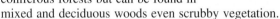

Nuthatches

RED-BREASTED NUTHATCH

Sitta canadensis

L: *111 mm   W: 11 g   Egg: 15 x 12 mm*

Etymology: *Sitta* (Gr.) - "a bird that pecks at trees;" *canadensis* (ML.) - "Canadian."

Status and Distribution: The Red-breasted Nuthatch is a common breeder in wooded areas in all natural regions. Its preference for conifers results in higher numbers in the mountains, foothills and boreal forest. If sufficient food is available, they will winter in the province but most individuals spend the winter farther south.

Field Checklist

✓**Habitat:** This nuthatch is found in mixed woods or coniferous forests, urban areas or at feeders.

✓✓✓**Sight:** It is distinguished from the White-breasted Nuthatch by its rust-colored underparts, white line over eye, stubby body and short tail.

✓✓**Sound:** It gives a nasal horn-like "yank-yank-yank-yank" call which is delivered at a constant pitch.

✓✓**Behavior:** The Nuthatch forages by patrolling down tree trunks and along branches often upside down. It flies wood-pecker-like with alternating flaps and glides resulting in a sinusoidal rather than straight-line path from one perch to the next. It mixes with other species including warblers during migration and through the winter.

Similar Species: White-breasted Nuthatch (vocally and visually).

Remarks: This species is highly detectable vocally but it can be overlooked as it moves down tree trunks foraging for seeds and insects. Reddish underparts and smaller size separate this from the White-breasted. The calls of the Red-breasted are higher-pitched and more nasal than those of the White-breasted.

Jan	Feb	Mar	Apr	May	Jun	Jul	Aug	Sep	Oct	Nov	Dec

216

RBNU ☐   Date: _____

WHITE-BREASTED NUTHATCH

Sitta carolinensis

L: 145 mm   W: 22 g   Egg: 19 x 14 mm

Etymology: *Sitta* (Gr.) - "a bird that pecks at trees;" *carolinensis* (ML.) - "of Carolina."

Status and Distribution: This nuthatch is an uncommon breeder and year-round resident in the parkland and southern boreal forest. Historically it was rare in Alberta but like several other species has expanded its range into Alberta from Saskatchewan.

Field Checklist

✓**Habitat:** The White-breasted Nuthatch prefers mature deciduous or mixed woods and urban areas.

✓✓**Sight:** Look for the large size, white face, neck and chest, variably rusty belly and undertail and relatively long pointed bill to separate this from the Red-breasted.

✓✓✓**Sound:** A nasal "who-who-who," that is less nasal than the call of the Red-breasted.

✓✓**Behavior:** They forage by patrolling down, around or along tree trunks. They can be heard tapping a tree trunk like a woodpecker. Nuthatches often stop with their head extended away from the tree trunk.

Similar species: Red-breasted Nuthatch (vocally and visually).

Remarks: Highly detectable vocally and reasonably so visually in Alberta but, nonetheless, it is not common. It is called a nuthatch for the way it hammers open seeds with its bill. Both species of nuthatches nest in cavities which they may excavate. The White-breasted consumes large quantities of insect pests. This may provide some economic benefit but the best foraging trees are ones that are beyond saving.

Jan	Feb	Mar	Apr	May	Jun	Jul	Aug	Sep	Oct	Nov	Dec

217   WBNU ❏   Date: _____

Creepers

BROWN CREEPER

Certhia americana

L: 133 mm   W: 8.4 g   Egg: 15 x 12 mm

Etymology: *Certhia* (L.) - "a creeper;" *americana* (ML.) - "for America."

Status and Distribution: The Brown Creeper is an uncommon breeder and permanent resident in the parkland, mountain and boreal forest regions. Its status is uncertain because it is inconspicuous. There are relatively few breeding records but undoubtedly estimates of the bird's distribution and abundance are conservative.

Field Checklist

✓**Habitat:** It is found in mature mixed woods but appears to prefer the coniferous portions.

✓**Sight:** Look for the curved bill, white underparts, streaked brown plumage on the back and yellowish bar across the wing.

✓✓**Sound:** It gives a high-pitched "see-see-see-tih-see" song or a simple "see" call. The call is faint and does not travel far. The pitch is such that even if the song reaches middle-aged ears, nothing registers.

✓✓**Behavior:** The Creeper climbs spiral-fashion up tree trunks as it forages, then flies to a low spot on neighboring trees. It is solitary. The Creeper uses its tail for support on tree trunks resulting in a completely different posture from that of nuthatches.

Similar species: Nuthatches (behaviorally).

Remarks: Small size, foraging behavior and weak call make the Brown Creeper inconspicuous and it is often overlooked. Look for a buff or yellow-colored wingpatch as the Creeper flies from high up one tree to a low perch on the next. Careful notes should be kept of breeding records of this species because it is important to know if it is rare or simply hard to detect. Take some youthful ears with you on your search.

Jan	Feb	Mar	Apr	May	Jun	Jul	Aug	Sep	Oct	Nov	Dec

BRCR ☐   Date: _____

ROCK WREN
Salpinctes obsoletus

L: 143 mm   W: 17 g   Egg: 19 x 15 mm

Etymology: *Salpinctes* (Gr.) - "a trumpeter (noisy);" *obsoletus* (L.) - "indistinct," for the dull coloration.

Status and Distribution: Rock Wrens breed in the grassland natural region with isolated breeding records from the foothills and mountains.

Field Checklist

✓✓✓**Habitat:** Very distinct preference for coulees and dry and rocky outcrops, generally in the southeast. They seem to be happy with little or no vegetation nearby.

✓**Sight:** A large wren by Alberta standards, the Rock Wren is generally brownish with a curved bill and a blackish subterminal and buff terminal tail band.

✓✓**Sound:** Males repeat a raspy "chee-urr, chee-urr" call and give a machine-like trill. They call frequently even in the afternoon.

✓✓**Behavior:** The Rock Wren walks a lot among rocks, bobs its head and peers over a ledge while singing. It is active during the heat of the day.

Similar species: All wrens visually, but habitat excludes all other Alberta species.

Remarks: Highly detectable vocally, sometimes a challenge to see. Quite active patrolling its rocky domain which includes outcrops, talus slopes, quarries and stone dams. The Rock Wren is a southern species that is at the northern edge of its range in Alberta. It is intriguing that individuals have managed to find suitable habitat in the mountains and foothills. Why did these birds venture so far from their southern home? This question could be asked of many species that somehow show up far from their normal breeding range. Late summer wandering is well documented for many species and likely leads to range expansion as individuals discover suitable new territories.

Jan	Feb	Mar	Apr	May	Jun	Jul	Aug	Sep	Oct	Nov	Dec

ROWR ☐   **Date:** _____

Wrens

HOUSE WREN

Troglodytes aedon

Photo: K.Morck

L: 120 mm W: 11 g Egg: 16 x 13 mm

Etymology: *Troglodytes* (Gr.) - "cave dweller," *trogle*, "hole" and *dytes*, "a diver;" *aedon* (Gr.) - " a songstress," Aedon was the Queen of Thebes.

Status and Distribution: The House Wren is a common breeder in southern and central Alberta and uncommon in the northern Rockies and the northern boreal forest.

Field Checklist

✓✓**Habitat:** House Wrens like thickets, coulees, suburban yards and river valleys. Look for them in cottonwood and aspen groves as they move about in bushes and undergrowth or low down in trees.

✓✓**Sight:** It has a curved bill and is squat-looking with generally dull, gray-brown plumage. Wren posture is distinctive primarily because the tail is held erect contributing to the overall stubby appearance of the bird.

✓✓✓**Sound:** Wrens have a bubbling noisy, almost explosive whistled song that is repeated endlessly, often very early in the morning.

✓✓**Behavior:** House Wrens are aggressive, curious, active and easily attracted by "pishing" calls. They will destroy other bird eggs in their quest to find and keep the best nesting sites.

Similar species: All wrens, but fortunately habitat differences separate all Alberta wren species.

Remarks: Highly detectable vocally and visually, this bird will find you if you wander into his territory. It nests in cavities and is a popular backyard nester. That is, they are popular until they begin singing at 4:00 a.m. Socially, all wrens are fascinating to watch; they are not well-liked by other birds. See if you can figure out why.

Jan	Feb	Mar	Apr	May	Jun	Jul	Aug	Sep	Oct	Nov	Dec

220   HOWR ☐   Date: _____

WINTER WREN
Troglodytes troglodytes

L: 99 mm   W: 9 g   Egg: 18 x 13 mm

Etymology: *Troglodytes* (Gr.) - "cave dweller," *trogle*, "hole" and *dytes*, "a diver."

Status and Distribution: There are scattered breeding records through-out the mountain and boreal forest natural regions. Despite their name, these birds normally leave Alberta in the fall. Their status is uncertain, but they may be suffering from habitat loss in the boreal forest.

Field Checklist

✓✓**Habitat:** Winter Wrens breed in dense brush in mature montane and boreal forests. Look along streams in the mountains and near water in boreal forest.

✓**Sight:** Our smallest wren, it sports a short erect tail and is basically chocolate brown on top and lighter underneath.

✓✓✓**Sound:** Males deliver a wonderful series of high-pitched musical trills often partially obscured by stream noises. The song can last ten seconds.

✓**Behavior:** Winter Wrens are shy, but active and difficult to get a close look at. Use "pishing" calls or song playback to draw the male into the open.

Similar Species: House Wren (vocally and visually) but there is little habitat overlap between these species.

Remarks: The mountain form of this species (*pacificus*) is buffier under-neath than the boreal forest form (*hyemalis*). The Winter Wren may be threatened by loss of mature forests to logging. Its status and distribution need to be documented. This is another species that may be considered uncommon because it is hard to census. Seeing a female Winter Wren is almost impossible unless you find her nest.

Jan	Feb	Mar	Apr	May	Jun	Jul	Aug	Sep	Oct	Nov	Dec

WIWR ☐   Date: _____

Wrens

SEDGE WREN

Cistothorus platensis

Photo: R.Gehlert

L: 101 mm W: 8 g Egg: 16 x 12 mm

Etymology: *Cistothorus* (Gr.) - *cistos*, "a shrub" and *thouros*, "leaping" or "running through;" *platensis* (Gr.) - *plates*, "flat, broad."

Status and Distribution: Sedge Wrens are scarce in the eastern parkland and southeastern boreal forest. Only a handful of records were confirmed in the breeding bird surveys for the Atlas. It is likely some Sedge Wren records were misidentified Marsh Wrens.

Field Checklist

✓✓**Habitat:** Its distinctive habitat preferences are for sedge- and grass-dominated sloughs and sphagnum bogs in central Alberta.

✓**Sight:** The crown and back are streaked and there is no distinct eye line. The underparts are mainly buffy. Like most wrens, it has a curved bill and holds its tail erect.

✓✓✓**Sound:** Their song begins with single chirps followed by a rattling trill.

✓**Behavior:** Both this species and the Marsh Wren are elusive and difficult to see. They will destroy other birds' eggs and nests.

Similar species: Marsh Wren (visually).

Remarks: Habitat, a streaked crown and the simpler song distinguish this species from the Marsh Wren. It is highly detectable vocally but hard to spot clearly in its habitat. This is another species needing better documentation. Historically it was considered rare in Alberta but systematic searches are producing many new records. Sedge Wrens live in habitat that is difficult to walk and search in, so the best advice is to learn their song.

Jan	Feb	Mar	Apr	May	Jun	Jul	Aug	Sep	Oct	Nov	Dec

SEWR ☐   Date: _____

MARSH WREN

Cistothorus palustris

Photo: K.Morck

L: 122 mm W: 12 g Egg: 16 x 12 mm

Etymology: *Cistothorus* (Gr.) - *cistos*, "a shrub" and *thouros*, "leaping" or "running through;" *palustris* (L.) - "marshy."

Status and Distribution: The Marsh Wren is a common breeder in central Alberta, less so in the boreal forest and grasslands. It is rare in the mountains. They are fairly early spring migrants and stay in Alberta well into the fall.

Field Checklist

✓✓**Habitat:** Unlike the Sedge Wren, the Marsh Wren likes cattail- and bulrush-dominated sloughs throughout the province. Their nests tend to be in cattails.

✓**Sight:** Its unstreaked crown and white eye-line are distinctive. Like the Sedge Wren, it is generally brownish and holds its tail erect. The underparts are mainly white.

✓✓**Sound:** The Marsh Wren gives a variety of chips and rattles normally ending in a buzz trill.

✓**Behavior:** It often perches sideways on reeds, is aggressive, noisy and responds well to "pishing." Seems to be at war with Red-winged Blackbirds. It will destroy other birds' eggs and nests.

Similar species: Sedge Wren (visually).

Remarks: Unstreaked crown, eyeline, habitat and song distinguish this species from the Sedge Wren. Highly detectable vocally and usually easy to spot but it rarely stays still. It is interesting to watch their relationship to other marsh songbirds. Most of them don't like Marsh Wrens and will pursue them if they show up near their nest. Like the House Wren, Marsh Wrens tend to come to you if you are patient and wait near the edge of cattail sloughs.

Jan	Feb	Mar	Apr	May	Jun	Jul	Aug	Sep	Oct	Nov	Dec

MAWR ☐   Date: _____

Dippers

AMERICAN DIPPER

Cinclus mexicanus

Photo: G. Beyersbergen

L: 177 mm   W: 55 g   Egg: 25 x 18 mm

Etymology: *Kinklos* (Gr.) - "a bird;" *mexicanus* (ML.) - "of Mexico."

Status and Distribution: Fairly common breeder in the Rocky Mountain region. Many individuals migrate but others remain through the winter in Alberta.

Field Checklist

✓✓✓**Habitat:** Look for Dippers in and along fast-flowing mountain streams, in both winter and summer. Great viewing areas are along the Bow River in Banff National Park.

✓✓**Sight:** This species is distinguished by its stubby body, short tail and slate-gray plumage.

✓**Sound**: Sometimes hard to hear against a background of noisy moving water but their song is long, melodious and wren-like. They give a "dzeet" call when flushed.

✓✓✓**Behavior:** The Dipper wades and swims in mountain streams and perches on ice at the edge of open water. It flies low over water when flushed.

Similar species: Rock Wren (vocally) but it would be extremely rare to find Rock Wrens and Dippers in the same area.

Remarks: Dippers depart when winter ice takes over the stream or river they have claimed as territory. Overwintering individuals have been reported along open water stretches at Jasper, Canmore, Banff, Sundre, Calgary, and the Sheep River near Okotoks. However, where the majority of Dippers winter is still unknown. Its nearest relative, the European Dipper (*Cinclus cinclus*) is known as the Water Ouzel. This is a bird that deserves to be watched, not just identified. Its remarkable underwater foraging habit and its predilection for mountain streams that are so cold almost defy belief. If you doubt their hardiness, step into a high mountain stream with bare feet and see how long you can stand it.

Jan	Feb	Mar	Apr	May	Jun	Jul	Aug	Sep	Oct	Nov	Dec

AMDI ☐   Date: _____

GOLDEN-CROWNED KINGLET

Regulus satrapa

L: 95 mm   W: 6 g   Egg: 13 x 10 mm

Etymology: *Regulus* (L.) - "Little king;" *satrapa* (Gr.) - *satrapes*, "a ruler," one who wears a golden crown.

Status and Distribution: A common breeder in the Rocky Mountain and foothills regions. There are regular breeding records throughout the western parkland and boreal forest.

• •

Field Checklist

✓**Habitat:** Golden-crowns seek out the conifers in mature mixed-wood in the mountains, foothills and boreal forests. Look for them in tall thick spruce.

✓**Sight:** This is a tiny bird. It is greenish overall with white wing bars and white and black border stripes on the golden-colored crown patch. A close look shows a red streak down the middle of the golden crown.

✓✓**Sound:** Their song is a very high-pitched group of "tsee tsee tsee" notes followed by a trill.

✓**Behavior:** Active, but difficult to see clearly as it moves through the branches and foliage of spruce trees. It occasionally moves down the trunk of trees like a nuthatch.

• •

Similar species: Ruby-crowned Kinglet (visually).

Remarks: Low detectability. Their high-pitched song and habit of hiding in thick spruces gives them a low detectability rating. Patience is the key to finding them once you have detected their song. Active in their quest for insects, they will group with other species outside the breeding season. They are often seen away from their breeding grounds in the spring and fall. Individuals may overwinter.

Jan	Feb	Mar	Apr	May	Jun	Jul	Aug	Sep	Oct	Nov	Dec

GCKI ☐   Date: _____

Kinglets

RUBY-CROWNED KINGLET

Regulus calendula

L: 106 mm W: 6 g Egg: 14 x 11 mm

Etymology: *Regulus* (L.) - "little king;" *calendula* (L.) - "glowing," in reference to crown patch.

Status and Distribution: A common breeder in the mountain, foothills and boreal forest regions. It is fairly common in the western parkland but only migratory through the grasslands.

• •

Field Checklist

✓**Habitat:** Ruby-crowned Kinglets are found in a variety of mixed wood habitats from burns to mature forests. Their preference is for areas with a high percentage of conifers. During migration they can be seen almost anywhere woody vegetation is found.

✓**Sight:** A tiny bird that is plump with grey-olive plumage. Note the white wing bars and eye-ring. The red crown patch is usually hard to see.

✓✓✓**Sound:** Kinglets produce a remarkably loud song for such a tiny bird. It begins with a few high notes followed by some lower-pitched notes ending in a loud, warbling three-note "too witchy too" phrase.

✓✓**Behavior:** This is an extremely active bird. It is constantly moving, calling, flycatching or fluttering its wings. It appears jumpy and nervous.

• •

Similar species: Golden-crowned Kinglet (visually).

Remarks: The Ruby-crowned Kinglet is a constant singer. Often it is one of the few species active during the day in coniferous forests. It is highly detectable vocally and its movement reveals its presence once you've found the source of the noise. The Kinglet responds well to "pishing" but rarely stays still long enough to give you a good look.

Jan	Feb	Mar	Apr	May	Jun	Jul	Aug	Sep	Oct	Nov	Dec

RCKI ☐   Date: _____

MOUNTAIN BLUEBIRD

Sialia currucoides

L: 174 mm   W: 29 g   Egg: 22 x 17 mm

Etymology: *Sialia* (Gr.) - *sialis,* "a kind of bird;" *currucoides* (Gr.) - *carruca* (L.), "carriage or posture," *oides,* "appearance."

Status and Distribution: The Mountain is a common breeder in central, southern and western Alberta. Its range extends north into the boreal forest at least up to the Caribou Mountains.

● ●

Field Checklist

✓**Habitat:** It prefers open country, coulees and river valleys. Look for it near nest boxes. It seems to be attracted to farmyards and ranches.

✓✓✓**Sight:** The all-blue male is unmistakable. Its color is best described as sky-blue. The female is duller grey-brown with bluish back and wings.

✓**Sound:** The Mountain's song is a series of fairly harsh single and double robin-like notes. Its call is a thin whistle.

✓**Behavior:** Look for it hovering when capturing insects. It is an early migrant and cavity nester favoring nest boxes. In spring the male often sits on nest boxes. The Bluebird tends to forage on the ground and return to its perch to consume prey.

● ●

Similar species: Eastern and Western bluebirds (vocally and visually).

Remarks: The Mountain is easily distinguished from the rare Eastern and Western Bluebirds by its all-blue male plumage. The other species show various amounts of brick-red on their underside. This species is highly detectable visually. Look for Mountain Bluebirds in late March and early April, as they return to Alberta a month before most migrants. Without doubt, the efforts of volunteers to erect and maintain nest boxes have significantly increased the abundance of this species in Alberta.

Jan	Feb	Mar	Apr	May	Jun	Jul	Aug	Sep	Oct	Nov	Dec

Order: Passeriformes - Family: Turdidae

TOWNSEND'S SOLITAIRE

Myadestes townsendi

L: 210 mm   W: 35 g   Egg: 23 x 17 mm

Etymology: *Myadestes* (Gr.) - *mya*, "fly" and *edestes*, "eater;" *townsendi* (ML.) - for John K. Townsend, a Philadelphia ornithologist and contemporary of Audubon.

Status and Distribution: The Solitaire breeds throughout Rocky Mountain and foothills natural regions. This includes the foothills outlier known as the Cypress Hills. The Solitaire wanders away from its breeding habitat and can be seen in spring and fall in the grasslands and parkland.

● ●

Field Checklist

✓**Habitat:** They prefer edges of coniferous forests in the mountains and foothills. Burned hillsides are favorites.

✓✓**Sight:** It is gray overall but look for the white eye-ring, buffy wing patches and white tail patches.

✓**Sound:** The Solitaire's call is a sharp, horn-like "peek." Its song is a complex finch-like warbling.

✓✓**Behavior:** This species forages like a bluebird pouncing on insects on the ground or taking them out of the air, then returning to a perch to enjoy the meal.

● ●

Similar species: Purple and Cassin's finches and Warbling Vireo (vocally), Northern Mockingbird (visually).

Remarks: The Townsend's Solitaire is similar in appearance to the Northern Mockingbird. However, these two species have provincial distributions that do not overlap. Regardless, the white eye-ring around the dark eye of the Solitaire looks completely different from the yellow eye of the Mockingbird. Although the Solitaire is a thrush, it behaves much like a flycatcher. Only moderately detectable, it is easily missed despite being a regular breeder in the mountains. A better name for this bird might have been Townsend's fly-catching Thrush.

Jan	Feb	Mar	Apr	May	Jun	Jul	Aug	Sep	Oct	Nov	Dec

TOSO ☐   Date: _____

Order: Passeriformes - Family: Turdidae

Thrushes

VEERY

Catharus fuscescens

L: 190 mm   W: 29 g   Egg: 22 x 17 mm

Etymology: *Catharus* (Gr.) - *katharos*, "pure," referring to its song; *fuscescens* (L.) - from *fuscus*, "dusky."

Status and Distribution: There are breeding records through the parkland, foothills and boreal forest regions. The concentration of these is in the parkland. Recent records extend the range of the Veery north to approximately Fort Vermilion.

• •

Field Checklist

✓**Habitat:** It is found in mature poplar-dominated woodlands, usually near water. Thick old woods with a damp interior are the Veery's favorite haunts. River valleys provide good homes.

✓**Sight:** The Veery has a dusky-brown back, light spotting on chest and no obvious eye-ring.

✓✓✓**Sound:** A descending series of flute-like plaintive "veer" notes. Like other thrushes, Veerys can sing "in harmony" by producing two notes simultaneously.

Behavior: The Veery is secretive. It uses its bill to uncover food on the forest floor where it spends most of the day.

• •

Similar species: Gray-cheeked, Hermit and Swainson's thrushes and Fox Sparrow (visually); Gray-cheeked Thrush (vocally).

Remarks: Highly detectable vocally but a challenge to find in its preferred mature forest habitat. The Veery in Alberta is not bright red-brown like the eastern form, so do not go looking for the bird pictured in eastern field guides. A slight difference in song, heavier spotting and southerly distribution separate it from the Gray-cheeked Thrush but additional sightings in the north move the Veery's distribution close to that of the Gray-cheeked Thrush.

Jan	Feb	Mar	Apr	May	Jun	Jul	Aug	Sep	Oct	Nov	Dec

VEER ❐   Date: _____

GRAY-CHEEKED THRUSH

Catharus minimus

L: 173 mm W: 31 g Egg: 23 x 17 mm

Etymology: *Catharus* (Gr.) - *katharos*, "pure," referring to its song; *minimus* (L.) - "smallest."

Status and Distribution: The Gray-cheeked Thrush breeds in the Caribou Mountains north of Fort Vermilion. This is a remarkably limited distribution and other high-latitude, high-elevation sites should be examined for evidence of this bird. Its normal breeding range is a vast area from Siberia to northern Quebec.

• •

Field Checklist

✓✓**Habitat:** High-latitude dwarf spruce and scrub willow. Look for it in the Caribou Mountains during the breeding season but anywhere during migration.

✓**Sight:** Both sexes are grayish-brown on the back with extensive spotting on the throat. There is no buffy eye-ring or buff-coloring on the face. The gray on the cheek is a subtle character.

✓✓**Sound:** Song is similar structurally to the Veery's. It is a series of fairly nasal, descending, variable notes often with a sharp up-slur at the end.

✓**Behavior:** Like all thrushes, it feeds and perches on or near the ground.

• •

Similar species: Other thrushes (vocally and visually).

Remarks: This species is distinguished from the Hermit Thrush by its lack of a rusty tail, from the Veery by its grayer upperparts and more heavily spotted breast, and from the Swainson's Thrush, which it most closely resembles, by its gray, not buffy, cheeks and a very light eye-ring. Song is still the best clue, as the Gray-cheeked can be confused vocally only with the Veery. Listen for the up-slur at the end but unfortunately it won't always be there. Range may overlap with the Veery's in the Buffalo Head Hills area, south of the Caribou Mountains.

Jan	Feb	Mar	Apr	May	Jun	Jul	Aug	Sep	Oct	Nov	Dec

GCTH ☐   Date: _____

SWAINSON'S THRUSH

Catharus ustulatus

L: *175 mm* W: *29 g* Egg: *22 x 17 mm*

Etymology: *Catharus* (Gr.) - *katharos,* "pure," referring to its song; *ustulatus* (L.) - "to singe."

Status and Distribution: Swainson's Thrush is widely distributed throughout the parkland, foothills, mountain and boreal forest regions. It is the most common of our "brown" thrushes and probably the easiest to see.

• •

Field Checklist

✓✓**Habitat:** It breeds in aspen-dominated forests of the parkland, mountains and boreal forest. It is usually found near standing water. It is not a deep forest bird to the extent that the Hermit Thrush is.

✓✓✓**Sight:** Look for the buffy eye-ring and buffy spotted throat. The upperparts are dull olive-brown.

✓✓✓**Sound:** Their song is an ascending series of whistles heard evening and morning in late May and early June. The beginning is guttural, the ending thin and high-pitched.

✓**Behavior:** Perches and forages low to the ground.

• •

Similar species: Hermit Thrush, Veery and Gray-cheeked thrushes (vocally and visually).

Remarks: Swainson's is highly detectable vocally and visually. It is not as secretive as other thrushes. Identification is confirmed by the buff around the eye and face. Swainson's are constant singers through the first month of the breeding season. Song can be initiated at any hour of the day or night. It helps to have a musical ear when separating thrush songs, but even with a tin ear you should be able to distinguish the ascending song of the Swainson's from the generally descending song of the Veery and Gray-cheeked Thrush.

Jan	Feb	Mar	Apr	May	Jun	Jul	Aug	Sep	Oct	Nov	Dec

Starlings

EUROPEAN STARLING

Sturnus vulgaris

L: 220 mm   W: 83 g   Egg: 30 x 21 mm

Etymology: *Sturnus* (L.) - "Starling;" *vulgaris* (L.) - "common."

Status and Distribution: The Starling breeds throughout the settled areas of Alberta. It is absent from the far north and high elevations of the mountains. It is primarily an urban breeder.

● ●

Field Checklist

✓✓**Habitat:** It is found in urban parks, suburbs, mature cottonwood, aspen and balsam groves usually with dead snags for nesting. Perfect habitat is the cottonwood islands along our southern rivers.

✓✓✓**Sight:** The Starling has a square tail, triangular-shaped wings, stocky body and yellow bill (spring). Its plumage is iridescent green and purple with brownish feather tips that fade through the spring.

✓✓**Sound:** A variety of calls includes imitations of other birds such as the Blue Jay and Red-tailed Hawk. It would not be described as musical.

Behavior: Starlings are gregarious in the breeding season and communal outside the breeding season.

● ●

Similar species: All blackbirds, Purple Martin, particularly the Cowbird (visually); Catbird (vocally).

Remarks: Highly detectable visually and vocally. Its body shape, especially in flight, yellow pointed bill and constant noises should separate the Starling from all blackbirds. A European immigrant, the Starling is an aggressive competitor for nest holes and likely reduces the population size of other cavity nesters like bluebirds, some swallows and woodpeckers. Not as urban as the House Sparrow, the Starling is nonetheless quite happy to nest in your house.

Jan	Feb	Mar	Apr	May	Jun	Jul	Aug	Sep	Oct	Nov	Dec

240

EUST ❏   Date: _____

AMERICAN PIPIT

Anthus rubescens

L: 157 mm   W: 18 g   Egg: 20 x 15 mm

Etymology: *Anthus* (Gr.) - *anthos*, "a kind of bird;" *rubescens* - "reddish."

Status and Distribution: This pipit breeds at high elevations in the mountain region. It migrates through southern and central Alberta where it is frequently seen, in spring, mixed with Horned Larks and Longspurs. It is considered common in the mountain parks.

● ●

Field Checklist

✓✓**Habitat:** The pipit is at home in high alpine meadows and tundra above the tree line. Other populations of this species breed in high arctic tundra.

✓**Sight:** It is generally gray-brown on the back. White outer feathers stand out against the black tail. It is buffy brown on the underparts, has a slim bill, black legs and a buffy eyebrow. The sexes are similar.

✓**Sound:** Listen for a sharp, repeated "pit-pit" call. Their song is a series of whistled one- or two-syllable notes.

Behavior: The pipit forages and spends considerable time on the ground, where it walks rather than hops and jerks its tail nervously.

● ●

Similar species: Vesper Sparrow, Sprague's Pipit, Horned Lark, longspurs (visually); Horned Lark (vocally).

Remarks: The Vesper Sparrow and some longspurs show white on the outer tail feathers, the American Pipit's slim bill separates it from those and other sparrows. The different breeding habitat and its black legs differentiate this species from Sprague's Pipit. Overall though, the Pipit has low detectability and is easily missed even on its breeding grounds. The Pipit is an insect eater which may benefit from warm air currents that transport insects from the valleys to their high-elevation homes.

Jan	Feb	Mar	Apr	May	Jun	Jul	Aug	Sep	Oct	Nov	Dec

AMPI ☐   Date: _____

Pipits

SPRAGUE'S PIPIT

Anthus spragueii

L: 154 mm   W: 24 g   Egg: 21 x 15 mm

Etymology: *Anthus* (Gr.) - *anthos*, "a kind of bird;" *spragueii* (ML.) - in honor of Isaac Sprague, botanical illustrator and colleague of Audubon.

Status and Distribution: Sprague's Pipit is a widespread breeder in the grassland and parkland regions. It's on the province's Blue List, considered at risk, with dramatic population declines documented.

Photo: T.Thormin

●●●

Field Checklist

✓✓✓**Habitat:** This pipit's preferred habitat is native grassland in extreme southeastern Alberta. It does not tolerate heavy grazing nor does it seem to accept tame pasture. Light grazing is not a problem.

✓**Sight:** Look for the dark eye in the buffy face, buffy streaked underparts and white outer feathers on a black tail and flesh-colored legs. It is paler overall than the American Pipit.

✓✓✓**Sound:** Song is the best identifier for this species. It is a thin, complex descending series of whistles given in flight.

✓✓**Behavior:** The male flies high, giving his song as he descends, only to swoop up and do it again. This bird is heard far more than it is seen.

●●●

Similar species: American Pipit (visually).

Remarks: The overall paleness of the plumage and the flesh-colored as opposed to dark legs separate this bird from the American Pipit. Although their breeding ranges do not overlap, they are both seen on the grasslands in the spring. Sprague's Pipit may be declining in numbers in southern Alberta from loss of habitat. It is rarely seen on the ground as the male spends early spring high in the air displaying and singing. Once on the ground, the bird blends in perfectly with its grassy background.

Jan	Feb	Mar	Apr	May	Jun	Jul	Aug	Sep	Oct	Nov	Dec

SPPI ☐   Date: _____

BOHEMIAN WAXWING

Bombycilla garrulus

L: 195 mm   W: 60 g   Egg: 25 x 17 mm

Etymology: *Bombycilla* (L.) - "silky-tailed;" *garrulus* (L.) - "talkative."

Status and Distribution: The Bohemian Waxwing breeds in the northern boreal forest and mountain regions. It winters mainly in the parkland and in river valleys in the grasslands. Much of its breeding range is north of Alberta.

Field Checklist

✓✓**Habitat:** Winters in urban regions particularly where Mountain Ash trees are common. Breeding habitat is mixed-wood or open coniferous forests usually near water.

✓✓**Sight:** Look for the crest and the yellow band at the tip of the tail. The Bohemian is distinguished from the Cedar Waxwing by yellow wing spots and cinnamon undertail coverts.

✓**Sound:** Singly, waxwings do not utter a notable sound but in a group they produce a chorus of high-pitched lispy whistles.

✓✓**Behavior:** Waxwings congregate in large flocks in winter and often stay flocked into June. They are tame and permit close approach.

Similar Species: Cedar Waxwing (vocally and visually).

Remarks: A distinctive winter sight is a large flock of Bohemian Waxwings flying like a cloud over houses and alighting on a tree. Their summer range overlaps with that of Cedar Waxwings and mixed groups can be seen. The best separator is the color of the undertail coverts. In heavily settled parts of the province, the winter waxwing is the Bohemian and the summer one, the Cedar. Farther north and in the mountains this nice distinction does not hold. This same species is common in Europe and Asia.

Jan	Feb	Mar	Apr	May	Jun	Jul	Aug	Sep	Oct	Nov	Dec

BOWA ☐   **Date:** _____

Wood-Warblers

ORANGE-CROWNED WARBLER

Vermivora celata

L: *120 mm* W: *9 g* Egg: *16 x 13 mm*

Etymology: *Vermivora* (L.) - *vermis,* "worm eater;" *celata* (L.) - "concealed," refers to the orange patch on crown.

Status and Distribution: There are breeding records for this species in the mountain, foothill, parkland and boreal forest regions. It is most common in the foothills and mountains.

Field Checklist

✓✓**Habitat:** The Orange-crowned is a bird of secondary growth, tangled thickets such as willow and alder bushes in the mountains, burns, beaver ponds in the north and riparian scrub along southern rivers.

✓**Sight:** It's olive green above and yellowish-white below. The male has a hint of a yellow eyebrow. The orange feathers on his head are mostly hidden. Females are grayer with yellow under tail coverts.

✓✓**Sound:** The male usually gives a weak trill that changes pitch from higher to lower towards the end of the call.

✓**Behavior:** An early spring migrant, the Orange-crowned is fairly secretive and correspondingly difficult to observe.

Similar Species: Palm Warbler (vocally); Tennessee Warbler (visually).

Remarks: The Orange-crowned is identified at times by its lack of characters - no prominent wing bars, eye-rings, flashes of color or distinctive song. It can be easily overlooked unless the song is learned. The yellow undertail coverts, as opposed to white, separate this species from the Tennessee. There is geographic variation in this species in Alberta. Birds in the mountains, *V.c.orestera,* show more yellow than these in the north, *V.c.celata.*

Jan	Feb	Mar	Apr	May	Jun	Jul	Aug	Sep	Oct	Nov	Dec

OCWA ☐   Date: _____

YELLOW WARBLER

Dendroica petechia

L: 119 mm   W: 10 g   Egg: 17 x13 mm

Etymology: *Dendroica* (Gr.) - *dendron*, "a tree" and *oica*, "inhabit;" *petechia* (L.) - "purplish spots," for reddish streaks or spots.

Status and Distribution: A common breeder throughout the province. The Yellow is the most easily spotted warbler in Alberta.

Field Checklist

✓**Habitat:** It can be found in virtually any shrubby habitat throughout the province, but prefers wetter habitats. Look for it near sloughs and ponds and in river valleys.

✓✓✓**Sight:** This is an all yellow bird. The upperparts are yellow-green. The dark eye stands out as do reddish streaks, which are distinctive on the breast of the male. Females are greener than males with no streaks.

✓✓**Sound:** Listen for its clear whistled "see-see-see, ti-ti-see" with the emphasis on the last three syllables.

✓**Behavior:** Yellow Warblers tolerate human presence. They approach "pishing" calls. Males sing frequently throughout the day, unlike many warblers, which are only early morning vocalists.

Similar species: Chestnut-sided Warbler, Magnolia Warbler (vocally).

Remarks: High detectability both vocally and visually. Unlike many warblers, the yellow is easily spotted patrolling or foraging in willows, alders and other wet bushes. It is a regular breeder in urban areas including backyards. Many people refer to the Yellow Warbler as the "Wild Canary" but of course it is unrelated to true European Canaries. Listen carefully to the call of the Yellow Warbler when you see the bird. When you hear one that has a different more emphatic ending, you may have a Magnolia or Chestnut-sided Warbler.

Jan	Feb	Mar	Apr	May	Jun	Jul	Aug	Sep	Oct	Nov	Dec

YEWB ☐   Date: _____

Wood-Warblers

CHESTNUT-SIDED WARBLER

Dendroica pensylvanica

L: 124 mm   W: 10 g   Egg: 17 x 22 mm

Etymology: *Dendroica* (Gr.) - *dendron*, "a tree" and *oica*, "inhabit;" *pensylvanica* (ML.) - "of Pennsylvania."

Status and Distribution: A rare breeder, it is localized in the Cold Lake area with scattered observations in the grasslands and parkland, including Long Lake, Lac la Biche, Edmonton and Pigeon Lake. During migration, particularly in the fall, it can be seen south and west of its breeding range.

Field Checklist

✓**Habitat:** The Chestnut-sided breeds in second growth deciduous bushes and thickets, cottonwood groves and aspen forests. It is not a deep forest bird.

✓✓**Sight:** The chestnut side, streaked back, yellow wing bars, yellow crown and black eye-line are distinctive. Females are duller and show less chestnut.

✓**Sound**: Males perform a slurred series of whistles, "pleased, pleased, pleased to meetcha." The ending is emphatic.

✓**Behavior:** A good look shows that it frequently flicks its tail.

Similar species: Yellow Warbler, Magnolia Warbler (vocally).

Remarks: The song of this species is very similar to that of the Yellow Warbler. Habitat is a help as the Chestnut-sided Warbler is found in drier upland sites. Moderately detectable overall, it will often flycatch in the open. This is an eastern species that is common in Manitoba and Saskatchewan but just crosses the border into Alberta near Cold Lake. Historically it was known from only a few sightings in central Alberta. It was likely never common in Alberta so a rare status may not be a cause for alarm. Records beyond the core Cold Lake area should be carefully documented.

Jan	Feb	Mar	Apr	May	Jun	Jul	Aug	Sep	Oct	Nov	Dec

248

CSWA ☐   Date: _____

MAGNOLIA WARBLER

Dendroica magnolia

L: 120 mm   W: 8 g   Egg: 17 x 12 mm

Etymology: *Dendroica* (Gr.) - *dendron*, "a tree" and *oica*, "inhabit;" *magnolia* (ML.) - for the Magnolia trees in which the species was first found on migration in 1810.

Status and Distribution: A summer breeder widespread in the northern parkland, boreal forest and northern Rockies. As a migrant, it is seen in the southern parklands and grasslands.

Field Checklist

✓**Habitat:** Magnolias prefer edges of aspen-dominated mixed forests, generally near standing water. They forage in the lower canopy, not near the tops of tall trees.

✓✓**Sight:** The Magnolia has a distinctive black band at the tip of the tail. It has a yellow rump, white tail patches, white wing patches, and is yellow underneath with black streaking. Females are duller with a gray cap.

✓**Sound**: Its call is a series of slurred whistles "wisha, wisha, wisha, witsy" rising and emphatic at the end. A metallic "tlep" is a call note

Behavior: This species forages amid dense foliage, remaining hidden. It gleans insects beneath bark.

Similar species: Yellow-rumped Warbler (visually); Yellow Warbler, Chestnut-sided Warbler (vocally).

Remarks: Moderately detectable (vocally) but harder to spot than the similar sounding Yellow and Chestnut-sided warblers. The best strategy for identifying these birds is to learn their songs. The Magnolia is hard to characterize, it can show up in a variety of boreal habitats and sounds similar to a Yellow Warbler. If you hear a "Yellow Warbler" calling from the edge of a forest, check it out, it may be a Magnolia.

Jan	Feb	Mar	Apr	May	Jun	Jul	Aug	Sep	Oct	Nov	Dec

MNWA ❐   Date: _____

Wood-Warblers

CAPE MAY WARBLER

Dendroica tigrina

L: 132 mm   W: 10 g   Eggs: 17 x 13 mm

Etymology: *Dendroica* (Gr.) - *dendron*, "a tree" and *oica*, "inhabit;" *tigrina* (L.) - "striped, like a tiger."

Status and Distribution: There are scattered breeding records for this species in the boreal forest. Its status is unknown. The Cape May might be rare or it just may be difficult to census.

Field Checklist

Habitat: The Cape May is a bird of mature coniferous forests.

✓**Sight:** The male has a chestnut patch on his yellow face, a streaked yellow belly, dark upperparts and a white wing patch. Females are duller.

✓**Sound**: The male's song is a very high, thin, short series of "seet" notes.

✓**Behavior:** This bird is difficult to see even if heard as its song provides little directionality. This is compounded by its habit of foraging in thick conifers.

Similar species: Black-throated Green Warbler (visually); Bay-breasted, Black-and-White and Blackpoll warblers (vocally).

Remarks: Low detectability, a challenge to hear and tough to see once heard. This species likes caterpillars and is most common during spruce budworm outbreaks. Females lack the white wing patch and the chestnut face patch. This is a species that needs better documentation in Alberta. Earlier publications on Alberta warblers show the Cape May breeding widely across northern Alberta. Only a few breeding records were confirmed during the 1986-91 census of the Alberta Bird Atlas project. The range map provided is based on relatively few documented observations and includes potential range based on habitat.

Jan	Feb	Mar	Apr	May	Jun	Jul	Aug	Sep	Oct	Nov	Dec

CMWA ❑   Date: _____

Order: Passeriformes - Family: Parulidae **Wood-Warblers**

YELLOW-RUMPED WARBLER

Dendroica coronata

L: 136 mm   W: 12 g   Egg: 17 x 13 mm

Etymology: *Dendroica* (Gr.) - *dendron*, "a tree" and *oica*, "inhabit;" *coronata* (L.) - "crowned," refers to the yellow crown patch.

Status and Distribution: The Yellow-rumped breeds throughout the boreal forest, mountain parks, and foothills and in the Cypress Hills. It can be seen anywhere in the province during migration.

Field Checklist

✓**Habitat:** It breeds in mixed or coniferous forests and black spruce bogs.The Yellow-rump is one of the few warblers that tolerates pine-dominated forests. This species could be seen in almost any habitat in the spring.

✓✓**Sight:** The male has a yellow rump and crown patch, white tail patches, white (Myrtle) or yellow (Audubon's) throat contrasting with dark head and throat. The female is brown rather than bluish gray.

✓✓**Sound**: Loose, musical trill, sometimes changing pitch (Audubon's).

✓**Behavior:** An active species, the Yellow-rumped moves throughout the forest canopy flycatching. It responds well to "pishing". The Yellow-rumped is an early spring and late fall migrant. It will flock with other species during migration.

Similar Species: Magnolia Warbler (visually); Dark-eyed Junco (vocally).

Remarks: Highly detectable, vocally and visually. The Yellow-rumped Warbler has two distinct forms in Alberta. The white-throated Myrtle and yellow-throated Audubon's. Myrtles breed throughout most of Alberta but pure Audubon's are found only in extreme southwestern Alberta and the Cypress Hills. In forested areas in Alberta, the Yellow-rumped is the most abundant warbler.

Jan	Feb	Mar	Apr	May	Jun	Jul	Aug	Sep	Oct	Nov	Dec

YRWA ☐   Date: _____

Order: Passeriformes - Family: Parulidae

TOWNSEND'S WARBLER

Dendroica townsendi

L: 125 mm   W: 9 g   Egg: 17 x 13 mm

Etymology: *Dendroica* (Gr.) - *dendron*, "a tree" and *oica*, "inhabit;" *townsendi* (ML.) - for John K.Townsend, a Philadelphia ornithologist.

Status and Distribution: Breeds in the Rocky Mountain region. Its status is uncertain but it can be found regularly in its forested mountain habitat.

Field Checklist

✓✓**Habitat:** Townsend's breeds in mature, dense, coniferous forests in the mountains, near water, particularly rivers.

✓**Sight:** The male has a dark ear patch bordered in yellow, a black throat and breast, black streaks on his flanks, white belly and white wing bars. The female (shown above) is duller with a yellow rather than a black throat.

✓✓✓**Sound:** The male sings a distinctive wheezy series of notes "zwee-zwee-zwee-zwee-zweeou" or "zweesy-zweesy-zweesy, zweesy, zeezee," that rises in pitch.

Behavior: Townsend's calls regularly but is often difficult to see as it moves slowly through thick coniferous foliage.

Similar species: Black-throated Green Warbler (vocally and visually).

Remarks: Highly detectable vocally but frustrating to spot. Look at the top of thick spruce trees for movement in the direction of the song. The distribution does not overlap with that of the Black-throated Green Warbler. This allows a preliminary identification based only on the characteristic wheezy song. The bulk of the breeding range of this species is in British Columbia but it comes across the border where it can find mature damp forests.

Jan	Feb	Mar	Apr	May	Jun	Jul	Aug	Sep	Oct	Nov	Dec

TOWA ☐   Date: _____

BLACK-THROATED GREEN WARBLER

Dendroica virens

L: *125 mm* W: *9 g* Egg: *17 x 13 mm*

Etymology: *Dendroica* (Gr.) - *dendron*, "a tree" and *oica*, "inhabit;" *virens* (L.) - "becoming green."

Status and Distribution: A regular breeder in the Cold Lake area. There are scattered breeding records elsewhere in the boreal forest. The status of this bird is uncertain but its preference for mature mixed woods may put it at risk.

Field Checklist

✓✓**Habitat:** It breeds and forages in mature spruce/fir stands in the boreal forest, usually near water.

✓**Sight:** The male's yellow face contrasts with its olive head and black throat. Look for white wing bars and white underparts. Females (pictured above) are similar but with a dirty yellow rather than a black throat.

✓✓**Sound:** Males give a wheezy, hoarse "zoo-zee-zoo-zoo-zee" call or a series of similarly pitched "zee" notes.

✓**Behavior:** More commonly heard than seen as it moves slowly through the tall spruces and firs of its preferred habitat.

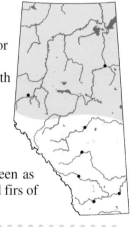

Similar species: Townsend's Warbler (vocally and visually); Cape May (visually).

Remarks: An eastern counterpart of the Townsend's but their ranges do not overlap. Good detectability vocally but a challenge to spot in tall, dense trees. Another warbler whose call should be learned, luckily it is quite distinctive. Historical breeding records for this species included Edmonton south to Battle Creek. With destruction of its habitat, the species is found breeding today only in northern Alberta. Even on migration it seems to prefer tall, thick conifers.

Jan	Feb	Mar	Apr	May	Jun	Jul	Aug	Sep	Oct	Nov	Dec

BGNW ☐ Date: _____

Wood-Warblers

BLACKBURNIAN WARBLER

Dendroica fusca

Photo: R.Gehlert

L: 121 mm   W: 10 g   Egg: 17 x 13 mm

Etymology: *Dendroica* (Gr.) - *dendron*, "a tree" and *oica*, "inhabit;" *fusca* (L.) - "dark, dusky." Anna Blackburn inspired the work of Johannes Gmelin who named the species from a specimen.

Status and Distribution: A regular breeder in the Cold Lake region; rare elsewhere in the boreal forest. Its status is uncertain overall in Alberta but it was never common. Historical records show breeding just to the north of Edmonton.

Field Checklist

✓**Habitat:** The Blackburnian breeds in mature mixed forests of spruce, fir and some birch.

✓✓✓**Sight:** The bright orange throat, orange and black striped back and broad white wing patch of males are conspicuous. Females are similar but yellow replaces the orange of the male.

✓**Sound:** Listen for a series of high, thin "seet-say" notes followed by a trill.

Behavior: The Blackburnian stays high in the canopy foraging on insects.

Similar species: Bay-breasted Warbler, Black-and-White Warbler (vocally).

Remarks: Only moderate detectability. Song is not distinctive and the bird tends to stay hidden in the foliage of the upper canopy. Once seen, however, identification is easy. Normally it gleans insects from branches of tall trees. The Blackburnian is considered at risk over much of its range. Like many warblers, it has fallen victim to habitat loss on both the breeding and wintering grounds. Cowbird parasitism, encouraged by forest clearing, may be a particular problem for this species.

Jan	Feb	Mar	Apr	May	Jun	Jul	Aug	Sep	Oct	Nov	Dec

BLWA ❑   Date: _____

PALM WARBLER

Dendroica palmarum

L: 126 mm   W: 10 g   Egg: 17 x 13 mm

Photo: R.Gehlert

Etymology: *Dendroica* (Gr.) - *dendron*, "a tree" and *oica*, "inhabit;" *palmarum* (L.) - "of palms," as it frequents saw palmetto in winter in Florida.

Status and Distribution: A regular breeder throughout boreal forest region but may be seen in the grassland and parkland regions during migration. Palm Warblers can be quite common in appropriate habitat.

Field Checklist

✓✓**Habitat:** One of the few species that enjoys black spruce bogs, it is also found in willow-alder margins beside boreal forest ponds and wet recent burns.

✓**Sight:** The male has a chestnut cap, bright yellowish eyebrow and throat, white belly, yellow undertail coverts and a streaked breast. An unusual warbler in that the sexes are quite similar.

✓✓**Sound**: Their song is a weak trill that generally fades in intensity towards the end.

Behavior: These birds wag their tails regularly as they forage in low bushes or on the ground.

Similar species: Yellow Warbler (visually); Swamp Sparrow, Chipping Sparrow, Dark-eyed Junco, Orange-crowned Warbler (vocally)

Remarks: One of five boreal forest birds that sings a monotonous trill. They do sound different but it takes practice to separate them. They are often found in the same habitat as the Swamp Sparrow but the Palm Warbler should be calling from bushes, the sparrow from wet grasses or sedges. The trill of the Palm Warbler seems to fade away at the end, that of the Swamp Sparrow just stops. Birds in eastern Canada have the entire underparts yellow, whereas ours has a white belly. The split occurs in northwestern Ontario.

Jan	Feb	Mar	Apr	May	Jun	Jul	Aug	Sep	Oct	Nov	Dec
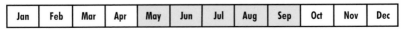

255   PAWA ❐   Date: _____

Wood-Warblers

BAY-BREASTED WARBLER

Dendroica castanea

Photo: R.Gehlert

L: 130 mm   W: 12 g   Egg: 18 x 13 mm

Etymology: *Dendroica* (Gr.) - *dendron*, "a tree" and *oica*, "inhabit;" *castanea* (L.) - "chestnut."

Status and Distribution: It is rare and localized in the boreal forest region and seen in the other regions on migration. It is on the Provincial Blue List as the status is unknown but populations are declining across North America.

● ●

Field Checklist

✓**Habitat:** The Bay-breasted breeds in mature, mixed, boreal forest containing spruce, fir and balsam poplar, generally near water.

✓✓**Sight:** The male shows a chestnut crown, throat and sides, black face, creamy neck patch and white wing bars. The female is duller and greenish.

✓**Sound**: High-pitched, whistled, rapid "suwee, suwee, suwee, sit a bit."

✓**Behavior:** A late spring migrant, the Bay-breasted tends to forage in a zone of dead or thinly leaved branches below the canopy.

● ●

Similar species: Chestnut-sided Warbler (visually); Black-and-White Warbler (vocally).

Remarks: It has low detectability, as the song is not distinctive and it is difficult to spot even if heard. The Bay-breasted prefers mature woods and can be lost in the canopy. Once seen it is easily identified. This is another warbler that increases in numbers with spruce budworm outbreaks. It can be numerous but it may also be declining in numbers overall from the same factors that plague all mature forest warblers. During migration, you can see the Bay-breasted Warbler in a variety of habitats. It tends to move through the parkland in mixed flocks of different warbler species.

Jan	Feb	Mar	Apr	May	Jun	Jul	Aug	Sep	Oct	Nov	Dec

BBWA ☐   Date: _____

Order: Passeriformes - Family: Parulidae

Wood-Warblers

BLACKPOLL WARBLER

Dendroica striata

L: 130 mm   W: 12 g   Egg: 18 x 13 mm

Etymology: *Dendroica* (Gr.) - *dendron*, "a tree" and *oica*, "inhabit;" *striata* (L.) - "striped."

Status and Distribution: The Blackpoll is widely distributed in the boreal forest and northern mountain regions. Its status is more secure in Alberta than the strictly mature-forest warblers, which are much harder to find.

Field Checklist

✓**Habitat:** Preferences for this species are variable from mature coniferous forests to burns, pond margins and river edges. It is most easily seen in riparian shrubbery.

✓**Sight:** Males have a black cap, white cheeks, bold streaking, white wing bars and light-colored legs. Females are duller and greenish.

✓✓✓**Sound**: Its song is a series of extremely high, thin, punctuated "seet" notes all given in the same pitch.

✓**Behavior:** The males often sing from an exposed perch or a dead snag or top of a bush.

Similar species: Black-and-White Warbler, Black-capped Chickadee (visually); Bay-breasted, Black-and-White, Cape May, and Blackburnian warblers (vocally).

Remarks: The highest-pitched warbler song. Surprisingly detectable, however, the song carries a long way and the bird sits in the open. The call is simple, monotonic and slower compared to other super-sopranos among warblers. It has the most distinctive song and is the one to learn first. The unstreaked crown, sharply demarcated face patch and flesh-colored legs separate this species from the Black-and-White Warbler. In eastern Canada, this is a mature forest species but it seems to tolerate a variety of habitats in Alberta.

Jan	Feb	Mar	Apr	May	Jun	Jul	Aug	Sep	Oct	Nov	Dec

257

BPWA ☐   Date: _____

Wood-Warblers

Order: Passeriformes - Family: Parulidae

BLACK-AND-WHITE WARBLER

Mniotilta varia

L: 123 mm W: 10 g Egg: 17 x 13 mm

Etymology: *Mniotilta* (Gr.) - *mnion*, "moss" and *tiltos*, "to pull out;" *varia* (L.) - "variable," refers to plumage.

Status and Distribution: The Black-and-White is widely distributed but uncommon throughout the boreal forest region and northern foothills. It is on the Provincial Yellow List because of population declines across the continent.

Field Checklist

✓**Habitat:** Its preferred breeding habitat is secondary deciduous growth 3 - 6 m high, usually near water.

✓✓✓**Sight:** The male's black throat and streaking separate this from any other warbler. Females (inset) and fall birds are similar but have a white rather than a black throat.

✓✓**Sound:** Song is a repeated "wee-zee, wee-zee, wee-zee," high-pitched and rolling throughout. It is distinctly lower-pitched than the song of the Blackpoll Warbler.

✓✓**Behavior:** The only warbler that moves nuthatch-like up and down tree trunks and along branches.

Similar species: Blackpoll Warbler (visually and vocally); Bay-breasted Warbler (vocally).

Remarks: The male sings frequently and is fairly easy to spot. Its preferred habitat is often wet, making approaches challenging. Another eastern Canadian forest species that seems at home in willow or alder bushes or young forests in Alberta. A streaked head separates this species from the Blackpoll Warbler. The Black-and-White Warbler can be seen in the grassland and parkland during migration often in the company of other warblers.

Jan	Feb	Mar	Apr	May	Jun	Jul	Aug	Sep	Oct	Nov	Dec

BAWW ☐   Date: _____

Order: Passeriformes - Family: Parulidae

Wood-Warblers

AMERICAN REDSTART

Setophaga ruticilla

L: *130 mm* W: *8 g* Egg: *16 x 12 mm*

Etymology: *Setophaga* (Gr.) - *setos*, "moth" and *phaga*, "to eat;" *ruticilla* (L.) - "red tail."

Status and Distribution: The Redstart breeds throughout the treed areas of the province but is most common in the boreal forest and northern parkland. It is also found in the Cypress Hills.

Field Checklist

✓**Habitat:** The Redstart is found in deciduous woods or the deciduous parts of mixed wood forests, with areas of dense undergrowth, with standing water usually nearby.

✓✓✓**Sight:** The male's bright orange-red wing and tail patches against his glossy black plumage are unmistakable. The belly is white. Females and immature males have yellow patches instead of orange or red ones.

✓✓**Sound:** The Redstart sings a series of thin, high notes followed by an emphatic down-slurred note "tzee-tzee-tzee-tzeeo."

✓**Behavior:** The male displays his color patches and often flycatches. He is always active, constantly fanning and fluttering his wings and tail.

Similar species: Magnolia and Black-and-White warblers (vocally).

Remarks: It is highly detectable both vocally and visually. The emphatic ending of the Redstart song is like that of the Magnolia but the notes of the Redstart have a pronounced slur. They forage by gleaning insects off leaves or catching them in mid-air. Their preference for flying insects means you will find Redstarts where mosquitoes are quite common! The delay in acquisition of full adult plumage is rare in small passerine birds. Young males are tolerated by older males perhaps because they resemble females.

Jan	Feb	Mar	Apr	May	Jun	Jul	Aug	Sep	Oct	Nov	Dec

259   AMRE ☐   Date: _____

Wood-Warblers

OVENBIRD

Seiurus aurocapillus

L: 146 mm   W: 18 g   Egg: 20 x 15 mm

Etymology: *Seiurus* (Gr.) - *seio*, "to shake" and *oura*, "tail;" *aurocapillus* (L.) - *aurum*, "gold" and *capillus*, "hair or crown."

Status and Distribution: It is a common breeder in the boreal forest and foothills regions. It is a migrant throughout the grasslands and parkland but a breeder in the Cypress Hills.

- -

Field Checklist

✓✓**Habitat:** It prefers dense aspen stands with a sparse shrub layer but a forest floor with thick leaf litter. Highest densities are seen in 30-year old aspen stands, where it is a ground nester.

✓**Sight:** Look for the black and orange streaks on the crown, streaked breast and sides, white eye ring and flesh-colored legs. The sexes are similar.

✓✓✓**Sound:** The Ovenbird's distinctive song is a loud, ringing "tee-cher, tee-cher, tee-cher, tee-cher, tee-cher" that increases in volume. Sometimes a one-syllable "teach" version is given.

✓**Behavior:** Elusive, often seen walking and scratching for insects among leaf litter.

- -

Similar species: Northern Waterthrush, Swainson's Thrush (visually); Yellowthroat, Connecticut Warbler (vocally).

Remarks: Highly detectable vocally, but a challenge to spot. Thrush-like behavior and mature forest habitat help it elude detection. Thrushes are larger with breast spots rather than streaks, they also hop rather than walk on the ground. The song of the Ovenbird is easily learned and won't be forgotten. The name of the species is due to the oven-like shape of its nest. Males respond strongly to song playback by approaching the source of the sound and singing loudly. Clear-cutting of mature aspen stands have major impacts on this species.

Jan	Feb	Mar	Apr	May	Jun	Jul	Aug	Sep	Oct	Nov	Dec

OVEN ☐   Date: _____

NORTHERN WATERTHRUSH

Seiurus noveboracensis

L: *146 mm*   W: *18 g*   Egg: *19 x 13 mm*

Etymology: *Seiurus* (Gr.) - *seio*, "to shake," and *oura*, "tail;" *noveboracensis* (L.) - "New York."

Status and Distribution: This species is common and widespread in the boreal forest and Rocky Mountain regions. It can be seen, as a migrant, in the parkland and grassland regions.

Field Checklist

✓**Habitat:** The Waterthrush is at home in riparian shrubs and forests, in flooded forests, around ponds, and woodland streams.

✓✓**Sight:** Both sexes show streaks on the breast, a buffy eyebrow and a grayish-green back.

✓✓**Sound:** The song is loud, somewhat slurred and staccato-like at the end. "Twit, twit, twit," "zeet-zeet-zeet," "chew, chew, chew, chew" is a reasonable representation.

✓**Behavior:** This bird bobs its head and tail constantly; it walks rather than hops.

Similar species: Ovenbird, Swainson's Thrush (visually); Connecticut Warbler (vocally).

Remarks: Good detectability as a consequence of its loud song and preference for fairly open habitat. The wetness of its preferred habitat makes close approach difficult. It gleans insects from leaf litter and fallen logs. Even more thrush-like than the Ovenbird but the call of the Waterthrush is completely different from that of any thrush. Look for this species in mosquito-infested habitats and watch it walk. The tail-twitching and head-bowing every few steps are important aids to identification.

Jan	Feb	Mar	Apr	May	Jun	Jul	Aug	Sep	Oct	Nov	Dec

NOWA ☐   Date: _____

Wood-Warblers

Order: Passeriformes - Family: Parulidae

CONNECTICUT WARBLER

Oporornis agilis

L: 137 mm   W: 14 g   Egg: 19 x 14 mm

Etymology: *Oporornis* (Gr.) - *opora,*
"autumn" and *ornis,* "bird;" *agilis* (L.)
- "nimble, active."

Status and Distribution: The Connecticut Warbler breeds in the southern
boreal forest, northern parkland and
foothills regions. Its status is uncertain. It is not common and not always
found from year to year in the same site.

Field Checklist

Habitat: Connecticuts prefer mature (open) aspen forests with
tall undergrowth but only a small percentage of appropriate
stands will have this species.

✓✓✓**Sight:** Males with their gray head, full
white eye-ring and yellow underparts are
distinctive. The bird seems large for a warbler. Females are olive-green on the top of the
head but they also have a complete eye-ring.

✓✓✓**Sound:** The male's song is a loud
emphatic "chip-chippety-chippety-chippety"
or "chippy chappy-chippy chappy-chippy-
chappy." In either case it increases in intensity
from beginning to end. The bird sounds angry.

✓**Behavior:** Males sing from the tops of trees. On the
ground it walks rather than hops.

Similar species: Mourning Warbler, MacGillivray's Warbler (visually);
Ovenbird, Northern Waterthrush (vocally).

Remarks: The Connecticut has a loud, distinctive song but it is not a
constant singer. The solid eye-ring is the best clue to separate this from the
Mourning Warbler. The ranges of the Connecticut and MacGillivray's do not
overlap so confusion should only occur during migration. Habitat preferences of this species are variable.

Jan	Feb	Mar	Apr	May	Jun	Jul	Aug	Sep	Oct	Nov	Dec

COWA ❑   Date: _____

MOURNING WARBLER

Oporornis philadelphia

L: *130 mm* W: *13 g* Egg: *18 x 14 mm*

Etymology: *Oporornis* (Gr.) - *opora*, "autumn" and *ornis*, "bird;" *philadelphia* (ML.) - named by Alexander Wilson who discovered it near the city.

Status and Distribution: The Mourning Warbler breeds throughout the southern boreal forest, northern parkland and northern foothills. It may overlap with MacGillivray's Warbler near Jasper, south to Rocky Mountain House.

Field Checklist

✓**Habitat:** The Mourning likes open aspen woods with a thick shrub layer. Look for it on forest edges, along cut lines and around interior forest clearings.

✓✓**Sight:** The male has a gray head and neck, no eye-ring, black on the throat and yellow underparts. The female shows a lighter gray head.

✓✓✓**Sound:** Its song is described as "churry-churry churry-cheerio," a fairly loud and slurred warble. It is a common call of television soundtracks when a suburban scene is presented.

Behavior: This species is secretive in its brushy habitat, but the male sings regularly.

Similar species: Connecticut Warbler (visually); MacGillivray's Warbler (visually and vocally).

Remarks: Song separates this species from the Connecticut Warbler. The ending of the Mourning song is not nearly as emphatic as that of the Connecticut. Their habitat overlaps considerably but the Mourning prefers shrubbery. Behaviorally, this species is identical to MacGillivray's. The name Mourning comes from the black crepe-like markings on the throat and the gray head, both symbols of sorrow. Look for this species fairly close to the ground; it should not be high in a tall tree.

Jan	Feb	Mar	Apr	May	Jun	Jul	Aug	Sep	Oct	Nov	Dec

MOWA ☐ Date: _____

Wood-Warblers

Order: Passeriformes - Family: Parulidae

MacGILLIVRAY'S WARBLER

Oporornis tolmiei

L: 131 mm   W: 12 g   Egg: 18 x 14 mm

Etymology: *Oporornis* (Gr.) - *opora*, "autumn," *ornis*, "bird;" *tolmiei* (ML.) - for Dr. William Frank Tolmie, Scottish medical officer with the Hudson's Bay Company.

Status and Distribution: This species breeds in the Rocky Mountain region. It is rare in the foothills, along southern river valleys and in the Cypress Hills.

Field Checklist

✓**Habitat:** MacGillivray's is found in aspen forests and willow-dominated riparian shrubs.

✓✓**Sight:** The white partial eye-ring stands out against the gray head and black throat of the males. Both sexes are yellow underneath and green on the back. The gray areas on females are duller.

✓✓**Sound:** It gives a loud, slurred, quick, "chiddle, chiddle, chiddle, churrie." The song is almost identical to that of the Mourning, whereas the ending of MacGillivray's song tends to be simpler, usually a one or two syllable phrase.

✓**Behavior:** Flies hesitantly and can pump tail in flight.

Similar species: Connecticut Warbler, Mourning Warbler (visually); Mourning Warbler (vocally).

Remarks: The Western counterpart of the Mourning Warbler, these two are known to hybridize. The distribution is the best first clue for identification. It forages low to the ground. The partial eye-ring is not a perfect character as fall Mourning Warblers can have an eye-ring. This species is not named for a co-author of this book but for William MacGillivray, a Scottish ornithologist and friend of Audubon who edited and corrected his original Birds of America. Better delineation of each species' range near the zone of contact would be valuable.

Jan	Feb	Mar	Apr	May	Jun	Jul	Aug	Sep	Oct	Nov	Dec

MGWA ☐   Date: _____

COMMON YELLOWTHROAT

Geothlypis trichas

L: 124 mm   W: 10 g   Egg: 17 x 13 mm

Etymology: *Geothlypis* (Gr.) - "earth finch;" *trichas* (Gr.) - "a kind of thrush."

Status and Distribution: This species breeds in all natural regions but is most common in the parklands. It is rare at high elevations and in the far north.

Field Checklist

✓✓**Habitat:** The Yellowthroat prefers alder and willow bushes along sloughs, marshes, bogs and beaver ponds.

✓✓✓**Sight:** The male's black mask provides a distinctive contrast with his greenish back and yellow underparts. Females lack the mask but show a pale eye-ring instead.

✓✓✓**Sound:** Their song is a loud, slurred "witchity, witchity, witchity, witch" that lasts about three seconds.

✓✓**Behavior:** Both sexes will approach "pishing" aggressively and give a "cluck" call when scolding. The Yellowthroat cocks its tail like a wren. It is in constant motion through its brushy habitat.

Similar species: Ovenbird (vocally).

Remarks: The Yellowthroat is highly detectable both vocally and visually. Usually detected first by song. The bird's foraging and exploration of its territory soon reveals its presence. Adult males are distinct; the wet habitat of the species and the behavior usually confirm the females' identification. The Wilson's and Yellow warblers can be found in the same habitat as the Common Yellowthroat, so be sure to listen for the song. The Ovenbird and Yellowthroat songs are among the easiest to recognize and should be learned quickly.

Jan	Feb	Mar	Apr	May	Jun	Jul	Aug	Sep	Oct	Nov	Dec

COYE ☐   Date: _____

Wood-Warblers

WILSON'S WARBLER

Wilsonia pusilla

L: 119 mm   W: 8 g   Egg: 16 x 12 mm

Etymology: *Wilsonia* (ML.) - for Alexander Wilson, an early American ornithologist; *pusilla* (L.) - "very small."

Status and Distribution: The Wilson's Warbler breeds in the mountains, foothills and boreal forest. It is most easily seen in the mountain parks and is a regular migrant through the parkland and grassland.

Field Checklist

✓**Habitat:** It prefers willow and alder thickets near water (boreal), alder and birch thickets (sub-alpine).

✓✓**Sight:** The male's dark tail, both above and below, and black cap contrast with his bright yellow face and underparts. The cap may be reduced or absent in females.

✓**Sound:** A series of rapid, staccato-like "chee" notes dropping in pitch towards the end. Call is a sharp "chip."

✓✓**Behavior:** A very active bird. It flycatches often and nervously twitches its tail.

Similar species: Yellow Warbler (visually); Tennessee Warbler (vocally).

Remarks: Described by most authors as a bundle of energy, the Wilson's is only moderately detectable. It is brightly colored but easily overlooked and its song is not highly distinctive. Be aware that the similarly yellow Common Yellowthroat and Yellow Warbler could be in the same habitat. Wait for the male to sing to confirm identification if you cannot get a good look. The birds of the boreal forest form *W. p. pusilla* are paler than the bright yellow *W. pusilla pileolata* of the mountains. Whether the two forms meet west of Edmonton, and what happens when they do, is not known.

Jan	Feb	Mar	Apr	May	Jun	Jul	Aug	Sep	Oct	Nov	Dec

WIWA ☐   Date: _____

CANADA WARBLER

Wilsonia canadensis

L: 133 mm   W: 10 g   Eggs: 17 x 13 mm

Etymology: *Wilsonia* (ML.) - for Alexander Wilson, an early American ornithologist; *canadensis* (ML.) - for Canada.

Status and Distribution: There are scattered breeding records throughout the boreal forest and northern parkland for the Canada Warbler. Its status is unknown. Like many birds, habitat availability rather than geography may be determining range.

Field Checklist

✓✓**Habitat:** It prefers heavy undergrowth in mature northern forests, but can be found along streams. Forest borders are preferred over interiors.

✓✓**Sight:** The male has bluish-gray upperparts, yellow underparts, yellow spectacles, white inner eye-ring and a distinctive black necklace. In females, the necklace is indistinct or missing.

✓✓✓**Sound:** The male's song is a jumble of slurred whistles initiated by a noticeable "chip."

Behavior: Forages by gleaning insects from leaves or by flycatching.

Similar species: None.

Remarks: Distribution and abundance of the Canada Warbler in Alberta is not well known. Often it cannot be found even in optimal habitat. As with most warblers, learning its song is the key to detection. Like the Wilson's and the Redstart, the Canada is an active flycatching species. It, too, likes mosquito-rich environments. Look for the Canada Warbler low in trees and bushes. Its nest is built on the ground. It is a late spring migrant and heads south early in the fall. The bulk of its breeding range is in eastern North America.

Jan	Feb	Mar	Apr	May	Jun	Jul	Aug	Sep	Oct	Nov	Dec

CAWA ❑   Date: _____

Wood-Warblers

Order: Passeriformes - Family: Parulidae

YELLOW-BREASTED CHAT

Icteria virens

L: 182 mm   W: 26 g   Egg: 22 x 17 mm

Etymology: *Icteria* (Gr.) - *ikteros*, "jaundice" (yellow); *virens* (L.) - "becoming green."

Status and Distribution: The Chat is restricted to the grassland and extreme southern parkland of Alberta. It is not common in Alberta because suitable habitat is not widely available.

Field Checklist

✓✓**Habitat:** Its favorite habitat is buckbrush, rose, buffaloberry and hawthorn thickets along rivers in southeastern Alberta.

✓✓✓**Sight:** Compared to the other warblers, it is identified by its large size, especially its tail, yellow throat and breast, thick bill and white spectacles. Females are similar.

✓✓✓**Sound:** The male has an extraordinary array of loud clucks, hoots, cackles, and whistles. They are reminiscent of the calls made by chimpanzees in early Tarzan movies.

✓**Behavior:** Males perform hovering display flights. They can sing from a conspicuous perch, but are difficult to approach. If disturbed, they disappear into deep brush and remain quiet.

Similar species: Northern Mockingbird, Catbird, Brown Thrasher (vocally).

Remarks: A true southern species that is a treat to encounter in southern Alberta. Highly detectable both vocally and visually but a challenge to approach in its almost impenetrable habitat. The name "chat" refers to the constant babble produced by the male. Look for the male's fluttering display flight, which he performs with his legs dangling as he rises up from a perch and then flutters back down. Writing-on-Stone or Dinosaur Provincial parks are great places to find this bird. Be careful poking about in bushes searching for Chats: their range almost perfectly matches the Alberta distribution of Prairie Rattlesnakes.

Jan	Feb	Mar	Apr	May	Jun	Jul	Aug	Sep	Oct	Nov	Dec

YBCH ☐   Date: _____

Order: Passeriformes - Family: Thraupidae   **Tanagers**

WESTERN
TANAGER
Piranga ludoviciana

L: 178 mm   W: 30 g   Egg: 23 x 17 mm

Etymology: *Piranga* (ML.) - South
American name for a bird; *ludoviciana*
(ML.) - of Louisiana, where it occurs
only rarely.

Status and Distribution: Widespread
and fairly common in the boreal forest,
mountains, foothills and northern parkland. On migration it can be seen
throughout southern Alberta.

Field Checklist

✓**Habitat:** The Western Tanager breeds in open coniferous and
mixed forests.

✓✓✓**Sight:** The combination of red, black and
yellow on the male is unmistakable. The
female is green with a yellow rump and
underparts. Both sexes have two wing bars, a
thick bill and chunky shape.

✓**Sound:** The male's song is a slurred, harsh
"pi-di-dik" or similar two-note phrase. It is
less musical with fewer pitch changes than
that of a Robin or Grosbeak.

✓**Behavior:** The male often sings from an exposed
perch at the top of a tall spruce. Follow the song until
you get a good look.

Similar species: Rose-breasted Grosbeak, Purple Finch (vocally). The
female resembles a female Baltimore Oriole, but the bill of the Tanager is
much heavier.

Remarks: The Tanager is more easily heard than seen. When seen it is often
flying. It's hard to spot sitting still. The similar-sounding Rose-breasted
Grosbeak prefers deciduous patches in the boreal forest. The amount of red
on the head of the male is variable and may vary with diet. A late migrant,
the Western Tanager eats insects and fruits. Look for it flycatching away
from its perch in a spruce or fir.

Jan	Feb	Mar	Apr	May	Jun	Jul	Aug	Sep	Oct	Nov	Dec

Sparrows

SPOTTED TOWHEE

Pipilo maculatus

L: *208 mm* W: *38 g* Egg: *23 x 17 mm*

Etymology: *Pipilo* (L.) - "to chirp or peep;" *maculatus* (L.) - "spotted."

Status and Distribution: The Spotted Towhee is a widespread breeder in the grasslands and southern parkland. It is most common in the grasslands.

● ●

Field Checklist

✓✓**Habitat:** This species frequents dense, brushy cover along coulees, rivers and undergrowth in open woodland.

✓✓✓**Sight:** Look for the bright red eyes that contrast with the black head, back and tail of the male and the brown of the female. Both sexes have white spotting on the wings, white underparts and rufous sides. The tail is tipped with white.

✓✓**Sound:** A single note followed by a buzzy trill and a single nasal alarm.

✓**Behavior:** The Towhee forages on or near the ground and is noisy and conspicuous.

● ●

Similar species: Catbird (vocally).

Remarks: A highly detectable, large, brightly-colored sparrow. Listen for scratching sounds as the Towhee rakes the leaf litter with both feet searching for food. Males sing from the tops of bushes then dive under cover to reappear at the top of another bush. Towhees are predominantly seed-eaters. Formerly, this species was combined with the eastern form and called the Rufous-sided Towhee *(Pipilo erythrophthalmus)*. Although they have now been separated, they will hybridize. The nasal alarm call of the Towhee is similar to the "mew" of a Catbird. As both can occur in the same habitat, try to find the source of the noise before confirming the identification.

Jan	Feb	Mar	Apr	May	Jun	Jul	Aug	Sep	Oct	Nov	Dec

SPTO ☐   Date: _____

AMERICAN TREE SPARROW

Spizella arborea

L: 150 mm W: 19 g Egg: 20 x 15 mm

Etymology: *Spizella* (Gr.) - "little finch;" *arborea* (L.) - pertaining to trees.

Status and Distribution: Common early spring migrant and rare breeder in the extreme north particularly, high elevation sites like the Caribou Mountains and the Cameron Hills.

Field Checklist

✓**Habitat:** In migration, the Tree Sparrow can be seen in fields, backyards, parks and slough edges. It prefers low shrubs or bogs in tundra for breeding.

✓✓**Sight:** Look for the rufous cap which can be streaked with gray, gray throat, black breast spot, two white wing bars and usually some yellow on the lower bill.

✓✓**Sound:** Their call is a whistled "tweedle-eet." The male's song is a warble preceeded by several clear, whistled "eet" notes.

✓**Behavior:** The Tree Sparrow is an early spring migrant, often seen flocked with other species.

Similar species: Chipping Sparrow (visually).

Remarks: The Tree Sparrow sings a rather musical call compared to Chipping or Clay-colored Sparrows. It spends virtually no time in trees. Look for it on or near the ground. Some individuals may overwinter and utilize feeders in southern Alberta. The song, black breast spot and lack of white eye-line separate this species from the Chipping Sparrow. Tree Sparrows pass through Alberta in April and may linger into May. They can overlap with Chipping Sparrows in April in central and northern Alberta, about the only time you could confuse the two species except in the fall when they all really do look alike.

Jan	Feb	Mar	Apr	May	Jun	Jul	Aug	Sep	Oct	Nov	Dec

ATSP ☐ Date: _____

Sparrows

CHIPPING SPARROW

Spizella passerina

L: 135 mm   W: 12 g   Egg: 18 x 13 mm

Etymology: *Spizella* (Gr.) - "little finch;" *passerina* (L.) - "a sparrow."

Status and Distribution: This is one of the most common breeders throughout Alberta. Its range runs from pure wilderness to suburban habitat.

Field Checklist

Habitat: Not a good clue for identification, Chipping Sparrows can be found virtually anywhere in the province including backyards, parks, fields and forests.

✓✓**Sight:** Look for the reddish cap, black line through the eye and white line above it and black bill.

✓✓**Sound:** Call "seep" or "chip" given frequently or a monotonic trill of unmusical "chip" notes.

✓**Behavior:** It calls and sings throughout the day. Migrates regularly in mixed flocks. These birds "chip" constantly and sit in the open if an intruder approaches their nest.

Similar species: Tree Sparrow (visually), Swamp Sparrow, Dark-eyed Junco (vocally).

Remarks: The most common sparrow in Alberta, highly detectable vocally and usually easy to spot. It takes practice to separate the songs of various species that trill, like the Chipping Sparrow. Fortunately the Dark-eyed Junco and the Chipping Sparrow can be found together so you can hear the differences in their songs. The Chipping Sparrow is comfortable in human presence and has adjusted well to urban life. It is interesting to speculate on the physiology of a species that has adapted to so many environments while a near relative such as the Brewer's Sparrow may be restricted to a narrow range of habitats.

Jan	Feb	Mar	Apr	May	Jun	Jul	Aug	Sep	Oct	Nov	Dec

CHSP ☐   Date: _____

CLAY-COLORED SPARROW

Spizella pallida

L: 132 mm   W: 12 g   Egg: 17 x 13 mm

Etymology: *Spizella* (Gr.) - "little finch;" *pallida* (L.) - "pale."

Status and Distribution: Found in all natural regions of Alberta. They are most common in the parklands, least common in the far north, and "at home" on the grasslands.

Field Checklist

Habitat: Anywhere in the province with shrubs. Generally the Clay-colored Sparrow prefers drier parkland and grassland environments.

✓Sight: Look for the whitish stripe on the crown, generally streaked back, unstreaked underparts and brownish face patch edged in gray. A classic "little brown bird."

✓✓✓Sound: Males give a unique slow series of dry "buzzes," usually monotonic and insect-like.

✓Behavior: It often calls from an exposed perch on top of its shrubby habitat.

Similar species: Brewer's Sparrow (visually and vocally).

Remarks: Clay-colored Sparrows can be found in a remarkable diversity of habitats from the open plains to urban backyards to high mountain slopes. One constant is its insect-like "buzz." Generally highly detectable both vocally and visually, the face pattern separates this species from the Brewer's Sparrow which shows more streaking overall on its head. For a species with such a wide tolerance for different environments, it is interesting that the Clay-colored does not cross the Rockies. It is rarely seen in any state west of the Rockies or in British Columbia. Its status in Alberta should be monitored as some reports suggest it is on the decline.

Jan	Feb	Mar	Apr	May	Jun	Jul	Aug	Sep	Oct	Nov	Dec

273   CCSP ☐   Date: _____

BREWER'S SPARROW

Spizella breweri breweri
Spizella breweri taverneri

L: 135 mm   W: 11 g   Egg: 17 x 12 mm

Etymology: *Spizella* (Gr.) - "little finch;" *breweri* - after Thomas Mayo Brewer, physician, ornithologist and friend of John James Audubon.

Status and Distribution: Brewer's Sparrow is restricted to the arid grasslands of the southeast (*breweri*) and high elevation slopes (*taverneri*) of the Rockies.

Field Checklist

✓✓✓**Habitat:** Throughout the southeast, it is always found in association with sagebrush (*Artemisia cana*). Sage grows well only in dry, often over-grazed sites. A separate form prefers dwarf birch (*Betula*) in the high alpine of the Rocky Mountains.

✓**Sight:** This species has virtually no distinctive markings. It has a streaked back, unstreaked underparts and is grayish-brown overall. The *taverneri* form is darker.

✓✓✓**Sound:** Call is two-part, the first is a whistle, the second ends in a buzzy trill. The song is an extraordinarily diverse and long series of chips, trills and buzzes. The song of *taverneri* is softer and more musical.

✓**Behavior:** Brewer's Sparrows are secretive but will sing frequently in the early morning. They are difficult to find if the male is not singing.

Similar species: Clay-colored Sparrow (visually and vocally), Lark Bunting (vocally).

Remarks: Genetic differences between *breweri* and *taverneri* suggest a split in their lineages from 5000 to 10,000 years ago. They have different habitats, migration dates and songs. They show statistically different size and coloration. Whether or not these two forms should be named as separate species is being studied currently.

Jan	Feb	Mar	Apr	May	Jun	Jul	Aug	Sep	Oct	Nov	Dec

BWSP ☐   Date: _____

Order: Passeriformes - Family: Emberizidae   **Sparrows**

VESPER
SPARROW

Pooecetes gramineus

L: 155 mm   W: 26 g   Egg: 18 x 13 mm

Etymology: *Pooecetes* (Gr.) - "grass dweller;" *gramineus* (L.) - "of grass."

Status and Distribution: Vesper Sparrows are widespread in the grassland and parkland but scattered in the foothills, mountains and open areas in the boreal forest.

Field Checklist

✓**Habitat:** The Vesper Sparrow breeds in open range, pasture, weedy fields, meadows and recent burns. It is more common in the parkland and grassland habitats than farther north.

✓✓**Sight:** Vespers are large relative to other sparrows. The white eye-ring, white outer tail feathers contrasting with the dark tail, chestnut shoulder patch and strongly streaked back are the best visual identifiers.

✓✓**Sound:** They have a melodic song which starts with two slurred whistles followed by a series of short notes and trills.

✓**Behavior:** Males sing in twilight (hence the name Vesper). They often perch on or near the ground. Look along the lowest strand of a barbed wire fence on the grasslands. Sometimes they will sing from an elevated perch.

Similar species: Song Sparrow (visually and vocally); female Lark Bunting (visually).

Remarks: Like all sparrows, a good sighting is needed to be sure of identification if the bird is not singing. The white outer tail feathers are the best field mark but you will need to learn to separate the tail patterns of Lark Sparrows, Longspurs and Horned Larks. Look for the range maps and habitat preferences for the similar species; context will help you narrow down the choices when you encounter an unknown sparrow.

Jan	Feb	Mar	Apr	May	Jun	Jul	Aug	Sep	Oct	Nov	Dec

275   VESP ☐   Date: _____

Sparrows

LARK SPARROW

Chondestes grammacus

L: 166 mm   W: 29 g   Egg: 20 x 16 mm

Etymology: *Chondestes* (Gr.) - "grain eater;" *grammacus* (Gr.) - "striped."

Status and Distribution: The Lark Sparrow is restricted to the grasslands natural region particularly in the eastern half of the province. It is not a common sparrow, even in its preferred habitat.

Field Checklist

✓✓**Habitat:** Look for it in sagebrush-dominated range and river valleys, sandhills and pasture in southeastern Alberta.

✓✓✓**Sight:** The white, black and chestnut head markings are unique; white-tipped and white outer tail feathers are conspicuous in flight; note the central black breast spot.

✓**Sound**: It issues sharp "tsip" calls and sings a series of fast and slow trills.

Behavior: It spends a lot of time on the ground but will fly up into trees when flushed.

Similar species: Horned Lark, Vesper Sparrow and Longspurs share some features and habitats. Care must be taken identifying grassland sparrows in flight.

Remarks: The white tips of the tail feathers of this large sparrow are distinctive; the Vesper Sparrow shows white only along the sides. The male sings in a flight display known as "larking," hence the common name of the bird. The Lark Sparrow uses treed habitats more than other grassland sparrows. Good detectability especially in the early evenings. Lark Sparrows may be monogamous or a male may have two mates with the nests fairly close together. Groups of Lark Sparrows can be seen even during the breeding season. The Lark Sparrow is considerably larger than most other sparrows that share its habitat.

Jan	Feb	Mar	Apr	May	Jun	Jul	Aug	Sep	Oct	Nov	Dec

LKSP ☐   Date: _____

Order: Passeriformes - Family: Emberizidae   **Sparrows**

LARK BUNTING
Calamospiza melanocorys

L: 172 mm   W: 39 g   Egg: 22 x 17 mm

Etymology: *Calamospiza* (Gr.) -
kalamos, "reed" and *spiza*, "a finch;"
melanocorys (Gr.) - "black lark."

Status and Distribution: The Lark
Bunting is restricted to the grasslands.
It is more common in the southeast,
particularly on arid overgrazed sites. It can be locally abundant but is
spottily distributed throughout its range.

Field Checklist

✓✓**Habitat:** Its favorite habitats are sagebrush-dominated
rangeland in southeastern Alberta.

✓✓✓**Sight:** Male: black with white wing and
undertail patches. Female: streaked, brown
and white. Both sexes are large for a sparrow
with a stocky build and thick bill.

✓✓✓**Sound:** The male's song is a rich,
variable series of whistles, trills, gurgles and
mechanical noises often given in flight.

✓✓**Behavior:** The male performs a conspicuous, hovering flight song rising above the sage and
floating noisily to a new perch. This species is
gregarious and aggressive near the nest.

Similar species: Brewer's Sparrow, Yellow-breasted Chat (vocally);
Bobolink, Chestnut-collared Longspur and female Vesper Sparrow (visually).

Remarks: Highly detectable, you will have little trouble hearing, seeing and
identifying this species. Male Bobolinks show more white and buff on the
upperparts and are not found in sagebrush. Longspurs are much smaller and
show other colors. The Lark Bunting is a polygynous breeder where one
male may be mated to several females. Seeing and hearing Lark Buntings
perform their noisy "lark" flight is a highlight of a visit to the southeast. In
some years, however, this species is rarely seen, only to return in large
numbers the next year.

Jan	Feb	Mar	Apr	May	Jun	Jul	Aug	Sep	Oct	Nov	Dec

LKBU ❏   Date: _____

Sparrows

SAVANNAH SPARROW

Passerculus sandwichensis

L: 134 mm   W: 18 g   Egg: 19 x 15 mm

Photo: K.Morck

Etymology: *Passerculus* (L.) - "little sparrow;" *sandwichensis* (ML.) - location in the Aleutian Islands where the first subspecies was named.

Status and Distribution: Savannahs are found in almost any grassy habitat in the province, but are least common in the boreal forest, and most abundant in the parklands and grasslands.

- -

Field Checklist

✓**Habitat:** All grassy and weedy habitats from prairie to parks and boreal forest meadows. Common along roads, Savannahs generally prefer dry to damp rather than wet habitats.

✓✓**Sight:** Savannah Sparrows are medium-sized, heavily streaked, often with a central breast spot. They have pink feet and a yellow stripe over the eye which is a distinctive feature compared to other grassland sparrows.

✓✓**Sound:** Their song is a sequence of short chips followed by a higher-pitched weak trill, "tsip-tsip tzee-ee."

✓**Behavior:** The Savannah Sparrow perches in low bushes, flies weakly when flushed, diving into cover after a short distance. It sings all day long.

- -

Similar species: Song Sparrow, Swamp Sparrow and Lincoln's Sparrow (visually); Baird's Sparrow and Grasshopper Sparrow (vocally).

Remarks: The Savannah Sparrow is our most common grassland sparrow. Its plumage is variable geographically in a variety of characteristics. Generally, the song is constant across the range. Although weak, the call carries a long way and can be heard throughout the day. Look for Savannah Sparrows perched on barbed-wire fences.

Jan	Feb	Mar	Apr	May	Jun	Jul	Aug	Sep	Oct	Nov	Dec

SVSP ❑   Date: _____

Sparrows

BAIRD'S SPARROW

Ammodramus bairdii

L: *139 mm*   W: *19 g*   Egg: *19 x 15 mm*

Etymology: *Ammodramus* (Gr.) - *ammos*, "sand" and *dramein*, "to run;" *bairdii* (ML.) - for Spencer F. Baird of the Smithsonian, named by Audubon.

Status and Distribution: Formerly considered rare, locally common and scattered in the grasslands and southern parkland regions. Its status is uncertain but suspected to be declining in numbers.

. . . .

Field Checklist

✓✓**Habitat:** Generally, Baird's is restricted to native prairie or ungrazed pasture in southern Alberta. It seems to require mid-height to tall grasses.

✓**Sight:** This bird is generously streaked, the head and breast are buffy, there is a prominent buffy stripe on the crown, and streaks form a necklace on the buffy breast band.

✓✓**Sound:** The song is several monotonic chips followed by a simple trill. It is a duller version of the Savannah Sparrow's song.

✓**Behavior:** A skulker, Baird's can sing from an exposed perch but is often hidden. If flushed, the bird hides after a short flight.

. . . .

Similar species: Savannah Sparrow, Grasshopper Sparrow (visually and vocally).

Remarks: The Baird's Sparrow's status fluctuates widely in Alberta. In the late 1980s it was considered endangered; five years later it was common. Its preference for tall native grass puts it at risk in Alberta from lack of habitat. The best identifier for the Baird's, Savannah and Grasshopper sparrows is song. With practice you can easily separate them. Learn the Savannah's, then listen for "odd sounding" ones in the southeast; these will be Baird's and Grasshopper Sparrows.

Jan	Feb	Mar	Apr	May	Jun	Jul	Aug	Sep	Oct	Nov	Dec

BDSP ☐   Date: _____

Sparrows

GRASSHOPPER SPARROW

Ammodramus savannarum

L: 129 mm   W: 17 g   Egg: 19 x 14 mm

Etymology: *Ammodramus* (Gr.) - *ammos*, "sand" and *dramein*, "to run;" *savannarum* (L.) - "of meadows."

Status and Distribution: It is found in the eastern half of the grasslands region. The status of this species in Alberta is uncertain. It is only locally common and often absent from seemingly suitable habitat.

● ●

Field Checklist

✓**Habitat:** Grasshopper Sparrows breed in abandoned pastures, sandhills, native prairie, potentially any tall-grass-dominated area in the arid southeast.

✓**Sight:** Look for the light central stripe on the crown, white eye-ring, generally streaked upperparts, unstreaked underparts, short tail and chunky overall appearance.

✓✓**Sound:** The male's song is a grasshopper-like buzz, preceded by several short chips. It is a buzzier version of the song of the Savannah Sparrow.

✓**Behavior:** It may fly low in a zig-zag fashion before dropping into the grass. Though secretive, the male sings occasionally from a tall grass stem.

● ●

Similar species: Baird's Sparrow, Le Conte's Sparrow (visually); Baird's and Savannah Sparrow (vocally).

Remarks: The Grasshopper Sparrow is named for the similarity of its song to the stridulations of grasshoppers. The lack of streaking on the breast and sides separates the species from the similar Baird's and Savannah Sparrows. Fairly low detectability, easily overlooked. Its song can be mistaken for an insect. In spring though, males sing regularly, usually from the top of a stem of grass.

Jan	Feb	Mar	Apr	May	Jun	Jul	Aug	Sep	Oct	Nov	Dec

GRSP ☐   Date: _____

LE CONTE'S
SPARROW

Ammodramus leconteii

L: *123 mm*   W: *13 g*   Egg: *18 x 14 mm*

Etymology: *Ammodramus* (Gr.) - *ammos*, "sand" and *dramein*, "to run;" *leconteii* (ML.) - named for John Le Conte, Philadelphia doctor, ornithologist and friend of Audubon.

Status and Distribution: Common and widespread in the parkland, southern boreal forest and foothills natural regions, but uncommon in the mountains.

Field Checklist

✓✓**Habitat:** Unlike its relatives, Le Conte's Sparrow prefers wet grasslands, slough and bog edges and roadside ditches. It is the wetland counterpart of the Baird's and Grasshopper sparrows.

✓**Sight:** Look for white and buffy crown stripes, buff-orange stripe over the eye, a streaked back and minimal streaking on the underparts.

✓✓**Sound:** The song is a short high-pitched buzz preceded by a "click." Both sexes utter "ticks" constantly when disturbed. Trying to find them while they are "ticking" at you can be extremely frustrating as the birds stay hidden and move freely in the thick grass.

✓**Behavior:** Highly secretive and difficult to flush, this bird often scurries in the grass rather than flying.

Similar species: Grasshopper Sparrow, Nelson's Sharp-tailed Sparrow (visually and vocally).

Remarks: A frustrating bird to spot. Its preferred wet habitat is difficult to walk in and affords many hiding places for the sparrows. They tend to sing from low perches on bushes above the grass but they flush easily to the security of the grass.

Jan	Feb	Mar	Apr	May	Jun	Jul	Aug	Sep	Oct	Nov	Dec

LCSP ❑   Date: _____

Sparrows

SONG SPARROW

Melospiza melodia

L: 156 mm   W: 21 g   Egg: 22 x 17 mm

Etymology: *Melospiza* (Gr.) - *melos*, "sing" and *spiza*, "finch;" *melodia* (L.) - "musical."

Status and Distribution: Song Sparrows are common in the parkland and southern boreal forest, but uncommon in the grasslands and at high elevation. During migration, however, the Song Sparrow can be found anywhere in the province.

Field Checklist

✓✓**Habitat:** The Song Sparrow breeds in shrubby growth along the edges of rivers, streams, ponds and lakes. Less frequently it occurs on the edges of fields and pastures away from water.

✓**Sight:** It is distinguished from other sparrows by its large size, long rounded tail, reddish brown back, heavily streaked underparts and a black central breast spot.

✓✓✓**Sound:** The characteristic song is a series of clear whistles, followed by a few short buzzy notes, then two-note phrases, "see, see, see, buzz, buzz, buzz, teeker, teeker, teeker." A good song to memorize early in a birding career.

✓**Behavior:** It scratches amid the leaf litter, sings frequently and pumps its tail up and down during flight.

Similar species: Fox, Lincoln's and Savannah sparrows (visually); Fox and Vespers sparrows (vocally).

Remarks: Tremendously variable geographically in coloration but their song is basically constant. Birds in southwestern Alberta are noticeably darker than those elsewhere in the province. Highly detectable vocally, the bird can be hard to spot in its brushy habitat. The Song Sparrow is an early migrant and can be heard singing in early April in central Alberta. For many it is as good a harbinger of spring as the first Robin.

Jan	Feb	Mar	Apr	May	Jun	Jul	Aug	Sep	Oct	Nov	Dec

SOSP ☐   Date: _____

LINCOLN'S SPARROW

Melospiza lincolnii

L: *139 mm*   W: *17 g*   Egg: *19 x 14 mm*

Etymology: *Melospiza* (Gr.) - *melos*, "sing" and *spiza*, "finch;" *lincolnii* (ML.) - for Thomas Lincoln, a young companion of Audubon on a trip to Labrador.

Status and Distribution: Lincoln's Sparrow is widespread in the boreal forest, northern parkland, mountains and foothills. Elsewhere in the province, it can be seen during migration.

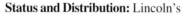

Field Checklist

✓**Habitat:** It is a denizen of bogs, wet meadows, willow, alder thickets and other wet and brushy areas in the mountains and northern half of the province.

✓**Sight:** Look for gray striping on the head, light streaking on the buffy breast band and the buffy eye-ring.

✓✓**Sound:** The song has a thrush or wren-like quality. It is an energetic series of warbles and trills. It gives the impression of producing two-note harmony, as a thrush song does.

✓**Behavior:** This sparrow chips incessantly when an intruder is near its nest.

Similar species: Song, Swamp Sparrow (visually); House Wren (vocally).

Remarks: The complexity of the song is reminiscent of that of a House Wren's but the habitat is wrong. Lincoln's Sparrows are in wet, grassy or shrubby areas, not necessarily near lakes or rivers. Good detectability vocally but hard to find. It responds aggressively to playback of its song. If disturbed, the bird may appear briefly only to disappear in a thick tangle of brush, not to be seen again. It is hard to chase in its wet habitat. Your best strategy is to learn its song.

Jan	Feb	Mar	Apr	May	Jun	Jul	Aug	Sep	Oct	Nov	Dec

285

LISP ☐   Date: _____

Sparrows

SWAMP SPARROW

Melospiza georgiana

L: 140 mm   W: 17 g   19 x 15 mm

Etymology: *Melospiza* (Gr.) - *melos*, "sing" and *spiza*, "finch;" *georgiana* (ML.) - "of Georgia."

Status and Distribution: Swamp Sparrows breed regularly in the boreal forest, northern parkland and foothills.

Photo: B.Carroll

Field Checklist

✓✓**Habitat:** Home for this bird is sedges and cattails on the edges of northern sloughs, ponds and along rivers.

✓**Sight:** Note the reddish cap, white throat, gray face and belly.

✓✓**Sound:** Once again, pay close attention to this bird's song. It is a monotonic trill, slow enough that individual notes are heard, but it ends abruptly.

Behavior: The Swamp Sparrow is wary and secretive. It hides even in response to playback of its song.

Similar species: Song and Lincoln's sparrows (visually); Chipping Sparrow, Palm Warbler and Dark-eyed Junco (vocally).

Remarks: Swamp Sparrows are a challenge for birders to identify because they are hard to see and their song resembles that of several other species. The slow speed of the Swamp Sparrow trill is diagnostic. Habitat usually eliminates confusion with the song of the Junco and Chipping Sparrow. Even though closely related to the Song Sparrow, the Swamp has uniform coloration across its range. Little is known about the breeding biology and behavior of this species in Alberta. Like many of our boreal forest birds, the challenge of studying the breeding ecology of the Swamp Sparrows in detail has yet to be overcome. Access to appropriate habitat is difficult, movement within the wet environment is almost impossible and you cannot study what you cannot see.

Jan	Feb	Mar	Apr	May	Jun	Jul	Aug	Sep	Oct	Nov	Dec

SWSP ☐   Date: _____

WHITE-THROATED SPARROW

Zonotrichia albicollis

L: 165 mm   W: 25 g   Egg: 21 x 15 mm

Etymology: *Zonotrichia* (Gr.) - *zono*, "belt" and *thrix*, "hair" (headstripes); *albicollis* (L.) - "white neck."

Status and Distribution: The "Canada" Sparrow is a common breeder in the foothills, parkland and boreal forest regions.

Field Checklist

✓**Habitat:** It prefers edges, burns, brushy margins along cutlines in aspen, coniferous or mixed forests.

✓✓**Sight:** Both sexes show a white (or tan) and black streaked crown, yellow in front of eye, white throat, streaked back and long tail.

✓✓✓**Sound:** This species is famous for its distinctive, clear, whistled song "O, sweet, Canada, Canada, Canada," and call note a sharp "chink."

✓**Behavior:** White-throated Sparrows are noisy foragers, scratching in the leaf litter and frequently uttering call notes. The male gives his full song throughout the day.

Similar species: White-crowned Sparrow (visually).

Remarks: Highly detectable vocally and visually. The song of the White-throated is a characteristic of northern woods. The birds are noisy foragers and seemingly curious about intruders. Regular members of mixed migrating flocks, the White-throat's distinctive call is heard constantly. A common migrant and breeder in Edmonton. Sexes do not differ in plumage - tan-striped birds possess a chromosomal variant different from white-striped individuals. Behaviorally, white-striped are dominant to tan-striped. Often, a pair has one of each, the white stripe is more aggressive and dominant regardless of its gender.

Jan	Feb	Mar	Apr	May	Jun	Jul	Aug	Sep	Oct	Nov	Dec

WTSP ☐   Date: _____

WHITE-CROWNED SPARROW
Zonotrichia leucophrys

L: 166 mm   W: 27 g   Egg: 21 x 16 mm

Etymology: *Zonotrichia* (Gr.) - *zono*, "belt" and *thrix*, "hair" (headstripes); *leucophrys* (L.) - *leukos*, "white" and *ophrys*, "eyebrow."

Status and Distribution: White-crowns are widely distributed in the mountains, foothills, Cypress Hills, Peace River parkland and northern boreal forest.

Field Checklist

✓**Habitat:** Its preference is for shrubby alpine areas, burns and bushes along water courses in the mountains and extreme north. During migration the White- crowned Sparrow can be seen any-where including urban sites.

✓✓**Sight:** It is identified by the strong black and white striping on top of the head, pink bill, gray face and generally gray underparts.

✓✓**Sound:** Listen for one clear whistle followed by a series of slurred whistles mixed with a trill. Their call note is a sharp "chink."

✓**Behavior:** These birds are noisy foragers. They respond aggressively to "pishing" and playback of their song.

Similar species: Golden-crowned Sparrow, White-throated Sparrow (visually); Fox Sparrow (vocally).

Remarks: The common mountain sparrow, it is highly detectable. The distribution of White-crowns is more erratic beyond the mountains and foothills. This is a geographically variable species for both song and plumage. Look at the white stripe nearest the eye and determine whether it extends forward to the bill (northern Alberta and the northern Rockies) or not (southwestern Alberta and Cypress Hills). Young White-crowns have reddish brown and buff stripes on their crowns.

Jan	Feb	Mar	Apr	May	Jun	Jul	Aug	Sep	Oct	Nov	Dec

GOLDEN-CROWNED SPARROW

Zonotrichia atricapilla

L: 171 mm   W: 34 g   Egg: 23 x 16 mm

Etymology: *Zonotrichia* (Gr.) - *zono*, "belt" and *thrix*, "hair" (headstripes); *atricapilla* (L.) - "black-haired," refers to black on sides of crown.

Status and Distribution: Fairly common in the main ranges of the northern Rocky Mountains, but locally distributed. Rarely seen away from the mountains.

Field Checklist

✓✓**Habitat:** The Golden-crowned breeds on high elevation mountain slopes and meadows with scattered, stunted fir and spruce (krummholz).

✓✓**Sight:** Note the yellow patch bordered by black on the head, gray face and throat, brown back and two white wing bars.

✓✓✓**Sound:** Their song is unique. It consists of three clear descending whistles, given in a minor key. The effect is a plaintive, mournful sound.

✓**Behavior:** The male is an energetic singer. Both sexes spend most of their time on the ground.

Similar species: White-crowned Sparrow (visually).

Remarks: High detectability given its song, size and preferred habitat. The male sings throughout the day even in poor weather. Its mournful call seems to mimic the often sombre weather conditions of its alpine environment. This bird is a fairly late migrant, arriving in Alberta in mid-May. Timing of breeding varies with depth of snow in its high-elevation home. The White-crowned can be found in the same habitat but its songs are easily separated from those of this species.

Jan	Feb	Mar	Apr	May	Jun	Jul	Aug	Sep	Oct	Nov	Dec

GCSP ☐   Date: _____

Order: Passeriformes - Family: Emberizidae

DARK-EYED JUNCO

Junco hyemalis

L: 151 mm   W: 19 g   Egg: 19 x 14 mm

Etymology: *Juncus* (L.) - "a rush;" *hyemalis* (L.) - "winter."

Status and Distribution: Juncos are common breeders in the mountains, foothills, northern parkland and boreal forest regions. In migration, both spring and fall, they can be seen anywhere including backyard feeders.

Field Checklist

✓**Habitat:** They like a variety of habitats including mixed woods, burns, cutlines, edges, city parks and suburbs.

✓✓✓**Sight:** Look for the white outer tail feathers that contrast with the gray or grayish-brown plumage. Their light bill contrasts with the dark head. This species has extremely variable plumage. Mountain forms have brown on the back and flanks rather than gray. Cypress Hills birds are lighter with pinkish sides.

✓✓**Sound:** Metallic trill, similar to that of a Chipping Sparrow.

✓**Behavior:** An active bird, it flashes its white outer tail feathers in flight.

Similar species: Chipping Sparrow (vocally).

Remarks: A welcome early spring migrant and active breeder in conifer-dominated woodlands. Its trills are similar to those of the Chipping Sparrow but are considered more musical. The direction the bird is facing relative to you, the wind, and the vegetation between you and the bird can radically change the character of a bird's call. Do not trust recordings to give you the sounds of birds in all situations in your region. A highly detectable species, look for at least two and sometimes three plumage variants in Alberta. Some individuals overwinter, thanks to urban feeders.

Jan	Feb	Mar	Apr	May	Jun	Jul	Aug	Sep	Oct	Nov	Dec

DEJU ☐   Date: _____

McCOWN'S LONGSPUR
Calcarius mccownii

L: 150 mm   W: 26 g   Egg: 20 x 15 mm

Etymology: *Calcarius* (L.) - "calcar (=spur);" *mccownii* - for J.P. McCown, a U.S. army captain who collected the first specimen in Texas.

Status and Distribution: Localized scattered breeding records throughout the grassland and southern parkland regions. It does not seem to be a common species anywhere in Alberta.

Field Checklist

✓✓**Habitat:** Its preferred breeding habitat is moderately or lightly grazed, shortgrass prairie.

✓✓**Sight:** Both sexes are identified by the distinctive black 'T' on the white tail when spread. Look for the male's black crown, black whisker stripe and chestnut wing patch. Females are brownish. Both have a large bill.

✓**Sound:** A series of warbles, chips and whistles are uttered in the male's flight song.

✓✓**Behavior:** Males sing in flight. This species is gregarious and often seen in mixed flocks with Horned Larks and Chestnut-collared Longspurs. They forage on the ground.

Similar species: Horned Lark, Chestnut-collared Longspur (visually); Horned Lark (vocally).

Remarks: Low detectability, not common and often mixed with other species in spring. The best technique for finding this species is to drive slowly along gravel roads in southeastern Alberta watching the tail markings of birds that you flush. Look for a "larking" display in spring when the male flies up and floats to the ground, holding his wings still while warbling and twittering. This is a common feature of grassland birds, thus we have many species with "lark" in their name that are not related to true larks.

Jan	Feb	Mar	Apr	May	Jun	Jul	Aug	Sep	Oct	Nov	Dec

Sparrows

Order: Passeriformes - Family: Emberizidae

LAPLAND LONGSPUR

Calcarius lapponicus

L: 155 mm   W: 31 g   Egg: 20 x 15 mm

Etymology: *Calcarius* (L.) - "calcar (=spur);" *lapponicus* - "of Lapland."

Status and Distribution: The Lapland Longspur is a spring and fall migrant throughout the grassland and parkland.

Field Checklist

✓✓**Habitat:** Look for this species in stubblefields and along the margins of prairie sloughs, lakes and weedy pastures.

✓✓**Sight:** In late spring, the males have black crowns, faces and necks. There is a white line behind the eye and down the neck, a chestnut collar, white underparts and a streaked back. Early spring colors may be muted as feathers have buffy tips. Females are considerably duller with a black triangle-like mark on the face.

✓**Sound:** Males give a series of slurred whistles reminiscent of a Western Meadowlark; a dry rattle is given in flight.

✓**Behavior:** It migrates in huge flocks sometimes mixed with Snow Buntings and Horned Larks.

Similar species: Harris's Sparrow, (visually); Chestnut-collared Longspur (visually and vocally). Winter birds resemble a variety of streaked sparrows.

Remarks: In early spring or fall, the plumage of the Lapland Longspur is well camouflaged in a field of stubble. A good identifier is the black almost triangular line of the face of females and winter birds. Adult males should not be confused with any other species. If you get a close look, you can see the long hind claw for which "Longspurs" are named.

Jan	Feb	Mar	Apr	May	Jun	Jul	Aug	Sep	Oct	Nov	Dec

LALO ☐   Date: _____

CHESTNUT-COLLARED LONGSPUR

Calcarius ornatus

Photo: T.Thormin

L: 146 mm W: 20 g Egg: 19 x 14 mm

Etymology: *Calcarius* (L.) - "calcar (=spur);" *ornatus* (L.) - "ornate, adorned."

Status and Distribution: A common breeder in the grasslands. It is more evenly distributed across southeastern Alberta than McCown's Longspur.

Field Checklist

✓✓**Habitat:** The Chestnut-collared breeds in variably grazed mixed and native grasslands; often it is seen with cattle. Sometimes it perches and sings from cow droppings.

✓✓✓**Sight:** The male has black and white head markings, black underparts, white outer tail feathers and a chestnut collar on the hind-neck. The female is buffy brown but with the same black triangle on the spread tail as the male.

✓**Sound:** Males give a Meadowlark-like rattle. Their song, a rapid warble, is often given in flight as part of a flight display.

✓**Behavior:** The male performs a flight song, calling while gliding to a new perch. This species is an early migrant and breeder.

Similar species: Lark Bunting, Bobolink (visually); Lapland Longspur (vocally and visually).

Remarks: The male's black breast may have various amounts of rust in the middle. A highly detectable species, the Chestnut-collared Longspur perches in the open on rocks or cowpies, performs a noisy song in flight and even nests in short grass. Males may mate with more than one female. One of the best ways of finding this species is to cruise gravel roads south of Medicine Hat. It won't be long before you flush this black-bellied Longspur from the side of the road.

Jan	Feb	Mar	Apr	May	Jun	Jul	Aug	Sep	Oct	Nov	Dec

CCLO ☐ Date: _____

SNOW BUNTING

Plectrophenax nivalis

L: 168 mm   W: 34 g   Egg: 23 x 17 mm

Etymology: *Plectrophenax* (Gr.) - *plectron*, a claw-like tool in reference to the bird's long hind claw and *phenax*, "false;" *nivalis* (L.) - "snow."

Status and Distribution: Winter visitor in southern Alberta but a spring and fall migrant elsewhere. It breeds in the high Arctic.

• •

Field Checklist

✓**Habitat:** Look for it in spring in open country, stubblefields and pastures.

✓✓✓**Sight:** The black and white pattern in the wings and tail is unmistakable. Winter birds show a brownish head, neck and upperparts. The birds are entirely black and white in breeding plumage.

Sound: All that we hear in spring are buzzes and rattles and occasional whistles.

✓**Behavior:** These birds travel in huge flocks in spring and fall. At times a field can seem to be alive with thousands of individuals.

• •

Similar species: None.

Remarks: The huge flocks that visit us in the spring are often mixed with Horned Larks and Lapland Longspurs. Their flight seems choreographed as flocks of Buntings turn and whirl in unison like flocks of sandpipers. This behavior makes it harder for predators to pick off individual birds. By mid-April, flocks are in northern Alberta heading north to their breeding grounds. Late stragglers give us a glimpse of the magnificent all black and white breeding plumage. Like Longspurs, Snow Buntings have a long hind-claw. Their common name describes their habit of migrating to southern Canada in advance of the first winter snows.

Jan	Feb	Mar	Apr	May	Jun	Jul	Aug	Sep	Oct	Nov	Dec

SNBU ❑   Date: _____

ROSE-BREASTED GROSBEAK

Pheucticus ludovicianus

L: 195 mm   W: 47 g   Egg: 25 x 18 mm

Etymology: *Pheucticus* (Gr.) - "shy, retiring;" *ludovicianus* (ML.) - of Louisiana.

Status and Distribution: The Rose-breasted Grosbeak breeds throughout the foothills, parkland and boreal forest regions. It is common in the northern parkland and southern boreal forest.

Field Checklist

✓✓**Habitat:** This grosbeak breeds in mature mixed woods or mature aspens, usually near edges.

✓✓✓**Sight:** The male is identified by his huge bill, black and white pattern with a rose breast and rose underwing lining. The female is brownish and streaked. She has yellow underwing linings.

✓✓**Sound:** The Rose-breasted Grosbeak's song is a series of warbling, melodic, slurred, Robin-like phrases. Its call is a sharp "peek."

Behavior: The male will respond aggressively to play back of song. He will approach the source of the song and call vigorously.

Similar species: Female: Black-headed Grosbeak, Purple and Cassin's finches (visually). Male: Robin, Western Tanager, Purple Finch, Warbling Vireo (vocally).

Remarks: The Rose-breasted Grosbeak presents a unique color combination that is unmistakable. In flight the black and white pattern is conspicuous. This species is highly detectable both vocally and visually. Listen for a variety of pitch changes in the whistled call. Males will sing from the nest and in flight. This species may hybridize with the Black-headed Grosbeak near Waterton. If you happen to take one of these birds in a mist net to band it, keep your fingers away from his beak.

Jan	Feb	Mar	Apr	May	Jun	Jul	Aug	Sep	Oct	Nov	Dec

RBGR ☐   Date: _____

Grosbeaks and Buntings

Order: Passeriformes - Family: Cardinalidae

BLACK-HEADED GROSBEAK

Pheucticus melanocephalus

L: 195 mm W: 48 g Egg: 28 x 18 mm

Etymology:*Pheucticus* (Gr.) - "shy, retiring;" *melanocephalus* (Gr.) - "black head."

Status and Distribution: This grosbeak is restricted to the extreme southwest corner of Alberta. It is not common even in suitable habitat. There are historical records for the Cypress Hills.

Field Checklist

✓✓**Habitat:** Its preference is for cottonwood groves, willows, riparian bushes and mature forests with thick undergrowth.

✓✓✓**Sight:** With his huge bill, cinnamon underparts and black and white markings, the male is distinctive. The female is buffy. Both sexes have yellow underwing linings.

✓**Sound:** Its song is very similar to that of the Rose-breasted Grosbeak. It is a series of slurred, warbling, Robin-like phrases. Call is a low pitched "eek."

Behavior: This species can hybridize with the Rose-breasted Grosbeak.

Similar species: Female: Rose-breasted Grosbeak, House and Cassin's finches (visually). Male: Robin, Warbling Vireo, finches (vocally).

Remarks: Its song is very difficult to distinguish from that of the Rose-breasted Grosbeak. In the southwest, make sure you see the singer for confirmation of identity. In the male of this species, cinnamon-brown replaces the pink and white of the Rose-breasted Grosbeak. Generally the female Black-headed is less streaked underneath than is the female Rose-breasted but otherwise they are similar. Hybridization between these species was facilitated by the urbanization of the prairies which resulted in patches of suitable habitat connecting the eastern and western grosbeak ranges.

Jan	Feb	Mar	Apr	May	Jun	Jul	Aug	Sep	Oct	Nov	Dec

BHGR ☐   Date: _____

LAZULI BUNTING
Passerina amoena

L: *136 mm* W: *14 g* Egg: *19 x 14 mm*

Etymology: *Passerina* (L.) - "sparrow-like;" *amoena* (L.) - "delightful, pleasant."

Status and Distribution: The Lazuli is not common but can be found in the mountains and along rivers in southern Alberta. It has been observed on occasion as far north as Sylvan Lake. Its status in the province is not well documented.

Field Checklist

✓✓**Habitat:** This bunting is found in riparian and coulee thickets of buckbrush, rose and willow, and on various shrubs in mountain valleys and aspen forests in the montane regions.

✓✓✓**Sight:** Look for the large conical bill. The male is bright turquoise on his head and throat. His breast is cinnamon, belly white and he has white wing bars. The female is grayish-brown with a bluish-gray rump.

✓✓**Sound:** Their song is rapid, jumbled, buzzy, phrases sounding something like "tree, tree, tree, trit-a-tree." The ending is buzzy.

Behavior: The male sings from an exposed perch or telephone wire.

Similar species: All bluebirds (visually). American Goldfinch, Indigo Bunting (vocally).

Remarks: Although similar in coloration to bluebirds, the bunting has a seed-eating bill, is lighter blue and has wing bars. A persistent singer, the male is easily detected by song. His appearance is distinctive. Females remain inconspicuous. The Lazuli eats a mixture of seeds and insects which it usually picks off or near the ground. Relatively few breeding records were confirmed during the 1986-91 censuses for the Alberta Bird Atlas. They are late migrants and may be hard to confirm as breeders in their thick habitat.

Jan	Feb	Mar	Apr	May	Jun	Jul	Aug	Sep	Oct	Nov	Dec

LZBU ☐ Date: _____

Rarities

NASHVILLE WARBLER

Vermivora ruficapilla

The Nashville Warbler is a rare migrant in the mountains, and rare vagrant in the Cold Lake and Cypress Hills regions. One confirmed breeding record is known from Alberta. There are populations of this species in Saskatchewan and Manitoba but also in British Columbia. Birds appear to be visiting Alberta from both directions. It is found in brushy secondary growth on the edges of deciduous or mixed woods but also can be seen in burns and bogs.

Look for the sharp contrast between the gray cap and bright yellow throat and underparts. The white eye-ring is distinctive. It has a reddish cap but like the orange patch on the Orange-crowned Warbler, it is rarely seen. The males give a series of clear, whistled, two-syllable chips followed by a trill on a lower pitch. It resembles the Tennessee Warbler song but it is shorter with two rather than three components.

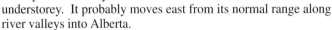

BLACK-THROATED BLUE WARBLER

Dendroica caerulescens

Photo: T.Thormin

The Black-throated Blue warbler is a rare vagrant with most records occurring in the fall, around Edmonton and Calgary. It breeds in deciduous and mixed woods usually with a heavy shrub understorey. It probably moves east from its normal range along river valleys into Alberta.

Spring males have a distinctive blue back, black throat and flanks, white underparts and a white wing patch. Females are greenish on the back and buffy underneath. They show an eye ring and eye line looking nothing like the males. This degree of sexual difference in plumage is unique among our warblers. Usually, females are simply a paler version of the males. Fall birds are duller. Their song is a wheezy set of four or more notes ending on an upslur "zu, zu, zu, zuzee." The song has the same wheezy quality which distinguishes the Townsend's and Black-throated Green Warbler songs.

HARRIS' SPARROW

Zonotrichia querula

The Harris' Sparrow is a relatively uncommon spring and more frequent fall migrant. It can be seen in fields, pastures, hedgerows and even at feeders during migration. It is told from other sparrows by its large size, pink bill, black cap, face and neck, grey cheeks and white underparts. Its song consists of three or four clear whistles on the same note or on a different pitch, usually in a minor key.

It moves through Alberta in early spring in flocks sometimes mixed with other sparrows. It behaves like the other members of the genus *Zonotrichia*, but the black on its head and its call are distinctive.

Harris' Sparrow breeds in the subarctic north and east of Alberta and passes the winter in the mid-western United States.

SMITH'S LONGSPUR

Calcarius pictus

Smith's Longspur is a scarce late (relative to migration patterns of Lapland Longspurs) spring and early fall migrant in eastern Alberta. Beaverhill Lake is an important stopping point in the spring. They do not linger long in Alberta and consequently, are easily missed.

Look for them in stubblefields, pasture or recently seeded croplands. Males in spring have bright black and white face markings, a white ear spot stands out, the underparts are buffy, and the tail is black and white. Females and fall birds are much duller but generally buffier than other Longspurs and sparrows. Males give five or six clear, short whistles. The common call is a soft rattle similar to the call of other longspurs.

They travel in large loose flocks that sometimes perform group aerobatics like shorebirds and Snow Buntings. Alberta is on the western edge of the migration route of this species, which breeds in the Arctic. Little is known about its breeding, wintering and migratory biology. This is a good species for a new graduate student to study.

Rarities

NORTHERN CARDINAL

Cardinalis cardinalis

The Northern Cardinal is a rare vagrant, which is seen mainly in winter at feeders in southern Alberta. Its normal habitat is open woodlands in eastern North America but it is also common in city parks and suburban areas. The Cardinal has expanded its range northwards in the east over the last 30 years and it clearly wanders in the west.

The male is bright red overall with a black face and red bill; the female is duller and generally brownish with red on the wings, tail and head. Both sexes have a conspicuous crest. There is nothing in our part of the world that could be confused with a Cardinal.

The male sings in loud, clear whistles "cheer, cheer, cheer, pretty, pretty, pretty." They begin to sing in late winter on sunny spring-like days. Cardinals are non-migratory and are common visitors to feeders, especially ones supplying sunflower seeds. Although seen yearly, there is no trend to increasing sightings of this species in Alberta.

BOBOLINK

Dolichonyx oryzivorus

L: 182 mm W: 34 g Egg: 22 x 16 mm

Etymology: *Dolichonyx* (Gr.) - *dolichos*, "long" and *onyx*, "claw;" *oryzivorus* (L.) - "rice-eating."

Status and Distribution: A local breeder in the central parkland and eastern grasslands. Never common in Alberta, Bobolink colonies seem to come and go for no apparent reason.

Field Checklist

✓**Habitat:** Bobolinks are found in moist meadows, pastures and hayfields in southeastern and east-central Alberta. Bobolinks do not like short dry grass.

✓✓✓**Sight:** Males are identified by their black underparts, white shoulders and rump, and buff back of the neck. The female has generally buffy streaked upperparts. Tail-feathers of both sexes are sharply pointed. This is especially noticeable when the tail is spread.

✓**Sound:** The male's song is a bubbly jumble of slurred, gurgled notes and warbles. The call is a typical blackbird sounding "chuck."

✓**Behavior:** The male often sings from an exposed perch or during a flight display. He is not shy about showing off his brightly colored back.

Similar species: Lark Bunting, Chestnut-collared Longspur (visually and vocally).

Remarks: The male Bobolink is polygynous. He uses song to attract females and a display of his colorful back to keep their interest. The song is often delivered in flight as the bird floats down 6 - 10 m to a perch. This same behavior is seen in Lark Buntings and Chestnut-collared Longspurs. Bobolinks are highly detectable but only found sporadically in suitable habitat. Loss of winter habitat (in Argentina) and problems during migration may be reducing its numbers. During fall migration, Bobolinks assume a rather dull plumage and feast in huge numbers on rice fields in the southern United States. Despite their name, they are mostly insectivorous in Alberta.

Jan	Feb	Mar	Apr	May	Jun	Jul	Aug	Sep	Oct	Nov	Dec

BOBO ☐   Date: _____

Blackbirds and Allies

RED-WINGED BLACKBIRD

Agelaius phoeniceus

L: *229 mm W: 70 g Egg: 25 x 18 mm*

Etymology: *Agelaius* (Gr.) - *agelaios,* "part of a flock;" *phoeniceus* (Gr.) - "deep red."

Status and Distribution: Red-wings are abundant everywhere in the province except localized in the far north. As forests are cleared in the north the Red-winged Blackbird will continue to expand its range.

. . . .

Field Checklist

✓**Habitat:** Reeds, cattails and bulrushes along sloughs, ponds and lakes throughout the province. Red-wings are perfectly content to nest in ditches as long as suitable nest sites are available.

✓✓✓**Sight:** In the male, red epaulets, tipped with yellow contrast with the all-black plumage. The female (inset) is heavily streaked, brown with a buffy head and throat.

✓✓**Sound:** The males give an unmistakable "o-ka-ree" song and a persistent "chuck" call.

✓✓**Behavior:** Red-wings are highly visible and aggressive in defence of nest. They readily perch in the open and tolerate human presence.

. . . .

Similar species: Brewer's and Rusty blackbirds, Brown-headed Cowbird (visually and vocally).

Remarks: Despite the territorial aggressiveness of males, studies have shown that the majority of Red-winged Blackbird clutches have mixed male parentage. Males are polygynous but not as efficient at keeping intruding males away as they would like. The differences between males and females are extreme, which is typical of polygynous species. This is a highly visible species, excellent for observing behavior. Watch for their interactions with other marsh birds such as Yellow-headed Blackbirds.

Jan	Feb	Mar	Apr	May	Jun	Jul	Aug	Sep	Oct	Nov	Dec

RWBL ❑   Date: _____

Blackbirds and Allies

WESTERN MEADOWLARK

Sturnella neglecta

Photo: K.Morck

L: 243 mm W: 111 g Egg: 28 x 29 mm

Etymology: *Sturnella* (L.) - diminutive of starling; *neglecta* (L.) - "overlooked," because of its resemblence to Eastern Meadowlark.

Status and Distribution: The meadowlark is common in the grasslands, less so in the parkland and southern boreal forest. Formerly it was more common in the north, foothills and mountains.

Field Checklist

✓**Habitat:** They prefer arid rangeland, coulees, river valleys, grazed pasture and road allowances primarily in the grasslands and parkland.

✓✓✓**Sight:** They have brilliant yellow underparts with a black breast 'V,' a brownish streaked back and white outer tail feathers which are visible in flight. The large pointed bill almost seems too big for their head.

✓✓**Sound:** The male's song, which is extremely loud and flute-like, rises initially then falls in pitch. Their call note is a loud "chuck" and a rattled "gurgle" is often given in flight.

✓**Behavior:** Males display and call prominently from fence posts, wires or rocks. Due to its fondness for wide open spaces, it is difficult to approach.

Similar species: Chestnut-collared Longspur (vocally).

Remarks: Its song carries a long distance and its open country habitat makes spotting a Meadowlark easy. In flight its white outer tail feathers are prominent. Western Meadowlarks spend much of their time on the ground, walking rather than hopping while foraging. Spring migrants arrive early but some individuals overwinter in southern Alberta. Given the amount of clearing of forests for agriculture in the north, Meadowlark range should be increasing. The opposite seems to be true as records are increasingly unusual beyond the grasslands.

Jan	Feb	Mar	Apr	May	Jun	Jul	Aug	Sep	Oct	Nov	Dec

WEME ☐   Date: _____

Blackbirds and Allies

YELLOW-HEADED BLACKBIRD

Xanthocephalus xanthocephalus

L: 260 mm   W: 93 g   Egg: 26 x 18 mm

Etymology: *Xanthocephalus* (Gr.) - *xanthos*, "yellow" and *kephale*, "head."

Status and Distribution: This blackbird is a common breeder throughout the grasslands, aspen parkland and southern boreal forest. There are scattered sightings farther north to the latitude of La Crete and in river valleys in the mountains.

Field Checklist

✓**Habitat:** It is found in cattail sloughs, marshes and lake edges throughout the eastern half of central and southern Alberta.

✓✓✓**Sight:** The bright yellow head and breast, black body, bill and eyepatch and white wing patches of the male are unique. The smaller female is brownish but with a yellow throat and breast and no white on the wing.

✓✓✓**Sound:** The male's song is a harsh unmusical, metallic, grinding complaint. Their call is a hoarse "croak."

✓✓**Behavior:** The male sings from an exposed perch, is aggressive, highly visible and noisy. Females tend to stay quiet except if there is an intruder near their nest.

Similar species: No similar species.

Remarks: The males of this species have to be the easiest bird to identify in the province. Their plumage and harsh vocalization are unique. They also have no interest in hiding which is a treat because they are interesting to watch. Males are aggressive and use a distinctive flight display to show their colors. See if you can find a good hiding place on the edge of a marsh, a great place to study bird behavior. How do the Yellow-heads interact with Red-winged Blackbirds - do they push them out of prime nesting habitat?

Jan	Feb	Mar	Apr	May	Jun	Jul	Aug	Sep	Oct	Nov	Dec

YHBL ❑   Date: _____

Blackbirds and Allies

RUSTY BLACKBIRD

Euphagus carolinus

L: 216 mm   W: 56 g   Egg: 25 x 19 mm

Etymology: *Euphagus* (Gr.) - *euphageen,* "to eat well;" *carolinus* (ML.) - "of Carolina."

Status and Distribution: The Rusty breeds primarily in the boreal forest. It may be in the northern parkland and foothills but it is easily confused with the Brewer's which is also in the same regions.

● ●

Field Checklist

✓**Habitat:** It is found around bogs, beaver ponds and lake edges in mixed-wood forests.

✓**Sight:** Males are dull black with yellow-white eyes. Females are brownish-gray but also with yellowish-white eyes. Their plumage is less glossy and less iridescent than that of Brewer's Blackbird.

✓✓**Sound:** The male's song is a squeaky, rapid version of the Red-wing's "o-ka-ree." Their call is a harsh "chuck."

✓✓**Behavior:** Rusty Blackbirds are often seen in forests, perching at the top of trees bordering water.

● ●

Similar species: Brewer's Blackbird, Red-winged Blackbird and Brown-headed Cowbird (visually and vocally).

Remarks: The northern counterpart to the Brewer's Blackbird but so similar that care must be taken when confirming identification everywhere, particularly south of the boreal forest. Rusty Blackbirds are solitary nesters, so are most likely seen in pairs and nest in trees near or over water. In the fall the Rusty is easily distinguished from the Brewer's by the reddish brown tips on its feathers. Habitat differences will give you 90% confidence in identification, its behavior and relatively dull plumage should be good for confirmation. During migration in the spring, both species can be found in central and southern Alberta.

Jan	Feb	Mar	Apr	May	Jun	Jul	Aug	Sep	Oct	Nov	Dec

RUBL ☐   Date: _____

Blackbirds and Allies

Order: Passeriformes - Family: Icteridae

BREWER'S BLACKBIRD

Euphagus cyanocephalus

L: 239 mm   W: 71 g   Egg: 25 x 18 mm

Etymology: *Euphagus* (Gr.) - *euphageen,* "to eat well;" *cyanocephalus* (Gr.) - *Kyanos,* "blue" and *kephale,* "head."

Status and Distribution: A common breeder in the grasslands, foothills, parklands and southern boreal forest. There are scattered records in the mountains and further north. Confusion with the Rusty makes range delimitation of both species problematic.

Field Checklist

✓**Habitat:** Look for it in pastures, ranchyards, prairies, aspen groves, burns, thickets and marshes in the southern half of the province.

✓**Sight:** It is easily confused with the Rusty. Look for glossy purple sheen on head and greenish tinge to the body. The female is browner, her eyes are brownish and not yellow like those of the female Rusty.

✓✓**Sound:** A wheezy, single note "zwee" followed by a "chuck" is the best the Brewer's can do for a song.

✓**Behavior:** A communal nester, it likes spruces planted as ranchhouse windbreaks in the grasslands and parkland.

Similar species: Rusty and Red-winged blackbirds, Common Grackle, Brown-headed Cowbird (visually and vocally)

Remarks: A gregarious species unlike the Rusty, and a communal nester, the Brewer's seems to be expanding northwards. Clearing of land and timber harvesting is creating Brewer's habitat perhaps at the expense of Rusty Blackbirds. With experience, you will notice the slightly longer tail and smaller head and bill of the Brewer's compared to those of the Rusty. Confirmed nesting records in the boreal forest would help demarcate the breeding range. Normally, Brewer's are monogamous but polygyny is not uncommon.

Jan	Feb	Mar	Apr	May	Jun	Jul	Aug	Sep	Oct	Nov	Dec

BRBL ❒   Date: _____

COMMON GRACKLE

Quiscalus quiscula

Photo: K.Morck

L: 305 mm   W: 122 g   Egg: 28 x 21 mm

Etymology: *Quiscalus* and *quiscula* (L.) - "quail."

Status and Distribution: A fairly common breeder in the parkland and scattered in the boreal forest and grasslands. Grackles are rare in the mountains and foothills. Highest densities are in the northern parkland and southern boreal forest.

Field Checklist

✓**Habitat:** Look for grackles in wet habitats, parks, golf courses, marshes and ditches.

✓✓✓**Sight:** Males have a long bill, yellow eyes, long keeled tail and are dark overall with purple iridescence on the head and bronze on the body. The female is duller, and much smaller than the male with a shorter tail.

✓**Sound:** Not a singer, a grackle produces squeaky "chucks," squeaks, wheezes and gurgles.

✓✓**Behavior:** Grackles forage by walking slowly on the ground on lawns, parks and in ditches. The tail can appear to droop in flight.

Similar species: Rusty and Brewer's blackbirds (vocally and visually)

Remarks: All male blackbirds are larger than females but the most pronounced differences in Alberta are between the male and female grackle. Common Grackles nest in small colonies of three to four pairs. The species is highly gregarious in eastern North America, migrating and wintering in huge flocks; this behavior is not as apparent in Alberta. Grackles are omnivores and are not shy about killing small birds and mammals for a living. The long tail of the males is obvious but in profile females are similar to Rusty's and Brewer's. Her bill is proportionally larger. Percy Taverner, an early ornithologist, described the walk of the male grackles as one of "comical pomposity." He also used the apt name "Crow Blackbird."

Jan	Feb	Mar	Apr	May	Jun	Jul	Aug	Sep	Oct	Nov	Dec

COGK ☐   Date: _____

Blackbirds and Allies

BROWN-HEADED COWBIRD

Molothrus ater

L: 191 mm   W: 46 g   Egg: 21 x 16 mm

Etymology: *Molothrus* (L.) - "a wanderer;" *ater* (L.) - "black."

Status and Distribution: The cowbird is abundant in all settled areas of the province and moving north as forests are cleared. The only habitat it cannot tolerate is dense forests.

● ●

Field Checklist

✓**Habitat:** The Cowbird can be found in any open country with suitable perches including burns, cutlines and roadsides in the north. It prefers to be near cattle.

✓✓**Sight:** Shorter and stubbier than other blackbirds, the brown head of the male is visible in good light. The female is brownish. Both sexes have a conical bill.

✓✓**Sound:** Surprisingly vocal, cowbirds utter squeaky rattles and liquid short trills.

✓✓**Behavior:** They are normally in groups with many males per female. They follow cattle when foraging. Both sexes perch high in trees or on posts to scan for hosts they can parasitize.

● ●

Similar species: Starling, Rusty and Brewer's blackbirds (visually).

Remarks: A social parasite, the female Brown-headed Cowbird lays her eggs in the nests of other species trusting the hosts to raise her young. Cowbirds have an extremely negative impact on the productivity of smaller passerines. A serious concern is that by opening the boreal forest, we are expanding the range of cowbirds and putting added pressure on already habitat-stressed warbler populations. In other parts of their range, Cowbird control programs have been needed to preserve breeding populations of a rare warbler and vireo. These programs pose a moral dilemma for environmentalists.

Jan	Feb	Mar	Apr	May	Jun	Jul	Aug	Sep	Oct	Nov	Dec

BHCO ❏   Date: _____

BALTIMORE ORIOLE

Icterus galbula

Blackbirds and Allies

L: 189 mm W: 35 g Egg: 23 x 15 mm

Etymology: *Icterus* (Gr.) - *ikteros*, "jaundice," name given to a small yellow bird which was believed to provide a cure; *galbula* (L.) - "a small yellow bird."

Status and Distribution: A common breeder in the parkland, grasslands and southern boreal forest. The Baltimore overlaps and hybridizes with the Bullock's in extreme southern Alberta.

Field Checklist

✓**Habitat:** It inhabits the edges of open poplar forests and groves and cottonwood groves along our southern rivers.

✓✓✓**Sight:** Males have a unique pattern of a black head, wings and central tail against a bright orange background. Females are yellow-brown underneath with brownish upperparts.

✓✓**Sound:** The oriole performs a flute-like series of whistled "doodle" notes. It also gives a rattle when alarmed.

✓**Behavior:** Look for their conspicuous hanging nests in aspens or cottonwoods usually near forest edges or in solitary trees.

Similar species: Bullock's Oriole (visually and vocally); Robin and Rose-breasted Grosbeak (vocally).

Remarks: Until recently, the Baltimore was combined with Bullock's as the Northern Oriole. It is moderately detectable, often seen flying between groves of trees, and males are fairly noisy in spring. North of Waterton and the Milk River virtually all Orioles are Baltimores but hybrids can be found farther south. Orioles are fond of caterpillars and eat a variety of insect pests making them beneficial to urban horticulturists. The Baltimore/Bullock's pair presents an interesting situation as, even though the forms interbreed, the "parent" populations of each species are not affected.

Jan	Feb	Mar	Apr	May	Jun	Jul	Aug	Sep	Oct	Nov	Dec

BAOR ☐   Date: _____

Blackbirds and Allies

BULLOCK'S ORIOLE
Icterus bullockii

L: 189 mm   W: 35 g   Egg: 23 x 15 mm

Etymology: *Icterus* (Gr.) - *ikteros*, "jaundice," name given to a small yellow bird which was believed to provide a cure; *bullockii* (ML.) - for father and son birders named Bullock.

Status and Distribution: Local and uncommon in extreme southern Alberta. Look along and south of the Milk River west to Waterton Lakes National Park.

• •

Field Checklist

✓**Habitat:** It is found in riparian forests, willow shrublands and urban areas.

✓✓✓**Sight:** The male has a bright orange eyebrow, cheek, underparts, rump and outer tail feathers, black throat, eye line, cap, back and central tail feathers and a large, white wing patch. The female has a dusky yellow face, throat and upper breast, gray underparts, olive-gray upperparts and tail, and small, white wing patches.

✓**Sound:** The male gives an accented series of 6-8 whistled, rich guttural notes.

✓**Behavior:** Similar to the Baltimore Oriole.

• •

Similar species: Baltimore Oriole (visually and vocally)

Remarks: Until recently, Bullock's was combined with the Baltimore as the Northern Oriole. The white patch on the wing is distinctive in flight, and the orange versus black head is easily seen if the bird is perched. Bullock's hybridizes with Baltimore's and understandably, they are similar species behaviorally. The adult female is more olive on the back and yellow on the throat than the Baltimore. Historical records show that Bullock's had an extensive distribution from the Red Deer River valley south. Recent data show that the Baltimore has occupied much of this range restricting Bullock's to the extreme southern part of Alberta.

Jan	Feb	Mar	Apr	May	Jun	Jul	Aug	Sep	Oct	Nov	Dec

BUOR ☐   Date: _____

Order: Passeriformes - Family: Fringillidae

Finches and Grosbeaks

GRAY-CROWNED ROSY FINCH

Leucosticte tephrocotis

Photo: K. Morck

L: 167 mm   W: 26 g   Egg: 22 x 16 mm

Etymology: *Leucosticte* (Gr.) - *leukos,* "white" and *stiktos,* "dappled;" *tephrocotis* (Gr.) - *tephros,* "gray" and *kotis,* top and back of head.

Status and Distribution: A common breeder in the mountain parks in summer. The Rosy Finch overwinters in mountain valleys and onto the grasslands and parkland. In the winter, it may wander well east of the mountains even as far as Manitoba.

• •

Field Checklist

✓✓✓**Habitat:** Summer habitat is tundra and heath meadows above timberline, grassy avalanche slopes, rock slopes and cliffs. In fall and in winter it can be east of the mountains at feeders or in fields.

✓✓**Sight:** Males are pinkish-brown on the wings and lower body. They have a unique gray cap and brownish upper body. Rosy Finches are sparrow-sized with an obvious seed-eating bill.

✓✓**Sound:** Their call is like the "chirp" of a House Sparrow or an Evening Grosbeak. The male's song is a rich warbling twitter.

Behavior: The Rosy Finch feeds on the ground, often in flocks, usually in open, exposed locations.

• •

Similar species: House Sparrow (vocally).

Remarks: A bird of alpine tundra in the summer, the Alberta form of this variable species was formerly known as the Rosy Finch. A good uphill hike or a chairlift is needed to bring you to the right habitat. Females are similar to males but slightly duller. Juveniles are basic brown with lighter wing bars. The weather poses a continuous challenge for this species: they can face snowstorms 12 months of the year. It is also a challenge for ornithologists who have not studied Rosy Finches extensively.

Jan	Feb	Mar	Apr	May	Jun	Jul	Aug	Sep	Oct	Nov	Dec

GCRF ☐   Date: _____

Finches and Grosbeaks

PINE GROSBEAK

Pinicola enucleator

Photo: E.Bowma

L: 226 mm   W: 64 g   Egg: 26 x 18 mm

Etymology: *Pinicola* (L.) - "pine" and *colere*, "to dwell;" *enucleator* (L.) - "to remove the seeds (nucleus)."

Status and Distribution: The Pine Grosbeak breeds in extreme northern Alberta and through the mountains. It winters throughout the province and is a regular visitor to urban feeders.

Field Checklist

✓✓**Habitat:** They prefer mature coniferous and mixed forests in the mountains and northern Alberta for breeding. Pine Grosbeaks can be almost anywhere, including feeders during migration and winter.

✓✓✓**Sight:** Male Grosbeaks are large and chunky with a huge black bill, reddish-pink head, back and breast and grayish wings and tail. Females are gray with an olive head. Both sexes have white wing-bars.

✓**Sound:** Flight call is a musical whistled "pui pui puia," reminiscent of the call of the Greater Yellowlegs. Their song is a soft warble.

✓**Behavior:** The Pine Grosbeak forms loose flocks in winter, feeding on mountain ash berries, other fruits, buds and seeds. Sunflower seeds are a favorite at feeders.

Similar species: Purple and Cassin's finches, White-winged Crossbill (visually).

Remarks: Other finches are smaller and generally lack wing bars. Noted for its tame almost sluggish movements, the Pine Grosbeak is highly detectable in winter but rare and difficult to find in the breeding season. Their distribution is affected by the richness of seed crops in their coniferous forest habitat. Absolute size is always a poor character for identification unless the forms being compared are side by side. The huge bill of grosbeaks, however, separates them from other finches.

Jan	Feb	Mar	Apr	May	Jun	Jul	Aug	Sep	Oct	Nov	Dec

Order: Passeriformes - Family: Fringillidae

PURPLE FINCH

Carpodacus purpureus

L: 151mm W: 26 g Egg: 20 x 15 mm

Etymology: *Carpodacus* (Gr.) - *karpos*, "fruit" and *dakos*, "bitter;" *purpureus* (L.) - "purple."

Status and Distribution: The Purple Finch breeds in the boreal forest, foothills and northern parkland. Most individuals leave the province in fall but some overwintering occurs.

Field Checklist

✓**Habitat:** Prime breeding habitat is mixed and open coniferous forests in central, northern and western Alberta. This finch nests in conifers but often forages in deciduous trees.

✓✓**Sight:** The male is rosy red on the head, hindneck, throat and breast, otherwise brown-ish-red above. The undertail coverts of both sexes are unstreaked and they have white underparts. The female is heavily streaked, brown and white overall except for the undertail coverts. She shows a distinctive, brown cheek patch outlined by whitish bars.

✓✓**Sound:** Their song is a rich, fast, bubbling warble. The call is a metallic "pit."

✓**Behavior:** Purple Finches are common visitors to suburban feeders during migration. They are energetic singers.

Similar species: Cassin's Finch and Pine Grosbeak (visually and vocally).

Remarks: An early spring migrant, the Purple Finch may visit urban feeders for weeks before moving north to breed. A difficult bird to spot, it is seen regularly flying high over the forest uttering its "pit" call. They often perch and sing from the tops of trees. Care should be taken identifying this species in or near the mountain range of Cassin's Finch. The "redness" of these finches is, in part, a function of diet. Caged Purple Finches, for instance, can turn yellowish. Do not make quick identifications by comparison to a photo; birds in the wild can be quite variable.

Jan	Feb	Mar	Apr	May	Jun	Jul	Aug	Sep	Oct	Nov	Dec

PUFI ☐   Date: _____

Finches and Grosbeaks

CASSIN'S FINCH

Carpodacus cassinii

L: 162 mm   W: 28 g   Egg: 20 x 15 mm

Etymology: *Carpodacus* (Gr.) - *karpos,* "fruit" and *dakos,* "bitter;" *cassinii* (ML.) - for the 19th century Philadelphia ornithologist, John Cassin.

Status and Distribution: Cassin's Finch breeds in montane regions south of Crowsnest Pass. There are scattered sightings north to Jasper.

Field Checklist

✓✓**Habitat:** It is found in high-elevation coniferous and mixed forests in extreme southwestern Alberta.

✓**Sight:** Males have a reddish cap and neck, brown back including nape and light underparts. The female is heavily streaked, brown and white. There is streaking on the underside of the tail in both sexes.

✓✓**Sound:** Their call is a two- or three- note slurred "kee-up," often given in flight. The male's song is a rich complex warble.

✓**Behavior:** Gregarious outside the breeding season.

Similar species: Purple Finch, Pine Grosbeak (visually and vocally).

Remarks: Overall, less red than the Purple Finch but best identified by its two-note call versus the single note "pit" of the Purple Finch. During the breeding season, there is little overlap between the species but during migration, the two finches can be found together. More study is needed to determine the northern limits of this species. Alberta is at the northern end of the range of this species. Elsewhere, it is the high-elevation finch as opposed to the low-elevation House Finch and middle-elevation Purple Finch. To a certain extent this division is true in Alberta as well.

Jan	Feb	Mar	Apr	May	Jun	Jul	Aug	Sep	Oct	Nov	Dec

CAFI ☐   Date: _____

Order: Passeriformes - Family: Fringillidae

RED CROSSBILL

Loxia curvirostra

L: 152 mm   W: 33 g   Egg: 22 x 16 mm

Etymology: *Loxia* (Gr.) - *loxos*, "crooked;" *curvirostra* (L.) - "curved bill."

Status and Distribution: A fairly common "resident" in the mountain and foothills regions, the Red Crossbill is uncommon in the boreal forest. "Resident" is used cautiously because Crossbill breeding and winter range are food dependent and hard to define.

Finches and Grosbeaks

Photo: K. Morck

• •

Field Checklist

✓✓**Habitat:** They are found in mature coniferous woods, particularly pine and mixed forests, although they can be seen anywhere, particularly in winter.

✓✓✓**Sight:** Males are generally reddish-scarlet to yellow except for their dark wings and tail. Their large bill is crossed at the tip. Females are yellow-olive rather than reddish.

✓**Sound:** Red Crossbills give a series of sharp "ju, ju, ju, jee, jee, jee" notes. Their song includes a warbled trill.

✓✓**Behavior:** Crossbills are irregular and irruptive breeders. They may invade an area in huge numbers then disappear for years. Crossbills often feed while hanging upside down from their feet. Their undulating flight is noticeable often at great heights.

• •

Similar species: White-winged Crossbill, Pine Grosbeak, Purple and Cassin's finches (visually and vocally).

Remarks: Heavy conifer seed crops can induce breeding at any time of year. Away from the breeding season, the birds are seen in substantial flocks foraging on seeds in cones of spruce and pine trees. Winter produces many sightings in the cities of the parkland. If you discover a flock, take the time to watch how they use their crossed bill and tongue to extract seeds from conifer cones. Learning the different call notes of finches is the best advice for identification. These birds are heard any time but only rarely do they present themselves in good light.

Jan	Feb	Mar	Apr	May	Jun	Jul	Aug	Sep	Oct	Nov	Dec

RECR ☐   Date: _____

Finches and Grosbeaks

Order: Passeriformes - Family: Fringillidae

WHITE-WINGED CROSSBILL

Loxia leucoptera

L: 152 mm   W: 26 g   Egg: 22 x 16 mm

Etymology: *Loxia* (Gr.) - *loxos,* "crooked;" *leucoptera* (Gr.) - "white wings."

Status and Distribution: A regular "resident" in the mountain, foothills and boreal forest. White-winged Crossbills wander into the parkland in winter.

● ●

Field Checklist

✓**Habitat:** Breeding is in spruce- or fir-dominated coniferous and mixed forests. Crossbills may be seen anywhere during winter.

✓✓✓**Sight:** The male is bright pink overall, with large white wing bars and a heavy bill that is crossed at the tips. The female is mottled, yellowish with white wing bars. Immatures are yellow with dark wings and tail.

✓**Sound:** Their flight call is a series of trilled "chit" or "chur" notes. Their song is a variable set of warbles, trills and rattles.

✓✓**Behavior:** This is an irruptive species, it may show up in large numbers one year and be absent the next. Flocks can congregate at mineral or road salt licks.

● ●

Similar species: Red Crossbill, Pine Grosbeak, Purple and Cassin's finches (visually and vocally).

Remarks: The white wingbars stand out in all plumages and are the best field mark along with the pink color of the males. All plumages and ages have the bright wing bars. Seed supply determines their winter range: if it is low, huge flocks can head south into the central United States. Flight, feeding and flocking behaviors of the two crossbill species are similar. Learning the calls can be an important aid to identification. Like the Red Crossbill, the White-winged is regularly seen away from its breeding habitat during winter.

Jan	Feb	Mar	Apr	May	Jun	Jul	Aug	Sep	Oct	Nov	Dec

WWCR ☐   Date: _____

COMMON
REDPOLL
Carduelis flammea

Photo: D. Wood

L: 126 mm W: 14 g Egg: 17 x 13 mm

Etymology: *Carduelis* (L.) -
carduus, "thistle;" *flammea* (L.) -
"flame," referring to the cap.

Status and Distribution: There are a
few breeding records for the province
but normal breeding range is in the
Arctic. The Common Redpoll is a winter visitor to much of the province.

Field Checklist

✓**Habitat:** It breeds in subarctic taiga vegetation (dwarf birch,
willow, patches of spruce). Any shrubby vegetation, backyards,
weedy pastures and woodlands will do for
migration and overwintering. They are particularly fond of the high energy seeds of
birch and alder.

✓**Sight:** Males have a bright red cap and
breast, black throat, whitish rump and generally streaked back. Females are similar but
have no red on the breast.

✓✓**Sound:** Listen for a slow, slurred, ascending "zwee-ee-eet" call. Their song is a mixture of
trills and twittering.

✓**Behavior:** Redpolls are highly gregarious and noisy,
their flight is undulating, not in a straight line.

Similar species: Hoary Redpoll (vocally and visually); Pine Siskin (vocally).

Remarks: Common Redpolls, occasionally mixed with some Hoary
Redpolls, visit Alberta during the winter. Some years they are everywhere,
other years they are scarce. As seed-eaters, they are regular visitors to
winter feeders. Some breeding records for Alberta may have resulted from
a late spring which precluded northward migration to normal breeding
areas. Most Redpolls have left the province for the north by mid-April.
Hoary Redpolls are whiter and show less red.

Jan	Feb	Mar	Apr	May	Jun	Jul	Aug	Sep	Oct	Nov	Dec

CORE ☐   **Date:** _____

Finches and Grosbeaks

PINE SISKIN
Carduelis pinus

L: 120 mm W: 13 g Egg: 17 x 12 mm

Etymology: *Carduelis* (L.) - *carduus*, "thistle;" *pinus* (L.) - "of pines."

Status and Distribution: The Pine Siskin breeds in the mountains and foothills. There are scattered records throughout the boreal forest and northern parkland. Some individuals overwinter in central and southern Alberta.

• •

Field Checklist

✓✓**Habitat:** Siskins prefer mixed coniferous and deciduous woods but are regular visitors to urban yards and parks.

✓✓✓**Sight:** Both sexes are generally brown and streaked, with yellow stripes on their wings and a yellow rump. The thin bill is distinctive compared to most other finches.

✓**Sound:** Their call is a rapid series of slurred whistles mixed with single longer ascending "zee-oop" slurs.

✓**Behavior:** Siskins are highly gregarious, tame, noisy and common at feeders during migration.

• •

Similar species: Yellow-rumped Warbler (visually), Common Redpoll (vocally).

Remarks: Pine Siskins are small compared to their large-billed relatives, this and the yellow streak on their wings are the best identifiers. Siskins are common in the mountains, but erratic elsewhere. Like many finches they appear in large numbers one year only to disappear the next. In some years, thousands have been banded in a single backyard. They will overwinter. Highly detectable birds, they forage on seeds in spruce and pine cones and various weedy plants. Like the Redpoll, they are fond of birch and alder seeds. Siskins are noisy year-round. Any significant patch of conifers in the province has the potential to house a Siskin nest.

Jan	Feb	Mar	Apr	May	Jun	Jul	Aug	Sep	Oct	Nov	Dec

PISI ☐   Date: _____

Order: Passeriformes - Family: Fringillidae

Finches and Grosbeaks

AMERICAN GOLDFINCH

Carduelis tristis

L: 124 mm   W: 13 g   Egg: 16 x 12 mm

Etymology: *Carduelis* (L.) - *carduus,* "thistle," for its favorite food; *tristis* (L.) - "sad," referring to its call.

Status and Distribution: Goldfinches are regular breeders in the grasslands, foothills, parkland and southern boreal forest with breeding records to Fort McMurray. Highest densities appear to be in the parkland.

• •

Field Checklist

✓**Habitat:** It is found in second growth in fields, cut lines, road allowances, along lake margins and burns. Weedy fields with thistles, dandelions and sunflowers are favorite haunts.

✓✓✓**Sight:** The male is brilliant yellow with a black cap, white rump, white wingbars and streaks on black wings and tail. The female is greenish-yellow with paler wing bars.

✓✓**Sound:** The male's "per-chick-oree" flight call is diagnostic. His song is a variable set of warbles, trills and twitters.

✓**Behavior:** Look for a distinctive low undulating roller-coaster flight, rarely in a straight line. The male calls in synchrony with his flight.

• •

Similar species: No similar species.

Remarks: American Goldfinches arrive late in the spring and breed in mid-to-late summer to ensure an adequate weed seed crop to feed their young. They depart early in the fall, which is interesting because the juveniles will not have been long out of the nest. The dull-plumaged young may remain until later in the fall but go unnoticed by birders. Their flight and flight call are the best identifiers although the highly detectable males are easily spotted while foraging. This is the only small, bright yellow bird in Alberta with a seed-eater's conical bill.

Jan	Feb	Mar	Apr	May	Jun	Jul	Aug	Sep	Oct	Nov	Dec

AMGO ☐   Date: _____

Finches and Grosbeaks

EVENING GROSBEAK

Coccothraustes vespertinus

Photo: K.Morck

L: *191 mm* W: *60 g* Egg: *24 x 17 mm*

Etymology: *Coccothraustes* (Gr.) - *cocco*, "kernel," and *thrauo*, "shatter seeds;" *verspertinus* (L.) - "evening."

Status and Distribution: Evening Grosbeaks have a variable breeding range in the foothills, northern parkland and southern boreal forest. The winter range is variable but includes much of southern Alberta.

• •

Field Checklist

✓**Habitat:** It summers in deciduous, mixed and coniferous forests in the mountains and the northern half of the province. It winters anywhere in central and southern Alberta and is a regular visitor to backyard feeders.

✓✓✓**Sight:** Look for the huge bill, yellow body, but darker head with bright yellow eyebrow and black wing with white patch. The female is similar, but paler. She has two white wing patches.

✓✓**Sound:** The call is a two- or three-note slurred "kee-up," often given in flight. It is similar to a House Sparrow's chirp. The male's song is a rich complex warble.

✓**Behavior:** Evening Grosbeaks are highly gregarious, staying in flocks outside the breeding season.

• •

Similar species: House Sparrow (vocally).

Remarks: The huge greenish-yellow bill is unique among our birds and the best visual identifier of this species. A common winter visitor to feeders, the Evening Grosbeak is becoming a more common breeder in the parkland. It enjoys sunflower seeds at feeders or the seeds of the Green Ash or Manitoba Maple, a common ornamental tree. The only similarly large-billed bird is the Pine Grosbeak but its pinkish plumage and black bill separate it easily from the Evening Grosbeak.

Jan	Feb	Mar	Apr	May	Jun	Jul	Aug	Sep	Oct	Nov	Dec

EVGR ☐   Date: _____

HOUSE SPARROW

Passer domesticus

Photo: K.Morck

L: 168 mm   W: 31 g   Egg: 23 x 16 mm

Etymology: *Passer* (L.) - "sparrow;" *domesticus* (L.) - "around houses."

Status and Distribution: A common resident in all settled areas of the province, it is rare in the far north away from towns.

Field Checklist

✓✓**Habitat:** Home for House Sparrows is backyards, parks, suburban fields, most urban areas and cultivated fields.

✓✓**Sight:** The male has a gray crown with a chestnut back and a black throat and bill. The female is brownish with a streaked back. Both are chunky compared to native sparrows.

✓✓**Sound:** The "song" given as "chiddik, chiddik, churk, churk" is a series of monotonous one- and two-syllable chirps. It also produces a noisy aggressive chatter near the nest or during courtship.

✓✓**Behavior:** They are aggressive, noisy and gregarious. They nest in boxes, spruce trees or crevices in buildings.

Similar species: The female can be confused with Chipping and Clay-colored Sparrows, but she is much larger. The male resembles the Harris's Sparrow and Lapland Longspur but his black bill is diagnostic. Confusion is only likely in rural areas.

Remarks: It has been in Alberta less than 100 years, but it is firmly established. Criticized for their noise, unsanitary habits and disruption of other hole nesters, they are nonetheless great subjects for learning avian social behavior. In the far north they use human-produced heat sources to survive the winter. In La Crete, in northern Alberta, pairs nest in the exhaust vents of a commercial laundromat. You have to admire their adaptability whatever you think of their faults.

Jan	Feb	Mar	Apr	May	Jun	Jul	Aug	Sep	Oct	Nov	Dec

HOSP ☐   Date: _____

HOARY REDPOLL

Carduelis hornemanni

The Hoary Redpoll is an uncommon to rare winter visitor, but it can be seen potentially throughout the province. The status of the species in the province is uncertain because most Hoarys are mixed in with flocks of Common Redpolls and go unnoticed. It is rare to see a flock containing only Hoary Redpolls.

Their favorite tree is a birch but Redpolls can be found in weedy fields, pastures, grain fields, parks and at backyard feeders. The Hoary is similar to the Common Redpoll but it is whiter especially on the rump and breast. The best way to find them is to look for the white-looking birds in a flock of Redpolls, these will likely be the Hoarys. Song is not a good way to distinguish between these species as they both make a combination of trills and twitters.

Hoary Redpolls appear in Alberta in October and stay through to April. Their normal breeding range is the high Arctic. Numbers seen each winter are variable but usually Hoarys are far less numerous than the Common Redpoll.

BIRDS OF ALBERTA SPECIES LIST

Order: GAVIIFORMES - Loons

Family: GAVIIDAE
Red-throated Loon	* - M	Gavia stellata	❏
Pacific Loon	* - M	Gavia pacifica	❏
Common Loon	*	Gavia immer	❏
Yellow-billed Loon	V	Gavia adamsii	❏

Order: PODICIPEDIFORMES - Grebes

Family: PODICIPEDIDAE
Pied-billed Grebe	*	Podilymbus podiceps	❏
Horned Grebe	*	Podiceps auritus	❏
Red-necked Grebe	*	Podiceps grisegena	❏
Eared Grebe	*	Podiceps nigricollis	❏
Western Grebe	*	Aechmophorus occidentalis	❏
Clark's Grebe	*	Aechmophorus clarkii	❏

Order: PELECANIFORMES - Pelicans and Cormorants

Family: PELECANIDAE
American White Pelican	*	Pelecanus erythrorhynchos	❏

Family: PHALACROCORACIDAE
Double-crested Cormorant	*	Phalacrocorax auritus	❏

Order: CICONIIFORMES - Herons, Egrets, Ibises, New World Vultures

Family: ARDEIDAE
American Bittern	*	Botaurus lentiginosus	❏
Great Blue Heron	*	Ardea herodias	❏
Great Egret	V	Ardea alba	❏
Snowy Egret	V	Egretta thula	❏
Little Blue Heron	V	Egretta caerulea	❏
Tricolored Heron	V	Egretta tricolor	❏
Cattle Egret	V	Bubulcus ibis	❏
Green Heron	V	Butorides virescens	❏
Black-crowned Night-Heron	*	Nycticorax nycticorax	❏

Species List

Family: THRESKIORNITHIDAE

White-faced Ibis	*	Plegadis chihi	❏

Family: CATHARTIDAE

Turkey Vulture	*	Cathartes aura	❏

Order: ANSERIFORMES - Ducks, Geese and Swans

Family: ANATIDAE

Greater White-fronted Goose	M	Anser albifrons	❏
Snow Goose	* - M	Chen caerulescens	❏
Ross's Goose	M	Chen rossii	❏
Canada Goose	*	Branta canadensis	❏
Brant	V	Branta bernicla	❏
Trumpeter Swan	*	Cygnus buccinator	❏
Tundra Swan	M	Cygnus columbianus	❏
Wood Duck	*	Aix sponsa	❏
Gadwall	*	Anas strepera	❏
Eurasian Wigeon	V	Anas penelope	❏
American Wigeon	*	Anas americana	❏
American Black Duck	*	Anas rubripes	❏
Mallard	*	Anas platyrhynchos	❏
Blue-winged Teal	*	Anas discors	❏
Cinnamon Teal	*	Anas cyanoptera	❏
Northern Shoveler	*	Anas clypeata	❏
Northern Pintail	*	Anas acuta	❏
Garganey	V	Anas querquedula	❏
Green-winged Teal	*	Anas crecca	❏
Canvasback	*	Aythya valisineria	❏
Redhead	*	Aythya americana	❏
Ring-necked Duck	*	Aythya collaris	❏
Tufted Duck	V	Aythya fuligula	❏
Greater Scaup	M	Aythya marila	❏
Lesser Scaup	*	Aythya affinis	❏
King Eider	V	Somateria spectabilis	❏
Harlequin Duck	*	Histrionicus histrionicus	❏
Surf Scoter	* - M	Melanitta perspicillata	❏
White-winged Scoter	*	Melanitta fusca	❏
Black Scoter	V	Melanitta nigra	❏
Oldsquaw	M	Clangula hyemalis	❏
Bufflehead	*	Bucephala albeola	❏
Common Goldeneye	*	Bucephala clangula	❏
Barrow's Goldeneye	*	Bucephala islandica	❏
Hooded Merganser	*	Lophodytes cucullatus	❏

Red-breasted Merganser	*	Mergus serrator	❏
Common Merganser	*	Mergus merganser	❏
Ruddy Duck	*	Oxyura jamaicensis	❏

Order: FALCONIFORMES - Hawks, Eagles and Falcons

Family: ACCIPITRIDAE

Osprey	*	Pandion haliaetus	❏
Bald Eagle	*	Haliaeetus leucocephalus	❏
Northern Harrier	*	Circus cyaneus	❏
Sharp-shinned Hawk	*	Accipiter striatus	❏
Cooper's Hawk	*	Accipiter cooperii	❏
Northern Goshawk	*	Accipiter gentilis	❏
Broad-winged Hawk	*	Buteo platypterus	❏
Swainson's Hawk	*	Buteo swainsoni	❏
Red-tailed Hawk	*	Buteo jamaicensis	❏
Ferruginous Hawk	*	Buteo regalis	❏
Rough-legged Hawk	M	Buteo lagopus	❏
Golden Eagle	*	Aquila chrysaetos	❏

Family: FALCONIDAE

American Kestrel	*	Falco sparverius	❏
Merlin	*	Falco columbarius	❏
Prairie Falcon	*	Falco mexicanus	❏
Peregrine Falcon	*	Falco peregrinus	❏
Gyrfalcon	M/WV	Falco rusticolus	❏

Order: GALLIFORMES - Pheasants, Grouse, Ptarmigan and Turkey

Family: PHASIANIDAE

Gray Partridge	*	Perdix perdix	❏
Chukar	E	Alectoris chukar	❏
Ring-necked Pheasant	*	Phasianus colchicus	❏
Ruffed Grouse	*	Bonasa umbellus	❏
Sage Grouse	*	Centrocercus urophasianus	❏
Spruce Grouse	*	Falcipennis canadensis	❏
Blue Grouse	*	Dendragapus obscurus	❏
Willow Ptarmigan	*	Lagopus lagopus	❏
White-tailed Ptarmigan	*	Lagopus leucurus	❏
Greater Prairie-Chicken	E	Tympanuchus cupido	❏
Sharp-tailed Grouse	*	Tympanuchus phasianellus	❏
Wild Turkey	*	Meleagris gallopavo	❏

Species List

GRUIFORMES - Rails, Coots, and Cranes

Family: RALLIDAE
Yellow Rail   *   Coturnicops noveboracensis   ❏
Virginia Rail   *   Rallus limicola   ❏
Sora   *   Porzana carolina   ❏
American Coot   *   Fulica americana   ❏

Family: GRUIDAE
Sandhill Crane   *   Grus canadensis   ❏
Common Crane   V   Grus grus   ❏
Whooping Crane   *   Grus americana   ❏

Order: CHARADRIIFORMES - Plovers, Sandpipers, Phalaropes, Jaegers, Gulls, and Terns

Family: CHARADRIIDAE
Black-bellied Plover   M   Pluvialis squatarola   ❏
American Golden-Plover   M   Pluvialis dominica   ❏
Mongolian Plover   V   Charadrius mongolus   ❏
Snowy Plover   V   Charadrius alexandrinus   ❏
Semipalmated Plover   * - M   Charadrius semipalmatus   ❏
Piping Plover   *   Charadrius melodus   ❏
Killdeer   *   Charadrius vociferus   ❏
Mountain Plover   *   Charadrius montanus   ❏

Family: RECURVIROSTRIDAE
Black-necked Stilt   *   Himantopus mexicanus   ❏
American Avocet   *   Recurvirostra americana   ❏

Family: SCOLOPACIDAE
Greater Yellowlegs   *   Tringa melanoleuca   ❏
Lesser Yellowlegs   *   Tringa flavipes   ❏
Solitary Sandpiper   *   Tringa solitaria   ❏
Willet   *   Catoptrophorus semipalmatus ❏
Wandering Tattler   V   Heteroscelus incanus   ❏
Spotted Sandpiper   *   Actitis macularia   ❏
Upland Sandpiper   *   Bartramia longicauda   ❏
Eskimo Curlew   M - E   Numenius borealis   ❏
Whimbrel   M   Numenius phaeopus   ❏
Long-billed Curlew   *   Numenius americanus   ❏
Hudsonian Godwit   M   Limosa haemastica   ❏
Marbled Godwit   *   Limosa fedoa   ❏
Ruddy Turnstone   M   Arenaria interpres   ❏

Surfbird	V	Aphriza virgata	❏
Red Knot	M	Calidris canutus	❏
Sanderling	M	Calidris alba	❏
Semipalmated Sandpiper	M	Calidris pusilla	❏
Western Sandpiper	M	Calidris mauri	❏
Least Sandpiper	M	Calidris minutilla	❏
White-rumped Sandpiper	M	Calidris fuscicollis	❏
Baird's Sandpiper	M	Calidris bairdii	❏
Pectoral Sandpiper	M	Calidris melanotos	❏
Sharp-tailed Sandpiper	V/M	Calidris acuminata	❏
Dunlin	M	Calidris alpina	❏
Curlew Sandpiper	V	Calidris ferruginea	❏
Stilt Sandpiper	M	Micropalma himantopus	❏
Buff-breasted Sandpiper	M	Tryngites subruficollis	❏
Ruff	V	Philomachus pugnax	❏
Short-billed Dowitcher	*	Limnodromus griseus	❏
Long-billed Dowitcher	M	Limnodromus scolopaceus	❏
Common Snipe	*	Gallinago gallinago	❏
Wilson's Phalarope	*	Steganopus tricolor	❏
Red-necked Phalarope	* - M	Phalaropus lobatus	❏
Red Phalarope	V	Phalaropus fulicaria	❏

Family: LARIDAE

Parasitic Jaeger	M/V	Stercorarius parasiticus	❏
Long-tailed Jaeger	V	Stercorarius longicaudus	❏
Franklin's Gull	*	Larus pipixcan	❏
Little Gull	V	Larus minutus	❏
Bonaparte's Gull	*	Larus philadelphia	❏
Mew Gull	*	Larus canus	❏
Ring-billed Gull	*	Larus delawarensis	❏
California Gull	*	Larus californicus	❏
Herring Gull	*	Larus argentatus	❏
Thayer's Gull	M	Larus thayeri	❏
Iceland Gull	V	Larus glaucoides	❏
Lesser Black-backed Gull	V	Larus fuscus	❏
Glaucous-winged Gull	V	Larus glaucescens	❏
Glaucous Gull	M	Larus hyperboreus	❏
Great Black-backed Gull	V	Larus marinus	❏
Black-legged Kittiwake	V	Rissa tridactyla	❏
Sabine's Gull	M	Xema sabini	❏
Caspian Tern	*	Sterna caspia	❏
Common Tern	*	Sterna hirundo	❏
Arctic Tern	M	Sterna paradisaea	❏
Forster's Tern	*	Sterna forsteri	❏
Black Tern	*	Chlidonias niger	❏

Species List

<u>Family: ALCIDAE</u>

Black Guillemot	V	Cepphus grylle	❏
Ancient Murrelet	V	Synthliboramphus antiquus	❏

Order: COLUMBIFORMES - Doves and Pigeons

<u>Family: COLUMBIDAE</u>

Rock Dove	*	Columba livia	❏
Band-tailed Pigeon	V	Columba fasciata	❏
Mourning Dove	*	Zenaida macroura	❏
Passenger Pigeon	E	Ectopistes migratorius	❏

Order: CUCULIFORMES - Cuckoos

<u>Family: CUCULIDAE</u>

Black-billed Cuckoo	*	Coccyzus erythropthalmus	❏
Yellow-billed Cuckoo	V	Coccyzus americanus	❏

Order: STRIGIFORMES - Owls

<u>Family: STRIGIDAE</u>

Eastern Screech-Owl	V	Otus asio	❏
Western Screech-Owl	V	Otus kennicottii	❏
Great Horned Owl	*	Bubo virginianus	❏
Snowy Owl	WV	Nyctea scandiaca	❏
Northern Hawk Owl	*	Surnia ulula	❏
Northern Pygmy-Owl	*	Glaucidium gnoma	❏
Burrowing Owl	*	Athene cunicularia	❏
Barred Owl	*	Strix varia	❏
Great Gray Owl	*	Strix nebulosa	❏
Long-eared Owl	*	Asio otus	❏
Short-eared Owl	*	Asio flammeus	❏
Boreal Owl	*	Aegolius funereus	❏
Northern Saw-whet Owl	*	Aegolius acadicus	❏

Order: CAPRIMULGIFORMES - Nightjars

<u>Family: CAPRIMULGIDAE</u>

Common Nighthawk	*	Chordeiles minor	❏
Common Poorwill	V	Phalaenoptilus nuttallii	❏

Order: APODIFORMES - Swifts and Hummingbirds

<u>Family: APODIDAE</u>

Black Swift	*	Cypseloides niger	❏
Vaux's Swift	V	Chaetura vauxi	❏

<u>Family: TROCHILIDAE</u>

Ruby-throated Hummingbird	*	Archilochus colubris	❏
Black-chinned Hummingbird	V	Archilochus alexandri	❏
Anna's Hummingbird	V	Calypte anna	❏
Costa's Hummingbird	V	Calypte costae	❏
Calliope Hummingbird	*	Stellula calliope	❏
Rufous Hummingbird	*	Selasphorus rufus	❏

Order: CORACIIFORMES - Kingfishers

<u>Family: ALCEDINIDAE</u>

Belted Kingfisher	*	Ceryle alcyon	❏

Order: PICIFORMES - Woodpeckers

<u>Family: PICIDAE</u>

Lewis's Woodpecker	* - V	Melanerpes lewis	❏
Red-headed Woodpecker	V	Melanerpes erythrocephalus	❏
Yellow-bellied Sapsucker	*	Sphyrapicus varius	❏
Red-naped Sapsucker	*	Sphyrapicus nuchalis	❏
Red-breasted Sapsucker	V	Sphyrapicus ruber	❏
Williamson's Sapsucker	V	Sphyrapicus thyroideus	❏
Downy Woodpecker	*	Picoides pubescens	❏
Hairy Woodpecker	*	Picoides villosus	❏
Three-toed Woodpecker	*	Picoides tridactylus	❏
Black-backed Woodpecker	*	Picoides arcticus	❏
Northern Flicker	*	Colaptes auratus	❏
Pileated Woodpecker	*	Dryocopus pileatus	❏

Order: PASSERIFORMES - Perching Birds

<u>Family: TYRANNIDAE - Flycatchers</u>

Olive-sided Flycatcher	*	Contopus cooperi	❏
Western Wood-Pewee	*	Contopus sordidulus	❏
Yellow-bellied Flycatcher	*	Empidonax flaviventris	❏
Alder Flycatcher	*	Empidonax alnorum	❏

Species List

Willow Flycatcher	*	Empidonax traillii	❑
Least Flycatcher	*	Empidonax minimus	❑
Hammond's Flycatcher	*	Empidonax hammondii	❑
Dusky Flycatcher	*	Empidonax oberholseri	❑
Cordilleran Flycatcher	*	Empidonax occidentalis	❑
Eastern Phoebe	*	Sayornis phoebe	❑
Say's Phoebe	*	Sayornis saya	❑
Great Crested Flycatcher	*	Myiarchus crinitus	❑
Western Kingbird	*	Tyrannus verticalis	❑
Eastern Kingbird	*	Tyrannus tyrannus	❑
Scissor-tailed Flycatcher	V	Tyrannus forficatus	❑

Family: LANIIDAE - Shrikes

Northern Shrike	*	Lanius excubitor	❑
Loggerhead Shrike	*	Lanius ludovicianus	❑

Family: VIREONIDAE - Vireos

Blue-headed Vireo	*	Vireo solitarius	❑
Cassin's Vireo	*	Vireo cassinii	❑
Warbling Vireo	*	Vireo gilvus	❑
Philadelphia Vireo	*	Vireo philadelphicus	❑
Red-eyed Vireo	*	Vireo olivaceus	❑

Family: CORVIDAE - Jays, Crows and Allies

Gray Jay	*	Perisoreus canadensis	❑
Steller's Jay	*	Cyanocitta stelleri	❑
Blue Jay	*	Cyanocitta cristata	❑
Clark's Nutcracker	*	Nucifraga columbiana	❑
Black-billed Magpie	*	Pica pica	❑
American Crow	*	Corvus brachyrhynchos	❑
Common Raven	*	Corvus corax	❑

Family: ALAUDIDAE - Larks

Horned Lark	*	Eremophila alpestris	❑

Family: HIRUNDINIDAE - Swallows

Purple Martin	*	Progne subis	❑
Tree Swallow	*	Tachycineta bicolor	❑
Violet-green Swallow	*	Tachycineta thalassina	❑
N. Rough-winged Swallow	*	Stelgidopteryx serripennis	❑
Bank Swallow	*	Riparia riparia	❑
Barn Swallow	*	Hirundo rustica	❑
Cliff Swallow	*	Petrochelidon pyrrhonota	❑

Family: PARIDAE - Chickadees

Black-capped Chickadee	*	Poecile atricapillus	❏
Mountain Chickadee	*	Poecile gambeli	❏
Chestnut-backed Chickadee	V	Poecile rufescens	❏
Boreal Chickadee	*	Poecile hudsonicus	❏

Family: SITTIDAE - Nuthatches

Red-breasted Nuthatch	*	Sitta canadensis	❏
White-breasted Nuthatch	*	Sitta carolinensis	❏

Family: CERTHIIDAE - Creepers

Brown Creeper	*	Certhia americana	❏

Family: TROGLODYTIDAE - Wrens

Rock Wren	*	Salpinctes obsoletus	❏
Carolina Wren	V	Thryothorus ludovicianus	❏
House Wren	*	Troglodytes aedon	❏
Winter Wren	*	Troglodytes troglodytes	❏
Sedge Wren	*	Cistothorus platensis	❏
Marsh Wren	*	Cistothorus palustris	❏

Family: CINCLIDAE - Dippers

American Dipper	*	Cinclus mexicanus	❏

Family: SYLVIIDAE - Gnatcatchers

Blue-gray Gnatcatcher	V	Polioptila caerulea	❏

Family: REGULIDAE - Kinglets

Golden-crowned Kinglet	*	Regulus satrapa	❏
Ruby-crowned Kinglet	*	Regulus calendula	❏

Family: TURDIDAE - Bluebirds and Thrushes

Northern Wheatear	V	Oenanthe oenanthe	❏
Eastern Bluebird	* - V	Sialia sialis	❏
Western Bluebird	* - V	Sialia mexicana	❏
Mountain Bluebird	*	Sialia currucoides	❏
Townsend's Solitaire	*	Myadestes townsendi	❏
Veery	*	Catharus fuscescens	❏
Gray-cheeked Thrush	*	Catharus minimus	❏
Swainson's Thrush	*	Catharus ustulatus	❏
Hermit Thrush	*	Catharus guttatus	❏
Wood Thrush	V	Catharus mustelina	❏
American Robin	*	Turdus migratorius	❏
Varied Thrush	*	Ixoreus naevius	❏

Species List

Family: MIMIDAE - Catbirds and Thrashers

Gray Catbird	*	Dumetella carolinensis	❏
Northern Mockingbird	*	Mimus polyglottos	❏
Sage Thrasher	*	Oreoscoptes montanus	❏
Brown Thrasher	*	Toxostoma rufum	❏
Bendire's Thrasher	V	Toxostoma bendirei	❏

Family: STURNIDAE - Starlings

| European Starling | * | Sturnus vulgaris | ❏ |

Family: MOTACILLIDAE - Pipits

| American Pipit | * | Anthus rubescens | ❏ |
| Sprague's Pipit | * | Anthus spragueii | ❏ |

Family: BOMBYCILLIDAE - Waxwings

| Bohemian Waxwing | * | Bombycilla garrulus | ❏ |
| Cedar Waxwing | * | Bombycilla cedrorum | ❏ |

Family: PARULIDAE - Woodwarblers

Tennessee Warbler	*	Vermivora peregrina	❏
Orange-crowned Warbler	*	Vermivora celata	❏
Nashville Warbler	* - V	Vermivora ruficapilla	❏
Northern Parula	V	Parula americana	❏
Yellow Warbler	*	Dendroica petechia	❏
Chestnut-sided Warbler	*	Dendroica pensylvanica	❏
Magnolia Warbler	*	Dendroica magnolia	❏
Cape May Warbler	*	Dendroica tigrina	❏
Black-throated Blue Warbler	V	Dendroica caerulescens	❏
Yellow-rumped Warbler	*	Dendroica coronata	❏
Black-throated Gray Warbler	V	Dendroica nigrescens	❏
Townsend's Warbler	*	Dendroica townsendi	❏
Black-throated Green Warbler	*	Dendroica virens	❏
Blackburnian Warbler	*	Dendroica fusca	❏
Pine Warbler	V	Dendroica pinus	❏
Palm Warbler	*	Dendroica palmarum	❏
Bay-breasted Warbler	*	Dendroica castanea	❏
Blackpoll Warbler	*	Dendroica striata	❏
Black-and-white Warbler	*	Mniotilta varia	❏
American Redstart	*	Setophaga ruticilla	❏
Ovenbird	*	Seiurus aurocapillus	❏
Northern Waterthrush	*	Seiurus noveboracensis	❏
Kentucky Warbler	V	Oporornis formosus	❏
Connecticut Warbler	*	Oporornis agilis	❏
Mourning Warbler	*	Oporornis philadelphia	❏
MacGillivray's Warbler	*	Oporornis tolmiei	❏
Common Yellowthroat	*	Geothlypis trichas	❏

Hooded Warbler	V	Wilsonia citrina	❏
Wilson's Warbler	*	Wilsonia pusilla	❏
Canada Warbler	*	Wilsonia canadensis	❏
Yellow-breasted Chat	*	Icteria virens	❏

Family: THRAUPIDAE - Tanagers

Scarlet Tanager	V	Piranga olivacea	❏
Western Tanager	*	Piranga ludoviciana	❏

Family: EMBERIZIDAE - Sparrows

Spotted Towhee	*	Pipilo maculatus	❏
Cassin's Sparrow	V	Aimophila cassinii	❏
American Tree Sparrow	*	Spizella arborea	❏
Chipping Sparrow	*	Spizella passerina	❏
Clay-colored Sparrow	*	Spizella pallida	❏
Brewer's Sparrow	*	Spizella breweri	❏
Vesper Sparrow	*	Pooecetes gramineus	❏
Lark Sparrow	*	Chondestes grammacus	❏
Lark Bunting	*	Calamospiza melanocorys	❏
Savannah Sparrow	*	Passerculus sandwichensis	❏
Baird's Sparrow	*	Ammodramus bairdii	❏
Grasshopper Sparrow	*	Ammodramus savannarum	❏
Le Conte's Sparrow	*	Ammodramus leconteii	❏
Nelson's Sharp-tailed Sparrow	*	Ammodramus nelsoni	❏
Fox Sparrow	*	Passerella iliaca	❏
Song Sparrow	*	Melospiza melodia	❏
Lincoln's Sparrow	*	Melospiza lincolnii	❏
Swamp Sparrow	*	Melospiza georgiana	❏
White-throated Sparrow	*	Zonotrichia albicollis	❏
Harris's Sparrow	M	Zonotrichia querula	❏
White-crowned Sparrow	*	Zonotrichia leucophrys	❏
Golden-crowned Sparrow	*	Zonotrichia atricapilla	❏
Dark-eyed Junco	*	Junco hyemalis	❏
McCown's Longspur	*	Calcarius mccownii	❏
Lapland Longspur	M	Calcarius lapponicus	❏
Smith's Longspur	M	Calcarius pictus	❏
Chestnut-collared Longspur	*	Calcarius ornatus	❏
Snow Bunting	WV	Plectrophenax nivalis	❏

Family: CARDINALIDAE - Cardinals, Grossbeaks and Buntings

Northern Cardinal	V	Cardinalis cardinalis	❏
Rose-breasted Grosbeak	*	Pheucticus ludovicianus	❏
Black-headed Grosbeak	*	Pheucticus melanocephalus	❏
Lazuli Bunting	*	Passerina amoena	❏
Indigo Bunting	V	Passerina cyanea	❏

Species List

| Dickcissel | V | Spiza americana | ❏ |

Family: ICTERIDAE - Blackbirds and Orioles

Bobolink	*	Dolichonyx oryzivorus	❏
Red-winged Blackbird	*	Agelaius phoeniceus	❏
Western Meadowlark	*	Sturnella neglecta	❏
Yellow-headed Blackbird	*	Xanthocephalus xanthocephalus	❏
Rusty Blackbird	*	Euphagus carolinus	❏
Brewer's Blackbird	*	Euphagus cyanocephalus	❏
Common Grackle	*	quiscalus quiscula	❏
Brown-headed Cowbird	*	Molothrus ater	❏
Baltimore Oriole	*	Icterus galbula	❏
Bullock's Oriole	*	Icterus bullockii	❏

Family: FRINGILLIDAE - Finches

Brambling	V	Fringilla montifringilla	❏
Gray-crowned Rosy-Finch	*	Leucosticte tephrocotis	❏
Pine Grosbeak	*	Pinicola enucleator	❏
Purple Finch	*	Carpodacus purpureus	❏
Cassin's Finch	*	Carpodacus cassinii	❏
House Finch	V	Carpodacus mexicanus	❏
Red Crossbill	*	Loxia curvirostra	❏
White-winged Crossbill	*	Loxia leucoptera	❏
Common Redpoll	* - WV	Carduelis flammea	❏
Hoary Redpoll	WV	Carduelis hornemanni	❏
Pine Siskin	*	Carduelis pinus	❏
American Goldfinch	*	Carduelis tristis	❏
Evening Grosbeak	*	Coccothraustes vespertinus	❏

Family: PASSERIDAE - Weaver finches

| House Sparrow | * | Passer domesticus | ❏ |

SPECIES WHOSE STATUS IS HYPOTHETICAL

Fulvous Whistling-Duck	Dendrocygna bicolor
Emperor Goose	Chen canagica
American Swallow-tailed Kite	Elanoides forfiatus
Red-shouldered Hawk	Buteo lineatus
Rock Ptarmigan	Lagopus mutus
Spotted Redshank	Tringa erythropus
Black Turnstone	Arenaria melanocephala
Rufous-necked Stint	Calidris ruficollis
Spoonbill Sandpiper	Eurynorhynchus pygmeus

American Woodcock	Scolopax minor
Pomarine Jaeger	Stercorarius pomarinus
Ross' Gull	Rhodostethia rosea
Ivory Gull	Pagophila eburnea
Barn Owl	Tyto alba
Whip-poor-will	Caprimulgus vociferus
Chimney Swift	Chaetura pelagica
White-throated Swift	Aeronautes saxatilis
White-headed Woodpecker	Picoides albolarvatus
Fork-tailed Flycatcher	Tyrannus savana
Pinyon Jay	Gymnorhinus cyanocephalus
Yellow-billed Magpie	Pica nuttalli
Pygmy Nuthatch	Sitta pygmaea
Canyon Wren	Catherpes mexicanus
White Wagtail/Black-backed Wagtail	Motacilla alba/M. lugens
Yellow-throated Vireo	Vireo flavifrons
Golden-winged Warbler	Vermivora chrysoptera
Virginia's Warbler	Vermivora virginiae
Black-throated Sparrow	Amphispiza bilineata

Alberta Birdlist

This birdlist is designed to be used for a one-day trip at one site. Some basic information will help make the data useful for scientific purposes. Record exact location providing longitude and latitude if available. Weather information should be noted on the accompanying tables. The actual number of individuals detected should be recorded in the abundance column (AB). To record breeding evidence (BR), use the most appropriate codes of those listed. Please record all habitats visited and indicate which of these habitats was dominant. **For species marked in bold or not included on the birdlist, you are asked to record detailed notes as these species may require completion of a rare bird form.**

Name _____

Address _____

_____

Ph: Home _____ Work _____

Other Observers _____

_____

Count Type: General _____

Specific (owl prowl, hawkwatch, waterfowl survey, etc) _____

Ability of observer(s) to detect and identify all species present (taking hearing into account) was: fair _____ good _____ excellent _____

Time Information

Date: ____ . ____ . _____ (dd/mm/yr)

Start Time: ____ : _____ (24-hr format)

End Time: ____ : _____ (24-hr format)

Duration: _____ hrs

Locality Information (to the nearest minute)

Locality _____

_____

Longitude: _____ ° _____ ' _____ "

Lattitude: _____ ° _____ ' _____ "

Please include any additional notes that may be of significance or interest

Return information to:
ALBERTA BIRDLIST PROJECT
c/o Federation of Alberta Naturalists
Box 1472
Edmonton, Alberta
T5J 2N5

This list can be photocopied for for use with the Alberta Birdlist project or contact FAN for additional copies. (FANCHK004a)

Habitat

Habitat	Habitats Visited	Dominant Habitat
Mixedwood Forest		
Coniferous Forest		
Deciduous Forest		
Grassland		
Alpine		
Creek		
River		
Pond/slough		
Lake		
Marsh		
Bog/fen		
Urban		
Cultivated		
Other(specify)		

Beaufort Wind Scale

Code	Speed	Conditions	✓
0	<2kph	smoke rises vertically	
1	2-5kph	some smoke drift	
2	6-11kph	leaves rustle	
3	12-19kph	leaves and twigs in motion	
4	20-29kph	raises dust, small branches move	
5	30-39kph	small trees sway, crested waves on water	
6	>40kph		

Sky Condition Codes

Code	Conditions	✓
0	clear, few clouds	
1	partly cloudy	
2	cloudy or overcast	
4	fog or smoke	
5	drizzle	
7	snow	
8	showers	

Species	AB	BR	Species	AB	BR	Species	AB	BR
Red-throated Loon			Greater Scaup			White-tailed Ptarmigan		
Pacific Loon			Lesser Scaup			Sharp-tailed Grouse		
Common Loon			Harlequin Duck			Wild Turkey		
Pied-billed Grebe			Surf Scoter			Yellow Rail		
Horned Grebe			White-winged Scoter			Virginia Rail		
Red-necked Grebe			Oldsquaw			Sora		
Eared Grebe			Bufflehead			American Coot		
Western Grebe			Common Goldeneye			Sandhill Crane		
Clark's Grebe			Barrow's Goldeneye			Whooping Crane		
American White Pelican			Hooded Merganser			Black-bellied Plover		
Double-crested Cormorant			Red-breasted Merganser			American Golden-Plover		
American Bittern			Common Merganser			Semipalmated Plover		
Great Blue Heron			Ruddy Duck			Piping Plover		
Cattle Egret			Osprey			Killdeer		
Black-crowned Night-Heron			Bald Eagle			Mountain Plover		
White-faced Ibis			Northern Harrier			Black-necked Stilt		
Turkey Vulture			Sharp-shinned Hawk			American Avocet		
Greater White-fronted Goose			Cooper's Hawk			Greater Yellowlegs		
Snow Goose			Northern Goshawk			Lesser Yellowlegs		
Ross's Goose			Broad-winged Hawk			Solitary Sandpiper		
Canada Goose			Swainson's Hawk			Willet		
Trumpeter Swan			Red-tailed Hawk			Spotted Sandpiper		
Tundra Swan			Ferruginous Hawk			Upland Sandpiper		
Wood Duck			Rough-legged Hawk			Whimbrel		
Gadwall			Golden Eagle			Long-billed Curlew		
Eurasian Wigeon			American Kestrel			Hudsonian Godwit		
American Wigeon			Merlin			Marbled Godwit		
American Black Duck			Prairie Falcon			Ruddy Turnstone		
Mallard			Peregrine Falcon			Red Knot		
Blue-winged Teal			Gyrfalcon			Sanderling		
Cinnamon Teal			Gray Partridge			Semipalmated Sandpiper		
Northern Shoveler			Ring-necked Pheasant			Western Sandpiper		
Northern Pintail			Ruffed Grouse			Least Sandpiper		
Green-winged Teal			Sage Grouse			White-rumped Sandpiper		
Canvasback			Spruce Grouse			Baird's Sandpiper		
Redhead			Blue Grouse			Pectoral Sandpiper		
Ring-necked Duck			Willow Ptarmigan			Dunlin		

Species	AB	BR	Species	AB	BR	Species	AB	BR
Curlew Sandpiper			Common Nighthawk			Blue Jay		
Stilt Sandpiper			BLACK SWIFT			Clark's Nutcracker		
BUFF-BREASTED SANDPIPER			Ruby-throated Hummingbird			Black-billed Magpie		
Short-billed Dowitcher			Calliope Hummingbird			American Crow		
LONG-BILLED DOWITCHER			Rufous Hummingbird			Common Raven		
Common Snipe			Belted Kingfisher			Horned Lark		
Wilson's Phalarope			Yellow-bellied Sapsucker			Purple Martin		
Red-necked Phalarope			Red-naped Sapsucker			Tree Swallow		
RED PHALAROPE			Downy Woodpecker			Violet-green Swallow		
PARASITIC JAEGER			Hairy Woodpecker			N.Rough-winged Swallow		
Franklin's Gull			Three-toed Woodpecker			Bank Swallow		
Bonaparte's Gull			Black-backed Woodpecker			Barn Swallow		
Mew Gull			Northern Flicker			Cliff Swallow		
Ring-billed Gull			Pileated Woodpecker			Black-capped Chickadee		
California Gull			Olive-sided Flycatcher			Mountain Chickadee		
Herring Gull			Western Wood-Pewee			Boreal Chickadee		
THAYER'S GULL			Yellow-bellied Flycatcher			CHESTNUT-BACKED CHICKADEE		
GLAUCOUS GULL			Alder Flycatcher			Red-breasted Nuthatch		
SABINE'S GULL			Willow Flycatcher			White-breasted Nuthatch		
CASPIAN TERN			Least Flycatcher			Brown Creeper		
Common Tern			Hammond's Flycatcher			Rock Wren		
Forster's Tern			Dusky Flycatcher			House Wren		
Black Tern			Cordilleran Flycatcher			Winter Wren		
Rock Dove			Eastern Phoebe			SEDGE WREN		
Mourning Dove			Say's Phoebe			Marsh Wren		
Black-billed Cuckoo			GREAT CRESTED FLYCATCHER			American Dipper		
Great Horned Owl			Western Kingbird			Golden-crowned Kinglet		
Snowy Owl			Eastern Kingbird			Ruby-crowned Kinglet		
Northern Hawk Owl			NORTHERN SHRIKE			EASTERN BLUEBIRD		
Northern Pygmy-Owl			Loggerhead Shrike			WESTERN BLUEBIRD		
Burrowing Owl			Blue-headed Vireo			Mountain Bluebird		
Barred Owl			Cassin's Vireo			Townsend's Solitaire		
Great Gray Owl			Warbling Vireo			Veery		
Long-eared Owl			Philadelphia Vireo			Gray-cheeked Thrush		
Short-eared Owl			Red-eyed Vireo			Swainson's Thrush		
Boreal Owl			Gray Jay			Hermit Thrush		
N.Saw-whet Owl			Steller's Jay			Varied Thrush		

Species	AB	BR	Species	AB	BR	Species	AB	BR
Gray Catbird			Brewer's Sparrow			Pine Grosbeak		
Northern Mockingbird			Vesper Sparrow			Purple Finch		
Sage Thrasher			Lark Sparrow			Cassin's Finch		
Brown Thrasher			Lark Bunting			House Finch		
European Starling			Savannah Sparrow			Red Crossbill		
American Pipit			Baird's Sparrow			White-winged Crossbill		
Sprague's Pipit			Grasshopper Sparrow			Common Redpoll		
Bohemian Waxwing			Le Conte's Sparrow			Hoary Redpoll		
Cedar Waxwing			Nelson's Sharp-tailed Sparrow			Pine Siskin		
Tennessee Warbler			Fox Sparrow			American Goldfinch		
Orange-crowned Warbler			Song Sparrow			Evening Grosbeak		
Yellow Warbler			Lincoln's Sparrow			House Sparrow		
Chestnut-sided Warbler			Swamp Sparrow					
Magnolia Warbler			White-throated Sparrow					
Cape May Warbler			Harris's Sparrow					
Yellow-rumped Warbler			White-crowned Sparrow					
Townsend's Warbler			Golden-crowned Sparrow					
Black-throated Green Warbler			Dark-eyed Junco					
Blackburnian Warbler			McCown's Longspur					
Palm Warbler			Lapland Longspur					
Bay-breasted Warbler			Smith's Longspur					
Blackpoll Warbler			Chestnut-collared Longspur					
Black-and-white Warbler			Snow Bunting					
American Redstart			Rose-breasted Grosbeak					
Ovenbird			Black-headed Grosbeak					
Northern Waterthrush			Lazuli Bunting					
Connecticut Warbler			Bobolink					
Mourning Warbler			Red-winged Blackbird					
MacGillivray's Warbler			Western Meadowlark					
Common Yellowthroat			Yellow-headed Blackbird					
Wilson's Warbler			Rusty Blackbird					
Canada Warbler			Brewer's Blackbird					
Yellow-breasted Chat			Common Grackle					
Spotted Towhee			Brown-headed Cowbird					
American Tree Sparrow			Baltimore Oriole					
Chipping Sparrow			Bullock's Oriole					
Clay-colored Sparrow			Gray-crowned Rosy-Finch					

Breeding Codes
Observed
X - species identified, but no indication of breeding.
Possible
H - species observed, or breeding calls heard, in suitable nesting HABITAT.
Probable
P - PAIR observed in suitable nesting habitat.
T - TERRITORY presumed through territorial nesting behavior.
C - COURTSHIP behavior between a male and a female.
V - VISITING probable nest site, but no further evidence obtained.
N - NEST-BUILDING or excavation of nest hole by wrens and woodpeckers.
Confirmed
NB - NEST-BUILDING or adult carrying nest material; used for all species except wrens and woodpeckers.
DD - DISTRACTION DISPLAY or injury feigning.
UN - USED NEST or eggshells found.
FL - recently fledged young or downy young.
ON - OCCUPIED NEST indicated by adult entering or leaving nest-site or adult seen incubating.
CF - CARRYING FOOD; adult seen carrying food or faecal sac for young.
NE - nest with EGGS.
NY - nest with YOUNG.

THE AUTHORS

W. Bruce McGillivray

Dr. McGillivray is the head of the Curatorial Section of the Provincial Museum of Alberta. He received his Ph.D in Ornithology from the University of Kansas in 1981. In 1983, he joined the Provincial Museum as Curator of Ornithology. Bruce has published numerous technical and popular articles on the birds of Alberta. His current related interests are determining the significance of geographic variations in Alberta birds and developing educational exhibits on the Web.

Glen P. Semenchuk

The Federation of Alberta Naturalists' Executive Director is also currently the Chairman of the Alberta Conservation Association. He received a Bachelor of Science degree from the University of Alberta in 1970 and has spent over twenty five years in the environmental consulting industry. In 1992 he edited *The Atlas of Breeding Birds of Alberta* which was the culmination of a five year field program, with over a thousand volunteers, which documented the distribution of breeding birds in the province. Currently he is involved in managing a large database on Alberta birds and the Alberta Birdlist Program, which encourages all birdwatchers to record their observations in a systematic manner and submit the records to the Federation of Alberta Naturalists.

Index

Index

344

Index

Index

Index